KU-211-319

Expertise and Decision Support

Expertise and Decision Support

Edited by

George Wright

University of Strathclyde
Glasgow, Scotland

and

Fergus Bolger

University College London
London, England

PLENUM PRESS • NEW YORK AND LONDON

Library of Congress Cataloging-in-Publication Data

Expertise and decision support / edited by George Wright and Fergus
  Bolger.
        p.   cm.
    Includes bibliographical references and index.
    ISBN 0-306-43862-3
    1. Expertise. 2. Judgment. 3. Decision support systems.
  4. Decision-making.   I. Wright, George, 1952-   . II. Bolger,
  Fergus.
  BF447.E97 1992
  153.8'3--dc20   91-37996
                                                                 CIP

ISBN 0-306-43862-3

© 1992 Plenum Press, New York
A Division of Plenum Publishing Corporation
233 Spring Street, New York, N.Y. 10013

All rights reserved

No part of this book may be reproduced, stored in a retrieval system, or transmitted
in any form or by any means, electronic, mechanical, photocopying, microfilming,
recording, or otherwise, without written permission from the Publisher

Printed in the United States of America

Contributors

Peter Ayton • Department of Psychology, City of London Polytechnic, Old Castle Street, London E1 7NT, England

Lee Roy Beach • Department of Management and Policy, College of Business and Public Administration, University of Arizona, Tucson, Arizona 85721

Fergus Bolger • Department of Psychology, University College London, Gower Street, London WC1E 6BT, England

Derek Bunn • London Business School, Sussex Place, Regent's Park, London NW1 4SA, England

Dominic A. Clark • Advanced Computation Laboratory, Imperial Cancer Research Fund, Lincoln's Inn Fields, London WC2 3PX, England

John Gammack • Bristol Business School, Coldharbour Lane, Frenchay, Bristol BS16 1QY, England

Gideon Keren • Department of Psychology, Free University of Amsterdam, 1081 HV Amsterdam, The Netherlands

Innes Newman • Bristol Business School, Coldharbour Lane, Frenchay, Bristol BS16 1QY, England

Peter Nicholls • Bristol Business School, Coldharbour Lane, Frenchay, Bristol BS16 1QY, England

Patricia Reagan-Cirincione • University Center for Policy Research, State University of New York at Albany, Albany, New York 12222

John Rohrbaugh • Graduate School of Public Affairs, State University of New York at Albany, Albany, New York 12222

Gene Rowe • Bristol Business School, Coldharbour Lane, Frenchay, Bristol BS16 1QY, England

James Shanteau • Department of Psychology, Kansas State University, Manhattan, Kansas 66506-5302

Andrew Sturdy • Bristol Business School, Coldharbour Lane, Frenchay, Bristol BS16 1QY, England

George Wright • Strathclyde Graduate Business School, 130 Rottenrow, Glasgow G4 0GE, Scotland

Preface

This volume brings together a range of contributors from Europe and North America. All contributions were especially commissioned with a view to elucidating a major multidisciplinary topic that is of concern to both academics and practitioners. The focus of the book is on expert judgment and its interaction with decision support systems. In the first part, the nature of expertise is discussed and characteristics of expert judges are described. Issues concerned with the evaluation of judgment in the psychological laboratory are assessed and contrasted with studies of expert judgment in ecologically valid contexts. In addition, issues concerned with eliciting and validating expert knowledge are discussed. Demonstrations of good judgmental performance are linked to situational factors such as feedback cycles, and measurement of coherence and reliability in expert judgment is introduced as a baseline determinant of good judgmental performance. Issues concerned with the representation of elicited expert knowledge in knowledge-based systems are evaluated and methods are described that have been shown to produce improvements in judgmental performance. Behavioral and mathematical ways of combining judgments from multiple experts are compared and contrasted.

Finally, the issues developed in the preceding contributions are focused on current controversies in decision support. Expert judgment is utilized as a major input into decision analysis, forecasting with statistical models, and expert systems. Should the role for judgment be minimized or should further "gateways" for judgment be opened? The overall conclusion is that expert judgment does and should play a major role in approaches to decision support—hence the importance of accurate evaluation of expertise.

This book will be of interest to those concerned with assessing and improving expert judgment in professional contexts, including academics in management science and psychology, software and knowledge engineers, decision analysts, and forecasting practitioners.

Contents

Chapter 3

Reliability and Validity in Expert Judgment   47

Fergus Bolger and George Wright

Chapter 4

On the Competence and Incompetence of Experts   77

Peter Ayton

Chapter 5

Epistemic Strategies: Causal Thinking in Expert and Nonexpert Judgment 107

Lee Roy Beach

Chapter 6

Sociological Perspectives on the Nature of Expertise 129

Andrew Sturdy, Innes Newman, and Peter Nicholls

PART II. ISSUES IN THE INTERACTION OF EXPERTISE
AND DECISION SUPPORT SYSTEMS

Chapter 10

**Human Expertise, Statistical Models, and Knowledge-Based
Systems**   227

Dominic A. Clark

Chapter 11

**Synthesis of Expert Judgment and Statistical Forecasting
Models for Decision Support**   251

Derek Bunn

Introduction

George Wright and Fergus Bolger

When is an expert *expert?* This question is becoming of increasing public interest. Our reliance upon specialists is growing rapidly due to—among other factors—ever more complex technological and social developments. It seems that we must constantly defer to expert judgment in our everyday affairs, but our dependence on expert judgment is more obvious when things go wrong. For example, at this time there is much public concern in the United Kingdom about the safety of eating beef from herds infected with "mad cow disease." "Expert" scientists have been called in by the government to reassure the public. However, not all experts agree that the disease cannot be conveyed to humans. Two quotations from the newspaper *The Independent* of 18 May, 1990, illustrate the point:

> The committee [which] advises the Ministry of Agriculture on bovine spongiform encephalopathy . . . said there was no scientific evidence to support calls for a ban on breeding from the offspring of BSE cattle.

while

> Agriculture ministers yesterday blamed alarmist reporting for public anxiety over "mad cow" disease (BSE) and . . . hoped the BBC and ITV would ask those whom it proposed to interview as "experts" whether they had published the evidence in journals their peers could check.

With expert judgment playing such a critical role in our lives, it is obviously of prime importance that we are able to assess the quality of this judgment. Over

George Wright • Strathclyde Graduate Business School, 130 Rottenrow, Glasgow G4 0GE, Scotland.   Fergus Bolger • Department of Psychology, University College London, Gower Street, London WC1E 6BT, England.
Expertise and Decision Support, edited by George Wright and Fergus Bolger. Plenum Press, New York, 1992.

1

30 years of laboratory research by cognitive psychologists has shown that judgment and decision making are often suboptimal relative to normative models, and decision analysis consultants have sought to improve judgment by providing formal techniques as decision support. However, the generalizability of this research to the quality of experienced decision making in the real world has been thrown into question. Recently, much research has studied the judgment and decision making of experts.

Another reason for the current interest in the quality of expert judgment is the result of recent developments in Artificial Intelligence. Here, Expert Systems and Intelligent Decision Support Systems are finding favor in industry and commerce. Given that such systems model aspects of expert judgment, it is evident that the quality of resulting systems is dependent upon the quality of the information originally elicited. Accurate identification of high-quality expertise is, therefore, essential.

Our book, *Expertise and Decision Support,* stems from the concerns expressed above.

Part I contains six chapters that analyze the nature of expertise. In the first four chapters, the nature of expertise is discussed and characteristics of expert judges are described. Issues concerned with the evaluation of judgment in the psychological laboratory are assessed and contrasted with studies of expert judgment in ecologically valid contexts. In addition, problems associated with eliciting, validating, and improving expert judgment are discussed. Demonstrations of good judgmental performance are linked to situational factors such as feedback cycles, while measurement of coherence and reliability in expert judgment is introduced as a baseline determinant of good judgmental performance.

One conclusion that emerges from these first four chapters, and that is highlighted in the last two chapters in this section, is that studies of performance measures of expertise may not have focused on the essence of the concept. Narrow, performance-oriented studies of judgment in the psychological laboratory contrast with a view of experts as having well-developed causal models of their domains and efficient problem-solving strategies which can be captured in knowledge-based systems. In addition, the preponderance of research studies on the quality of *probabilistic* judgment contrast with another—perhaps more populist—view of expertise, as that of providing definitive answers or solutions to problems. More broadly, attributions of expertise are nested within social and political relationships, such that claims to expertise may legitimate power and authority. Clearly, a priori identification of *valid* expertise if fraught with difficulty.

Part II contains five chapters that look at issues in the interaction of expertise and decision support systems. How should differences between individual experts' judgments and opinions be resolved? How should expertise be represented in expert systems? Do expert systems have advantages over statistical models of expert judgment? What is the role of expert judgment in forecasting with statistical models? These chapters concern themselves with the variety and depth of expert knowledge and evaluate ways in which this richness can be elicited and captured. Once captured, expert knowledge may be integrated with statistical models with the aim of improving over both judgmental and statistical performance, taken separately.

We turn next to give a detailed overview of the contents of this book. In Chapter 1, James Shanteau reviews studies of the quality of expert judgment. One result of behavioral research is a view that experts are inadequate decision makers who show poor quality in their judgments. However, in cognitive science, which is oriented to representing human knowledge for practical application, expert performance is viewed as superior to that of novices. Shanteau's view, based on his own research, is that the quality of expert performance depends on task factors. In addition, Shanteau distinguishes those psychological characteristics or traits that experts hold in common and which, indirectly, tend to facilitate a positive public image. Finally, Shanteau argues, experts follow problem-solving strategies that help overcome any cognitive limitations.

Following up on the issue of the quality of expert judgment, in Chapter 2 Gideon Keren analyzes whether or not it is possible to define and identify deficient and flawed decisions. What skills are required for good decisions? Is there a general skill or are more specific skills required? Should decisions be evaluated in terms of process or outcome? Many real-life decisions are ill-defined and have multiple, often ambiguous goals. In such circumstances, judging a decision by its outcome is difficult. Indeed, favorable outcomes can occur by chance—as can unfavorable outcomes. For a bridge player, a disappointing outcome of a *single* hand may not indicate an inadequate strategy or reasoning process.

Keren notes that decision analysis provides a support for the *process* of decision making, allowing systematic consideration of structural interrelationships, actions, outcomes, and uncertainties. However, it offers little help in option and event generation. Good intuition and creativity are also necessary inputs. Keren argues that further advancement in developing methods for aiding and improving decisions will require a better descriptive theory of decision making. Finally, Keren argues that decisions are best improved by *structure-modifying* techniques that lead to revisions in the *internal* representation of decision problems and result in new insights. Such techniques are likely to improve the process of judgment compared to more mechanistic and superficially internalized methods of debiasing faulty judgment.

Continuing on the theme of the quality of expert judgment, in Chapter 3 Fergus Bolger and George Wright focus on the *methods* that have been used to assess the reliability and validity of expert judgment. A major research concern has been judgments about the likelihood of events occurring. Bolger and Wright distinguish three stages in the judgment process that need to be considered in any evaluation of the quality of probabilistic judgment. These stages are subject to the influence of the domain of judgment, the judge, the elicitation method, and the assessment process. These influences impact upon any evaluation of judgmental responses. Next, Bolger and Wright turn to evaluate the quality of nonprobabilistic expert judgment and use reliability and validity as a focus for analysis. From their analyses, these authors propose a strategy for eliciting reliable and valid judgments from experts.

A general view of expert judgment that arises out of the first three chapters is rather positive: experts, have special characteristics that permit improved performance relative to nonexperts, if given an appropriate task. Further, any failings in expert judgment are correctable.

At the start of Chapter 4, Peter Ayton argues the case for the quality of expert judgment in a similar fashion. He discusses the concept of expertise in relation to problem-solving behavior and choice of strategy, concludes that experts approach problems differently from novices, and argues that experts are able to provide definitive answers to problems that may be solved with the application of relevant knowledge. However, Ayton develops the argument that experts are also called upon to give judgments where the necessary knowledge to specify the answer is not possessed by *anyone*. Expert advice, Ayton posits, often consists of domain knowledge *and* probabilistic judgment of likelihoods. Ayton evaluates studies of medical and legal judgment and questions whether the possession of domain expertise improves *probabilistic* reasoning. Ayton's conclusion regarding the quality of expert judgment is therefore rather more pessimistic than that of the preceding chapters in that there are situations when expert *probability* judgment is likely to be seriously flawed, perhaps *as a direct consequence* of experience. Further, such biases are likely to be incorrigible.

Next, in Chapter 5, Lee Roy Beach provides an evaluation of studies of probabilistic judgment. Beach reviews laboratory studies of human judgment and argues that subjects and experimenters often view the experimental problems differently. It follows that attributions of bias and faulty reasoning should be reevaluated. From his discussions, Beach develops a contingency model of judgment where judges use different strategies for different tasks that are encountered in different environments. His major distinction is between *aleatory* and *epistemic* reasoning. The first is the logic of gambling and probabilistic reasoning. The second links to specific domain knowledge and knowledge of causal relationships. Little research has been conducted on the second sort of reasoning. More generally, Beach argues, task and environment factors determine strategy selection. For example, the higher the perceived benefits of being accurate, and the more that task is seen to be within the expert's area of competence, then the greater the striving for accuracy.

Beach evaluates the nature of epistemic strategies and illustrates epistemic, causal reasoning in medical diagnosis. He contends that expert knowledge far more frequently involves causal thinking than it does aleatory thinking and that efforts to understand and improve expert judgment must begin with this fact. However, most of the research to date, which we have comprehensively documented in the first four chapters of this book, has been within an aleatory framework. Could it be that these performance-based studies of expertise have defined expertise so narrowly that they have missed the true nature of the concept?

Part I is concluded by yet another perspective on the nature of expertise. In Chapter 6, Andrew Sturdy, Innes Newman, and Peter Nicholls place the concept of expertise in a *broader* sociological context. Attention is focused on societal power relationships. Is expertise objective and measurable? Claims to expertise may legitimate the right of monopoly in professional activity, e.g., in accountancy. Sturdy et al. first evaluate functional, critical, and processual approaches within sociology in relation to their usefulness in helping us understand the nature of expertise in society. They turn next to a case study of management consultants who as an occupation, claim management expertise. Management consultants may be viewed as challenging or competing with the identity of managements (their clients) as "experts." The technical expertise that management consultants offer is inextricably linked with their political skills. Management consultants, Sturdy et al. argue, conduct a dialogue of standardization that emphasizes technicity, structured methodologies, and corporate models, yet in practice they are sensitive to the limitations of the rational approaches. Management consultants sell their services on the basis of techniques but employ substantively *different* methods in order to deal with the complex reality of client environments. Expertise, these authors contend, has tacit and political dimensions that cannot be captured neatly by rule-based representations and modeled in expert systems.

In Part II we move on from the debates surrounding the nature and quality of expertise to practical issues concerning the interaction of expert judgment with decision supporting systems.

In Chapter 7, Gene Rowe discusses mathematical and behavioral methods of aggregating individual expert opinions. He argues that use of aggregating techniques stems from our inability to select the "best" judge. The a priori identification of experts is a major bottleneck in the practical application of differential weighing in the mathematical aggregation of opinion. The basic idea behind behavioral aggregation is that the potential information available to the group must be at least as great as that available to the individuals therein; hence it is assumed that the transfer of this extra information will aid in the production of a more valid response.

Rowe notes that the greatest potential for behavioral aggregation is where there is a *heterogeneity* of group members with varying opinions and low agreement. However, unstructured group interaction may result in "process loss" by, for example, social pressures to conformity and the presence of talkative and dominant individuals. Rowe advocates a "mixed" approach of mathematical and behavioral aggregation and critically examines Delphi and the Nominal Group Technique as ways of avoiding process loss and enhancing process gain. Rowe concludes with a consideration of practical problems in implementing the variety of ways of aggregating the opinions of individual experts.

Continuing on the theme of harnessing group expertise, in Chapter 8 Patricia Reagan-Cirincione and John Rohrbaugh describe a new generation of group process techniques called "decision conferencing." Here, information technology, collective feedback, consensus building, and experienced group facilitators encourage effective communication within a group of experts. Using a case study analysis, they describe how decision conferencing was used to estimate parameters for a simulation model of a recently adopted alcoholism treatment system for New York State. The successful development of the plan hinged on the accurate assessment of the level of need for the various programs.

Reagan-Cirincione and Rohrbaugh argue that decomposition of decision problems to reveal areas of "cognitive conflict" between individuals is extremely useful as a means of better articulating the reasons for systematic differences between expert estimates. The authors argue that the use of decomposition to investigate the nature of cognitive conflict and the facilitation of in-depth discussions, between experts, of alternative problem decompositions will improve the level of accuracy achieved through behavioral aggregation. However, given the relative newness of the decision conferencing technique, no comparative studies of this method and other behavioral/mathematical approaches to the aggregation of expert opinion have yet been undertaken.

In Chapter 9, John Gammack describes knowledge elicitation techniques for eliciting expertise for subsequent representation in expert systems. He concludes that the knowledge elicitated is contingent on the properties of the elicitation task. Gammack analyzes the need to validate knowledge-based systems and notes that, no matter how many rules and conditions are included, there is always the possibility of unforeseen circumstances which qualify the utility of a rule. Validation of knowledge represented in expert systems may be as informal as looking at user satisfaction and managerial take-up or as formal as verification of the sequence of rule-testing within a system by the expert who is modeled therein.

Validity requirements for stand-alone expert systems may be more onerous than for other decision support systems. If systems can explain their reasoning to the user, the credibility and implementation of advice giving may be enhanced. Opaque systems without explanation facilities are, Gammack argues, unlikely to be fully implemented. Finally this author discusses the usefulness of decision tree and matrix-based representations of knowledge and argues, from a case example, that experts, in practice, follow "holistic" strategies rather than apply their knowledge in the serial fashion that conventional knowledge representation methods, such as decision trees, emphasize and facilitate.

Expert systems, as discussed by Gammack, may represent the "state of the art" in decision support, in many eyes. But how do expert systems compare with more traditional forms of decision support, such as Bayesian and regression models?

In Chapter 10, Dominic Clark contrasts statistical modeling of judgment with the modeling of judgment in knowledge-based or expert systems. Clark outlines the basis of both approaches and reviews comparisons that have been made between these two representations of expert judgment and with holistic expert judgment. Clark notes that rule-based systems facilitate representation of reasoning under uncertainty. This, he argues, gives expert systems their potential utility.

Given that both statistical models and expert systems can outperform experts, which should we choose in developing a decision support system? Expert systems, in contrast to statistical models of judgment, can frequently make decisions on the basis of *partial* information and are able to function in situations where there is a nonmonotonic relation between two or more predictors and the predicted outcome. But, as Gammack argued in Chapter 9, these nonmonotonic relationships are often difficult to uncover using conventional knowledge elicitation practice. However, statistical models provide an opaque representation of the prediction/outcome relationship, whereas expert systems can provide explanations of advice and decisions. Such transparent and credible advice may be more likely to be utilized in practical situations.

This issue is elaborated in Chapter 11, where Derek Bunn analyzes the role of expert judgment in statistical forecasting models. Surveys of the practical use of such models has invariably shown a managerial inclination to use relatively simple models and subject them to considerable judgmental adjustment. In both business and economic forecasting, adjustment is part of the forecaster's craft. Bunn develops a case that the quality of the expert judgmental input should be improved by becoming less casual. He argues that a documented audit trail should at least be recorded and, better, that adjustment decomposition structures should be developed. Finally, he considers issues in the combination of judgmental and statistical forecasts and notes that the methodology of combining forecasts represents a pragmatic response to a form of modeling failure. A combination does not embody a single theory and does not provide an internally consistent casual model relating all the inputs to the output variable.

The authors represented in this volume come from a variety of different backgrounds, and their contributions cover a number of disparate topics; however, a uniting theme is their desire to understand the nature of expert judgment so as to enable more adequate provision of decision support. But what are the practical lessons to be derived from the research reported here?

From the definitions and analyses presented in the part entitled "On the Nature of Expertise," we saw that caution must be exercised in attributing expertise, and that a complex mix of psychological, social, and situational factors contribute to individually and/or organizationally defined expertise. However, despite the complexity, we now have a clearer conceptualization of individual, task, small group, and organizational influences on both attributions of expertise and on performance measures of expert judgment and decision making. This enhanced understanding will permit intervention via decision support to be managed more effectively in the future.

PART I

ON THE NATURE OF EXPERTISE

CHAPTER 1

The Psychology of Experts
An Alternative View

James Shanteau

"Trust one who has gone through it" (Virgil).

"No lesson seems to be so deeply inculcated by the experience of life as that you never should trust experts" (Lord Salisbury).

"There are not competent people enough in the world to go round" (George Bernard Shaw).

These quotes illustrate two facts: First, the topic of experts and expertise is of interest to many writers, both in literature and in science. Second, these writers disagree about the value of advice from experts. The goal of this paper is to explore the issue of expertise from a psychological perspective and to use that perspective to provide insights into the differing views of experts.

The paper is organized into five sections. The first section describes the prevailing view of experts in judgment and decision-making research. The second outlines the view on experts in cognitive science research. The next describes a "third view" based, in part, on my studies of experts. The fourth contains some observations about common psychological characteristics and strategies of experts. The final section considers implications of these observations for expert systems.

James Shanteau • Department of Psychology, Kansas State University, Manhattan, Kansas 66506-5302. The research described in this chapter was supported in part by grants from the Army Research Institute, the Department of Health and Human Services, and the Bureau of General Research at Kansas State University. This chapter was prepared while the author was serving as Director of the Decision, Risk, and Management Science Program at the National Science Foundation. Copies of cited research available from author.

Expertise and Decision Support, edited by George Wright and Fergus Bolger. Plenum Press, New York, 1992.

EXPERTS AS VIEWED IN DECISION-MAKING RESEARCH

The first known analysis of experts was by Hughes in 1917 for agricultural judges. He found that grain rated highest by corn judges did not always produce the highest crop yields (a result largely supported in a later reanalysis by Wallace, 1923). More recently, Trumbo, Adams, Milner, and Schipper (1962) studied the *validity* (accuracy) and *reliability* (repeatability) of wheat judges. Nearly one-third of the samples were misgraded and more than one-third of the samples were graded differently when judged a second time. Finally, more experienced judges were more confident but not necessarily any more accurate.

Comparable findings were reported in studies of soil judges by Shanteau and Gaeth (1981; also see Foss, Wright, & Coles, 1975; Gaeth & Shanteau, 1979). Slightly less than half the assessments agreed with laboratory results (where chance is roughly 8%). Reliability of repeated judgments was 50%.

Such validity and reliability results are not unique to agricultural judgments. Psychological analyses of medical diagnosticians (Einhorn, 1974), clinical psychologists (Oskamp, 1962), parole officers (Carroll & Payne, 1976), and court judges (Ebbesen & Konecni, 1975) show that experts are often inaccurate and unreliable. Moreover, the experience of judges is not related to their judging ability (Meehl, 1954).

The conclusion from this research is that experts are inadequate decision makers. That has been reinforced in recent studies (e.g., Chan, 1982) which have reported deficiencies in *calibration* (subjective-objective comparability) and *coherence* (internal consistency) of probability judgments. Furthermore, experts are apparently unaware of these various shortcomings.

Another approach to characterizing expert judgment has been to look at the *amount of information* used in making decisions. Presumably, experts should use all relevant information. Many studies, however, have reported that expert judgments are based on surprisingly little information. Court judges, for instance, have been observed to use only one to three factors in sentencing defendants (Ebbesen & Konecni, 1975); medical pathologists have been reported to be equally limited (Einhorn, 1974).

One reason for the limited use of relevant information is that experts are often influenced by *irrelevant information*. Soil judges, for example, have been observed to be influenced by irrelevant materials in soils (Gaeth & Shanteau, 1984). Similar findings have been reported in studies of nurses (Shanteau, Grier, Johnson, & Berner, 1991) and personnel selection (Nagy, 1981). This implies that decisions are made without an adequate differentiation between what is relevant and what is irrelevant. If so, it should not be surprising that expert decisions are often inaccurate, unreliable, and biased.

One frequent explanation for this low level of performance is that experts reportedly rely on *heuristics* (mental rules of thumb) in making judgments. These heuristics often lead to *biases* or judgmental errors. Similar biases have been observed for both novice and expert decision makers (Kahneman, Slovic, & Tversky, 1982). "Numerous studies show that people—including experts—have great difficulty judging probabilities, making predictions, and otherwise attempting to cope with uncertainty. Frequently these difficulties can be traced to the use of judgmental heuristics" (Slovic, Fischhoff, & Lichtenstein, 1985).

Altogether, previous decision-making research has painted a bleak picture of the abilities of experts. It is difficult to find studies cited in the literature which have anything positive to say about experts (Christensen-Szalanski & Beach, 1984).

EXPERTS AS VIEWED IN COGNITIVE SCIENCE RESEARCH

A quite different view of experts has emerged from research in cognitive psychology (Anderson, 1981). Studies within this tradition have revealed novice-expert differences in nearly every aspect of cognitive functioning, from memory and learning to problem solving and reasoning. Chess masters, for instance, have been found to perceive patterns of play more effectively (deGroot, 1965) and to have superior memory for chess positions (Chase & Simon, 1973). Analyses of experts in mathematics, physics, and computer programming produced similar demonstrations of expert skill (Mayer, 1983).

Three general themes have emerged from this body of research. First, expertise is *domain-specific*. Any special skills of an expert are lost outside his/her area of expertise. An expert's cognitive processes are tailored to the unique characteristics of a particular problem area. For instance, novices have been found to reason backwards from the unknowns to the givens. Experts, in contrast, reason forward using stored "functional units" from the givens to the goal (Larkin, 1979). This forward reasoning ability only develops in specific domains. Thus, the thinking of experts becomes "domain-adapted" (Slatter, 1987).

Second, the thinking of experts relies more on *automated processes* (Shiffrin & Schneider, 1977). Automated processes are often parallel and function independently, somewhat like visual perception or pattern recognition. Controlled processes, on the other hand, are linear and sequential, more like deductive reasoning. With practice, some control processes may become automatized over time (Larkin, McDermott, Simon, & Simon, 1980). As they gain experience, experts come to rely less on deductive thinking and more on pattern recognition-like thinking.

Third, expert thinking is reflected by and can be studied through *verbal protocols*. By asking experts to think aloud, qualitatively rich accounts of an expert's reasoning becomes available (Ericsson & Simon, 1980). Protocol analysis is commonly used to provide raw data for the construction of expert systems. A verbal protocol of an expert, for example, can be used to infer (1) factual relationships and (2) production rules. In expert systems, these correspond to (1) the knowledge base and (2) the inference engine (Slatter, 1987).

In total, the cognitive science view is that experts within their domains are skilled, competent, and think in qualitatively different ways than novices (Anderson, 1981; Chi, Glaser, & Farr, 1988). This skill provides a sufficient basis for building expert systems (Coombs, 1984).

A THIRD VIEW OF EXPERTS

My research on expert decision makers began in the mid-1970s with analyses of livestock judges (Phelps & Shanteau, 1978; Shanteau & Phelps, 1977). Based on previous decision research, my expectation was that these judges would be as limited as other experts had been reported to be. Indeed, this research showed that the decisions of livestock judges were sometimes unreliable and did not always match up to standards.

Nonetheless, livestock judges were careful, skilled, and knowledgeable decision makers. Despite the evidence of cognitive limitations, these experts seemed able to make effective judgments. Since then, my emphasis has been on exploring the factors that lead to competent performance in experts. The research question has been: Under what conditions do experts do well and under what conditions do they do poorly?

My research on this question has examined a variety of experts: auditors, personnel selectors, registered nurses, soil judges, and business managers. Although this research has led to many insights about experts (e.g., Ettenson, Shanteau, & Krogstad, 1987; Krogstad, Ettenson, & Shanteau, 1984), it is not the goal here to review specific research findings. Rather, the present paper reflects observations and insights gained about experts while conducting these studies.

My view is that experts are neither as deficient as suggested in the decision making literature nor as special as implied by the cognitive science perspective. Instead, the skills and abilities that emerge (or don't emerge) in experts depends on the situation in which they work. Experts sometimes perform competently and make difficult decisions well, as is true of weather forecasters (Murphy & Winkler, 1977). At other times, experts seem incapable of performing much above the level of novices, as is reportedly the case of clinical psychologists (Oskamp, 1962).

The relationship between topic area and decision performance is illustrated in Table 1. The left side of the table lists judgment domains in which good performance has been observed. The right side lists domains in which poor or

Table 1. Domains in Which Good Decision Performance Has Been Observed and in Which Poor Performance Has Been Observed

Domains with	
Good performance	Poor performance
Weather forecasters	Clinical psychologists
Livestock judges	Psychiatrists
Soil judges	Court judges
Auditors	Student admissions
Chess masters	Behavioral researchers
Physicists	Counselors
Mathematicians	Personnel selectors
Accountants	Parole officers
Insurance analysts	Stockbrokers
Physicians	Physicians

deficient performance has been reported. Except for physicians (shown on both sides), the literature in each field is clear about the level of competence. The question then is: What is in common about the tasks listed on each side?

My original answer (Shanteau, 1987) was that domains where good performance has been observed involve decisions about objects or things. Thus, the experts are being asked to evaluate and make decisions about something that is relatively constant. Where poor performance is observed, the decisions involve human behavior. Thus, experts are being asked to evaluate and decide about what is, in effect, a moving target.

Other insights have been offered about this table. Dawes (personal communication, November 1987), for instance, observed that predictability is different for the two sides: human behavior is inherently less predictable than physical stimuli. Dawes also noted that the level of competence expected by clients (or the public) varies for the two sides. Clinical psychologists, for example, are expected to be always correct, whereas weather forecasters are allowed to make an occasional mistake. Paradoxically, in the less predictable behavior domains, experts often are held to a higher standard of performance.

One final distinction involves the opportunity to improve based on feedback. With domains on the left side, there are more chances to learn from past decisions. Based on previous successes and failures, an expert can better his/her decisions. With right-side domains, in contrast, there appear to be fewer chances to learn. Thus, the opportunity to improve is less.

In summary, the alternative third view holds that the performance of experts is not uniformly good or bad. Rather, the level of performance depends on the problem type and the task constraints. Any conclusions about the skills of experts must take domain into account.

PSYCHOLOGICAL CHARACTERISTICS OF EXPERTS

From studying and interacting with experts, my students and I observed that experts in various domains often display similar psychological characteristics. These appear to reflect what Goffman (1959) described as "self-presentation"— the creation and maintenance of a public image. Beyond that, these characteristics are part of a decision style common to many experts. This section contains a description of several of these psychological traits (see also Shanteau, 1984, 1987, 1989).

Without exception, every expert we have studied has an extensive and up-to-date *content knowledge*. They know a lot and pride themselves on keeping up with the latest developments in their field. One recently retired agronomy expert commented that he felt unqualified to help on a research project because he had not kept up in the past few months (Gaeth, 1980). This despite his having been a leading expert for nearly 40 years!

The two prevailing views of experts offer differing perspectives on knowledge. In judgment/decision making, the role of knowledge is seldom mentioned in discussions of the processing limitations of experts. The cognitive science literature, in contrast, focuses almost exclusively on expert knowledge in various forms. The alternative view is that knowledge is a necessary, but not sufficient condition for expertise. The rest of this section examines nine other characteristics of experts.

First, experts have highly developed *perceptual/attention* abilities. They can extract information that nonexperts either overlook or are unable to extract. When Phelps (1977) presented already detailed information to novice livestock judges, they made decisions that were nearly as good as experts'. The difference was that expert livestock judges could see patterns of information that novices could not.

Second, experts have a sense of what is *relevant* when making decisions. The assessment of relevance can be quite difficult and experts have been observed to use irrelevant information to their detriment. Nonetheless, expert soil judges are better than novices in distinguishing relevant from irrelevant materials (Shanteau & Gaeth, 1981). When trained to make explicit distinctions between relevant and irrelevant, the decisions of novice soil judges were found to improve (Gaeth & Shanteau, 1984).

Third, experts have an ability to *simplify complex problems*. As one medical specialist commented, "An expert is someone who can make sense out of chaos." In part, this is related to the superior pattern-recognition abilities reported for game-playing experts, such as chess masters (deGroot, 1965). There is more involved, however. Professional personnel selectors, for example, have an enhanced ability to get at the crux of an issue (Shanteau & Nagy, 1984). This allows experts to deal more effectively with the cognitive limitations experienced by all humans.

Fourth, experts can *communicate* their expertise to others. An expert's credibility depends on the ability to convince others of that expertise. As one manager put it, "An expert is anyone who can persuade someone else that he (she) is an expert" (Dino & Shanteau, 1984). In fact, experts who are unable to communicate their expertise are viewed as inferior. This can be self-fulfilling because poor communicators are not given the opportunity to make decisions and to show their skills.

Fifth, experts *handle adversity* better than nonexperts. Even when things are not going well, experts continue to make effective decisions. Novices have yet to learn the saying of professional musicians: "If you are going to make a mistake, make a good one and get on with it." That is, there is no point in worrying about past errors, you have to keep functioning (Shanteau, 1987). This may account for the superior ability of experts to work under stressful conditions (Shanteau & Dino, in press).

Sixth, both experts and novices can follow established strategies when the decision problems are straightforward. Experts, however, are better at identifying and adapting to *exceptions*. Shanteau and Phelps (1977) found that expert livestock judges were likelier to have single-case deviations in their decision patterns. When exceptions are encountered, experts could generate meaningful special-situation strategies. In contrast, novices often persist in following well-established rules, even when inappropriate.

Seventh, almost all experts show strong *self-confidence* in their decision making. One widely respected agricultural judge, when confronted with an inconsistent decision about which of two animals was best-of-show, said: "There must have been two grand champions." That is, the source of any inconsistency resides elsewhere than in the expert (Shanteau & Phelps, 1977). Although this might be viewed as arrogance, it comes across more as a highly developed faith in one's own abilities. Experts really do believe in themselves and their capacity to make good decisions.

Eighth, experts know how and when to *adapt* their decision strategies to changing task conditions. A well-regarded agricultural judge noted that one of the biggest difficulties in teaching students is "their persistence in using inflexible and outdated standards" (Phelps, 1977). Expert decision makers, in contrast, recognize that conditions change and that they may need to adapt their strategies accordingly. Of course, changing strategies prematurely can be just as bad as being resistant to change. The key is to know when to adapt and when not to.

Finally, experts have a strong *sense of responsibility* and a willingness to stand behind their recommendations. Experts make it clear to others—"This is what I have decided." Of course, experts must live at times with decisions that are shown later to be incorrect. However, the sense of responsibility helps expert nurses, for instance, avoid letting bad outcomes disrupt later decisions. Novice nurses, in contrast, often have difficulty continuing after a decision turns out poorly.

PSYCHOLOGICAL STRATEGIES OF EXPERTS

In our studies of experts, we have observed the use of various formal and informal decision strategies. Although many of these strategies are domain or problem-specific, several have been found in common use. These strategies have the effect of helping experts overcome cognitive limitations. Five such strategies are described here.

First, experts are willing to make *continuous adjustments* in initial decisions. They use feedback in dynamic environments to avoid adherence to rigid decision strategies (see also Hogarth, 1981). Blind commitment to initial choices is characteristic of nonexperts. The best decision makers have learned that making improvements is more important than being consistent.

Second, experts get *help from others* to make better decisions. They seldom work in isolation, but either operate in a group or seek out feedback from others. This leads to consultation with colleagues and subordinates to gain added insights, especially for tough cases. Group interaction has been reported by Sniezek and Henry (1990) to increase judgmental accuracy and confidence. Experts seem aware that isolation from associates can lead to inferior decisions.

Third, experts often make use of formal or informal *decision aids*. These aids help avoid the biasing effects associated with judgment heuristics. Livestock judges, for instance, keep written records of prior decisions (Shanteau & Phelps, 1977); this has the effect of reducing hindsight biases resulting from memory errors (Fischhoff, 1975). Edwards and von Winterfeldt (1986) argue that experts, of necessity, will adopt whatever aids are needed to assist their decision making. The "unaided expert" may be an oxymoron.

Fourth, although experts may make small errors, they try to *avoid making large mistakes*. They operate as though coming close is generally good enough. The focus is not on being exactly right, but on avoiding making bad decisions. Experts often use a dual strategy of first making a ballpark estimate, and then conducting a more careful analysis. By concentrating on getting close, experts avoid making sizable errors. The loss function for experts apparently is flat around the maximum, but falls off rapidly for larger deviations (Shanteau, 1989).

Finally, experts follow some sort of *divide-and-conquer* strategy. They break large problems into simpler parts, work on the parts, and then put the pieces back together. The specifics depend on the domain; but all the types of experts we have studied have developed ways of separating complex decisions into manageable parts. Interestingly, although this approach is prescribed in decision analysis (e.g., Gardiner & Edwards, 1975), experts appear to have developed this strategy on their own.

IMPLICATIONS FOR EXPERT SYSTEMS

Using techniques from artificial intelligence, expert systems are increasingly being proposed to aid or even replace skilled decision makers. According to Kolodner (1984), the goal is to build systems that "contain all or most of the compiled knowledge an expert has." Some argue that eventually expert systems will provide "replacements for humans" (Cebrzynski, 1987).

However, getting experts to interact with these systems has proved difficult (Michie, 1982). There are several potentially valuable expert systems, such as MYCIN, which are either unused or misused by the very people the systems were designed to help (Ham, 1984). Other examples involve extended efforts to develop expert systems that had to be abandoned, in part because of questions about the cooperativeness of experts (Rose, 1988).

At the same time, there has been debate about whether computer systems can mimic experts successfully (e.g., Graubard, 1988). Most investigators see great potential for expert systems (Barrett & Beerel, 1988; Slatter, 1987), although others question whether that potential can ever be realized (Dreyfus & Dreyfus, 1986; Haugeland, 1985).

The analyses of experts here may contribute to a greater understanding of when and where expert systems are likely to be useful. Domain knowledge and experience are clearly necessary for expertise; having the facts and relevant experience are essential for any expert (Naylor, 1987). Nonetheless, knowledge is not sufficient for expertise. By concentrating on knowledge and production rules, other aspects of expertise might be overlooked by cognitive scientists and builders of expert systems.

There is something more to experts, something that the writer Tom Wolfe (1979) described as the "Right Stuff." According to Wolfe's account of test pilots, "the idea was to prove . . . that you might be able to join the special few at the very top, that elite who had the capacity to bring tears to men's eyes, the very Brotherhood of the Right Stuff itself."

What is the "Right Stuff"? Chuck Yeager (1985) answers as follows: "The question annoys me because it implies that a guy who has 'the right stuff' was born that way. . . . All I know is I worked my tail off to learn how to fly, and worked at it all the way." Beyond these descriptions, both Wolfe and Yeager leave the question of defining "Right Stuff" unanswered.

I believe the psychological characteristics and strategies described here are major components of the right stuff. Without these, an expert could not function and would not be recognized as an expert. Others have come to similar conclusions from different perspectives (Benner, 1984).

Can an expert system be built that incorporates these characteristics? Not enough is known yet to answer this question. But the following, at least, would seem necessary to build such a system. First, expertise must be looked at from the perspective of experts, not as something to be defined within the constraints of available hardware and software. Second, experts cannot be expected to explain everything they do; verbal protocols are inefficient (Hoffman, 1987) and may be misleading when capturing expertise. Third, more emphasis should be placed on the psychology of experts when building expert systems; characteristics such as confidence and communication must be incorporated into these systems, not removed from them. Lastly, as suggested by Table 1, different types of expert systems may be needed to reflect object expertise (left side) and behavior expertise (right side). The traditional knowledge-engineering methods may be well suited for the former, while linear decision models may be better suited for the latter.

CONCLUSIONS

In his insightful book, Golde (1970) states that "we seem to expect too much and the wrong things of our experts." We expect that experts will "know just what's wrong and exactly what to do about it," i.e., that experts can find the right answers. The power of professionals, according to Golde, is "much less than we believe. . . . Miracles are rare and difficult problems cannot be made simply to disappear." Although "an expert does sometimes make decisions, his role is usually much more that of an advisor." A more realistic view of what an expert can do is the following:

> He'll attempt to uncover the real problem, which is probably different and more complex than I imagined. He ought to develop some alternative courses of action and outline their relative merits or risks. He won't be able to do everything himself, but he'll let me know the kinds of decisions or actions I must take. (Golde, 1970)

This view of experts describes what they do and how they perceive themselves. For the most part, such a view has yet to be reflected in the scientific literature on experts.

ACKNOWLEDGMENTS

I wish to thank Gary Gaeth, Geri Dino, and Richard Ettenson for their insightful contributions during the initial phases of this research.

REFERENCES

Anderson, J. R. (1981). *Cognitive skills and their acquisition*. Hillsdale, N.J.: Erlbaum.

Barrett, M. L., & Beerel, A. C. (1988). *Expert systems in business: A practical approach*. Chichester: Ellis Horwood (Halsted).

Benner, P. (1984). *From novice to expert: Excellence and power in clinical nursing practice*. Reading, MA: Addison-Wesley.

Carroll, J. S., & Payne, J. W. (1976). The psychology of parole decision process: A joint application of attribution theory and information-processing psychology. In J. S. Carroll & J. W. Payne (Eds.), *Cognition and social behavior*. Hillsdale, N.J.: Erlbaum.

Cebrzynski, G. (1987, February 27). Experts systems are seen as replacements for humans. *Marketing News, 21* (5), 1.

Chan, S. (1982). Expert judgments made under uncertainty: Some evidence and suggestions. *Social Science Quarterly, 63*, 428–444.

Chase, W. G., & Simon, H. A. (1973). Perception in chess. *Cognitive Psychology, 4*, 55–81.

Chi, M. T. H., Glaser, R., & Farr, M. J. (1988). *The nature of expertise*. Hillsdale, N.J.: Erlbaum.

Christensen-Szalanski, J. J. J., & Beach, L. R. (1984). The citation bias: Fad and fashion in the judgment and decision making literature. *American Psychologist, 39*, 75–78.

Coombs, M. J. (1984). *Developments in expert systems*. London: Academic Press.

deGroot, A. D. (1965). *Thought and choice in chess*. The Hague: Mouton.

Dino, G. A., & Shanteau, J. (1984). *What skills do managers consider important for effective decision making?* Paper presented at the Psychonomic Society meeting, San Antonio.

Dreyfus, H. L., & Dreyfus, S. E. (1986). *Mind over machine*. New York: The Free Press.

Ebbesen, E., & Konecni, V. (1975). Decision making and information integration in the courts: The setting of bail. *Journal of Personality and Social Psychology, 32*, 805–821.

Edwards, W., & von Winterfeldt, D. (1986). On cognitive illusions and their implications. *Southern California Law Review, 59*(2), 401–451.

Einhorn, H. (1974). Expert judgment: Some necessary conditions and an example. *Journal of Applied Psychology, 59*, 562–571.

Ericsson, K., & Simon, H. A. (1980). Verbal reports as data. *Psychological Review, 87*, 215–251.

Ettenson, R., Shanteau, J., & Krogstad, J. (1987). Expert judgment: Is more information better? *Psychological Reports, 60*, 227–238.

Fischhoff, B. (1975). Hindsight ≠ foresight: The effect of outcome knowledge on judgment under uncertainty. *Journal of Experimental Psychology: Human Perception and Performance, 1*, 288–299.

Foss, J. E., Wright, W. R., & Coles, R. H. (1975). Testing the accuracy of field textures. *Soil Science Society of American Proceedings, 39*, 800–802.

Gaeth, G. J. (1980). *A comparison of lecture and interactive training designed to reduce the influence of interfering materials: An application to soil science*. Unpublished masters' thesis, Kansas State University.

Gaeth, G. J., & Shanteau, J. (1979). *Analysis of the Soil Survey Laboratory data and description for some soils of Kansas: Validity of the soil texture-classifications*. (Tech. Rep. 79–11). Kansas State University, Department of Psychology.

Gaeth, G. J., & Shanteau, J. (1984). Reducing the influence of irrelevant information on experienced decision makers. *Organizational Behavior and Human Performance, 33*, 263–282.

Gardiner, P. C., & Edwards, W. (1975). Public values: Multi-attribute utility measurement in social decision making. In, M. Kaplan & S. Schwartz (Eds.), *Human judgment and decision processes*. New York: Academic Press.

Goffman, E. (1959). *The presentation of self in everyday life*. Garden City, N.Y.: Doubleday-Anchor.

Golde, R. A. (1970). *Can you be sure of your experts?* N.Y.: Award Books.

Graubard, S. R. (Ed.). (1988). *The artificial intelligence debate: False starts, real foundations.* Cambridge, MA: MIT Press.

Ham, M. (1984, January). Playing by the rules. *PC World,* 34–41.

Haugeland, J. (1985). *Artificial intelligence: The very idea.* Cambridge, MA: MIT Press.

Hoffman, R. R. (1987, Summer). The problem of extracting the knowledge of experts from the perspective of experimental psychology. *AI Magazine,* 53–67.

Hogarth, R. M. (1981). Beyond discrete biases: Functional and dysfunctional aspects of judgmental heuristics. *Psychological Bulletin, 90,* 197–217.

Hughes, H. D. (1917). An interesting corn seed experiment. *The Iowa Agriculturalist, 17,* 424–425.

Kahneman, D., Slovic, P., & Tversky, A. (1982). *Judgments under uncertainty: Heuristics and biases.* Cambridge: Cambridge University Press.

Kolodner, J. L. (1984). Towards an understanding of the role of experience in the evolution from novice to expert. *Developments in Expert Systems,* 95–116.

Krogstad, J. L., Ettenson, R. T., & Shanteau, J. (1984). Context and experience in auditor's materiality judgments. *Auditing: A Journal of Practice and Theory, 4,* 54–73.

Larkin, J. H. (1979). Information processing and science instruction. In J. Lochhead & J. Clement (Eds.), *Cognitive process instruction.* Philadelphia: Franklin Institute Press.

Larkin, J. H., McDermott, J., Simon, D. P., & Simon, H. A. (1980). Expert and novice performance in solving physics problems. *Science, 208,* 1335–1342.

Mayer, R. E. (1983). *Thinking, problem solving, cognition.* New York: Freeman.

Meehl, P. (1954). *Clinical versus statistical prediction: A theoretical analysis and a review of the evidence.* Minneapolis: University of Minnesota Press.

Michie, D. (1982). *Introductory readings in expert systems.* New York: Gordon & Breach.

Murphy, A. H., & Winkler, R. L. (1977). Can weather forecasters formulate reliable forecasts of precipitation and temperature? *National Weather Digest, 2,* 2–9.

Nagy, G. F. (1981). *How are personnel selection decisions made? An analysis of decision strategies in a simulated personnel selection task.* Unpublished doctoral dissertation, Kansas State University.

Naylor, C. (1987). *Build your own expert system.* (2nd ed.). New York: Halsted Press.

Oskamp, S. (1962). The relationship of clinical experience and training methods to several criteria of clinical prediction. *Psychological Monographs, 76.*

Phelps, R. H. (1977). *Expert livestock judgment: A descriptive analysis of the development of expertise.* Unpublished doctoral dissertation, Kansas State University.

Phelps, R. H., & Shanteau, J. (1978). Livestock judges: How much information can an expert use? *Organizational Behavior and Human Performance, 21,* 209–219.

Rose, F. (1988, August 12). Thinking machine: An "electronic clone" of a skilled engineer is very hard to create. *The Wall Street Journal,* 14.

Shanteau, J. (1984). Some unasked questions about the psychology of expert decision makers. In M. E. El-Hawary (Ed.), *Proceedings of the IEEE Conference on Systems, Man, and Cybernetics.* New York: IEEE.

Shanteau, J. (1987). Psychological characteristics of expert decision makers. In J. L. Mumpower, O. Renn, L. D. Phillips, & V. R. R. Uppuluri (Eds.), *Expert judgment and expert systems.* Berlin: Springer-Verlag.

Shanteau, J. (1989). Psychological characteristics and strategies of expert decision makers. In B. Rohrmann, L. R. Beach, C. Vlek, & S. R. Watson (Eds.), *Advances in decision research.* Amsterdam: North Holland.

Shanteau, J. & Dino, G. A. (in press). Environmental stress effects on creativity and decision making. In O. Svenson & A. J. Maule (Eds.), *Decision making under stress.* New York: Plenum Press.

Shanteau, J., & Gaeth, G. J. (1981). *Evaluation of the field method of soil texture classification: A psychological analysis of accuracy and consistency.* (Tech. Rep. 79-1). Kansas State University, Department of Psychology.

Shanteau, J., Grier, M., Johnson, J., & Berner, E. (1991). Teaching decision making skills to student nurses. In J. Baron & R. V. Brown (Eds.), *Teaching decision making to adolescents*. Hillsdale, N.J.: Erlbaum.

Shanteau, J., & Nagy, G. F. (1984). Information integration in person perception: Theory and application. In M. Cook (Ed.), *Issues in person perception*. London: Methuen.

Shanteau, J., & Phelps, R. H. (1977). Judgment and swine: Approaches and issues in applied judgment analysis. In M. F. Kaplan & S. Schwartz (Eds.), *Human judgment and decision processes in applied settings*. New York: Academic Press.

Shiffrin, R. M., & Schneider, W. (1977). Controlled and automatic human information processing: II. Perceptual learning, automatic attending, and a general theory. *Psychological Review, 84,* 127–190.

Slatter, P. E. (1987). *Building expert systems: Cognitive emulation*. Chichester: Ellis Horwood.

Slovic, P., Fischhoff, B., & Lichtenstein, S. (1985). Regulation of risk: A psychological perspective. In R. Noll (Ed.), *Social science and regulatory policy*. Berkeley: University of California Press.

Sniezek, J. A., & Henry, R. A. (1990). Revision, weighting, and commitment in consensus group judgment. *Organizational Behavior and Human Decision Processes, 45,* 66–84.

Soil Survey Laboratory. (1966). *Soil survey data and descriptions for some soils of Kansas*. (Soil Survey Investigation Report 4). Washington, D.C.: USDA.

Trumbo, D., Adams, C., Milner, M., & Schipper, L. (1962). Reliability and accuracy in the inspection of hard red winter wheat. *Cereal Science Today, 7.*

Wallace, H. A. (1923). What is in the corn judge's mind? *Journal of the American Society of Agronomy, 15,* 300–324.

Wolfe, T. (1979). *The right stuff*. New York: Farrar, Straus, & Giroux.

Yeager, C., & Janos, L. (1985). *Yeager: An autobiography*. Toronto: Bantam Books.

CHAPTER 2

Improving Decisions and Judgments
The Desirable versus the Feasible

Gideon Keren

The purpose of this chapter is to assess the conditions and the extent to which decisions and judgments can be modified, and eventually improved. Before such an assessment can be made, however, two basic questions have to be raised. An obvious underlying assumption in the present context is that decisions are not invariably perfect, and consequently do not always lead to the desired goals. The first question then concerns a metadecision question: How should one judge the quality of decisions? Is it possible to define and identify deficient and flawed decisions, and what criteria should be used in such a process? In the first part of this chapter I will briefly address one of the more fundamental (and at the same time one of the most difficult) questions in decision sciences, namely, what constitutes a good or a poor decision and how could it be measured and assessed.

Given that some distinctions can be made between good and poor decisions, the second question concerns the skills (if any) that are required for making good decisions. Several relevant questions can be raised in this context: What kind of skills are involved in the process of making decisions and judgments, and how can they be identified? (Or, alternatively, perhaps decision making is more of an art?) If skills are involved, is there a general skill of making good decisions, or are more specific skills required for different tasks? Whatever skills are involved, can they be learned in a systematic manner? These and related questions are treated in the second part of this chapter.

Gideon Keren • Department of Psychology, Free University of Amsterdam, 1081 HV Amsterdam, The Netherlands.
Expertise and Decision Support, edited by George Wright and Fergus Bolger. Plenum Press, New York, 1992.

The answers to the above two questions should provide the necessary background for assessing the extent to which decision processes can be improved by corrective procedures. This topic is addressed in the last part of this chapter. A sample of corrective procedures is briefly described, and the characteristics and potential limitations of such procedures are discussed.

ASSESSING THE QUALITY OF JUDGMENTS AND DECISIONS

An essential question in decision sciences is what constitutes a good decision, and how could it be measured. This metadecisional question (which will be referred to as a second-order decision) received relatively little attention in the relevant literature (for exceptions, see Mitroff & Betz, 1972; Vlek, Edwards, Kiss, Majone, & Toda, 1984). Several reasons may account for the relative reluctance of researchers to address the question directly. First, it could be argued that the question is too broad, ill-defined (e.g., Simon, 1973), and consequently cannot be treated in a concise manner. Second (and related to the above), it may be claimed that the question is meaningless since decision problems can be classified into various categories (e.g., von Winterfeldt, 1980); evaluation criteria for different decision classes may not necessarily be the same. Third, it can be asserted that a second-order decision could be associated with a third-order decision, and so on, ad infinitum. This argument is similar to the one raised against the use of second-order probabilities (Goldsmith & Sahlin, 1983). Finally, one may simply state that a satisfactory answer to the question does not exist. Pessimists may also extend this claim to the future.

Despite the above difficulties, the question of what constitutes a good decision is central and cannot be ignored. From a theoretical perspective the question is a cornerstone for any normative theory of decision making. From an applied viewpoint, this is the ultimate question that any practitioner will be interested in, and consequently it has direct bearing for any descriptive theory.

Like many first-order decisions, second-order or metadecisions are also multidimensional. In principle, the process underlying the metadecision problem is quite similar to that underlying first-order decisions: the relevant dimensions have to be identified (and eventually weighted), their values have to be assessed, corresponding uncertainties have to be estimated and, finally, the entire information has to be integrated to yield what would be hoped to be an unambiguous decision. A multiattribute utility analysis (e.g., Keeney & Raiffa, 1976), that is often employed with first-order decisions, should be equally applicable to second-order decisions.

The simplicity of such a procedure, however, is more apparent than real. To begin with, the application of multiattribute utility analysis (even to first-order decisions) is accompanied by many difficulties (e.g., Beach & Barnes, 1983;

Keeney, 1977; Keeney & Raiffa, 1976). In addition, judgments concerning second-order decisions carry their own difficulties: in particular, as mentioned, it is not clear what relevant dimensions should be adopted for such an analysis. The purpose of the present section is not to provide an exhaustive discussion regarding the original question, namely, how to define and assess what is a good decision. Rather, some of the more central aspects pertinent to the above question are briefly discussed. These may eventually serve as tentative initial guidelines for the development of desired evaluation procedures. The following exposition is also essential for the construction and evaluation of cognitive aids that may modify and improve decision quality, which is the central topic of this chapter.

NORMATIVE, DESCRIPTIVE, AND PRESCRIPTIVE CONSIDERATIONS

A conventional distinction made in decision theory is between the normative and the descriptive facets. Descriptive decision theory is mainly concerned with how decisions are actually made; its goal is to uncover the strategies and cognitive processes underlying decision behavior. Normative decision theory deals with optimal rather than actual decisions, and assumes an "ideal" decision maker that is not confined by natural human limitations.[1] Given underlying assumptions and some external constraints, it attempts to find out the best solution to a decision problem, regardless of how such decisions are made in practice.

As pointed out, however, by Coombs, Dawes, and Tversky (1970) "descriptive and normative theories are deeply interrelated in most applications" (p. 114). On one hand, in many situations people strive to obtain the optimum and, even if not always successful, it clearly shapes their behavior. Thus, an implicit normative element exists in almost any descriptive theory of decision making. On the other hand, optimality is not always easily defined, and may involve considerations such as fairness (e.g., Kahneman, Knetch, & Thaler, 1986), reputation, and morale. In such instances, a descriptive analysis of the goals may be a prerequisite for the application of the normative analysis (Coombs et al., 1970).

Despite the close link between descriptive and normative theories, they are nonetheless different and often also incompatible. Indeed, there is ample research to suggest that, at least in certain domains, normative theories cannot adequately serve the descriptive facets; the two types of theories are often not

---

[1]This is similar to the "ideal" observer assumption that is adopted in signal detection theory.

exchangeable, and the differences between them cannot be reconciled (e.g., Tversky & Kahneman, 1986).

The discrepancy between the normative and the descriptive facets is, at least partly, explained by the unequivocal fact concerning the human's limited memory and processing capacity. This conclusion is strongly supported by empirical studies in the paradigmatic framework of information processing. In addition, humans are error-prone (e.g., Perrow, 1984; Rasmussen & Rouse, 1981), and vulnerable to both emotional and motivational states (e.g., Janis & Mann, 1977) that may affect their performance. Given these natural constraints, Keeney and Raiffa (1976) proposed to further distinguish between a normative and a prescriptive approach. The normative approach is used with reference to the development and acceptance of the axiomatic basis (or fundamental assumptions) of decision theory, and as such is designed for an idealized ("superrational") human being. In contrast, the prescriptive approach, while still aimed at optimization, is more tuned to the human's limitations to process information, and may take into account emotional, motivational, and other potential nonrational effects.

The distinction between normative, prescriptive, and descriptive facets is in particular important in the present context, not just for the purpose of evaluating the quality of decisions, but also in setting guidelines for the development of possible corrective procedures for modifying decision processes. For the purpose of improving decisions, the most appropriate criteria would be ones that are prescriptive (rather than normative) in nature.

Establishing such prescriptive guidelines is certainly not an easy task. Notwithstanding, it is important that such criteria be stated unambiguously, and well in advance, before the decision(s) and the corresponding outcome(s) are taking place. In practice, however, there is a strong tendency to establish the criteria for evaluating decisions after the corresponding events have occurred and the outcomes are known. People are notoriously creative in providing explanations for past events (Fischhoff, 1982). The study by Wholstetter (1962) on the Pearl Harbor affair offers an excellent real-life illustration. Wholstetter reviewed and analyzed the debates of different congressional committees that were investigating the affair, and concluded that people are unable to ignore outcome knowledge, and thus cannot place themselves in the same conditions as the decision maker who did not have that knowledge. Evidently, outcome knowledge changes the entire mental model. With wisdom of hindsight, one is free to ignore all the "noise" created by irrelevant or unreliable cues. Knowledge based on hindsight may occasionally hinder the development of appropriate decision processes. As noted by Fischhoff (1982), "the very outcome which gives us the feeling that we understand what the past was all about may prevent us from learning anything from it" (p. 343). It is worthwhile to emphasize, in particular in the present context, that attempts to modify and reduce this bias have been met with relatively little success (Fischhoff, 1982).

JUDGMENTS AND DECISIONS: OUTCOME VERSUS PROCESS

It was proposed above that the standards for evaluating decision quality should be set in advance. But what should appropriate standards be, and what aspects of the decision should be evaluated? A fundamental question in this respect is whether a decision should be appraised according to the process by which it has been obtained, or by the corresponding outcome. There is no normative or prescriptive rule that determines whether decisions should be judged by process or outcome. It stands to reason that both are relevant, though the relative weights of these two types of considerations may vary depending on the nature of the decision and the goals to be achieved.

Most researchers suggest, at least implicitly, that the quality of a decision should be based on the inferred process by which it is made. Simon (1978), for instance, submitted that "Economics has largely been preoccupied with the *results* of rational choice rather than the process of choice" (p. 2). Similar views were expressed by Majone (1979, and in Vlek et al., 1984) and Wright and Murphy (1984). A somewhat different view has been recently presented by Christensen-Szalanski (1985): He proposed that whereas researchers are mainly interested in the process, most practitioners are concerned with outcomes. Casual observations may suggest that practitioners are primarily interested in outcomes and judge decisions accordingly. Yet, as will be shown below, despite the intuitive appeal to judge decision quality by outcomes, there are several reasons for avoiding such a procedure.

EVALUATION OF DECISIONS BY OUTCOME

Several questions can be raised when outcome is used as the evaluation criterion: What is a "good" (or desired) outcome and how should it be determined? Are all possible outcomes well-defined? Are they measurable? What legitimate inferences can be drawn from the outcome with regard to the preceding decision process?

Evaluating by outcome presupposes the existence of an objective and unambiguous criterion of evaluation (Majone, 1979). Many real-life decisions imply ill-defined problems and multiple, often ambiguous, goals for which there is no normative solution. Under such circumstances, judging by outcome may be extremely difficult and contain a large component of arbitrariness.

In most real-life situations, certainly the more complex ones, determining the relevant outcomes to be observed is not a trivial matter. A major characteristic of ill-structured problems (e.g., Simon, 1973) is uncertainty concerning the final product. Even when the outcome to be observed is rather well-defined, it is not always possible to record the outcome in an objective way. In particular, in complex situations, people often develop different mental models (e.g., Gentner & Stevens, 1983) and a considerable gap may exist between the real outcome of the decision and the way it is perceived by different actors. Possible disagreements may also arise concerning what parts of an outcome are relevant, and how they should be interpreted and measured. It is important that these issues be resolved in advance before the outcome is known.

An initial input requirement for any decision problem is a statement regarding the goals that should be achieved. This task is usually far from being trivial: to begin with, ill-defined problems are frequently associated with ill-defined goals. In addition, there are often several desired goals to be achieved, some of which may even be conflicting, and their relative priority may not be clear. Also, as noted by Fischhoff, Slovic, and Lichtenstein (1979), the values expressed by people seem to be highly labile: people do not always know what they want, not to mention change of goals and values in the course of time.

A fundamental distinction in decision theory is between resolving issues concerning uncertainty and issues concerning preferences. A decision involves two guesses, one concerning future outcomes and consequences, and one concerning future preferences (March, 1978). These two aspects are deeply interwoven, and the failure to separate between these two aspects is often a major source of ambiguity. Special care should be exercised not to confound two related yet essentially different questions: one is whether the goals that were set by the decision maker were indeed the desired ones, and whether they were realistic and attainable. Given the answer to this question, the following question is whether subsequent decisions that were made were indeed the best ones to achieve these goals (given the restrictions imposed by the environment).

Another potential problem concerns the possible inferences one can draw from outcome knowledge to the decision process preceding it. Such inferences are vulnerable to two types of potential errors: a favorable outcome could occur resulting from chance factors and thus does not necessarily imply that the preceding decision process was indeed the appropriate one. The other type of error may occur when an unfavorable outcome, again due to chance factors, is interpreted as evidence for an inappropriate decision process.

An important aspect of the above analysis is the frequency with which the decision (and the event following it) occurs. For example, imagine a bridge player who plays thousands of hands. For such a player, a disappointing outcome of a single hand does not indicate that his reasoning and strategies are not optimal, and thus inadequate. Bridge, like most real-life situations, contains a large element of uncertainty due to random noise.[2] Our bridge player may further

---

[2]Uncertainty in bridge is caused by two sources: one which is exposed by the physical environment, namely the random distribution of cards, and one due to human interaction, that is, the uncertainty about the opponents' reactions.

test his decision strategy in subsequent games, that is, increase his sample size, before making any inferences regarding his strategy. If he indeed adopts optimal decision strategies, then he should expect on the long run outcomes that are on the average favorable and optimal. The same player facing a decision in a large investment is in a completely different situation since his sample size in this instance may be reduced to a single case. We should thus distinguish between unique decisions that take place only once (or are very infrequent), and repeated decisions that occur quite often. Inferences about the decision process, derived from outcomes, can only be justified in the case of repeated events. In addition, and probably more important in the present context, the decision process may be fundamentally different for unique and repeated events (e.g., Keren & Wagenaar, 1986; Lopes, 1981). Consequently, possible modifications and attempts to improve the decision process should take this distinction into account.

Finally, even when possible outcomes are well-defined and a normative criterion is available, deviations from the normative prescriptions can occur in different directions. For instance, a poor outcome can be due to either choosing an inappropriate action or to lack of action. The underlying psychological mechanisms leading to each of these two decisions may be different, and consequently require different corrective procedures.

I have outlined some of the major problems involved in using outcomes as a criterion for evaluating decisions. Although the above list is not meant to be exhaustive, it is sufficient to point out the dangers involved in judging decisions solely by outcomes. Judgments of outcomes usually contain a large subjective component. This is particularly true for unique decisions, decisions that are being made only once and in which the outcome is highly vulnerable to different kinds of chance factors.

EVALUATION OF DECISIONS BY PROCESS

Research in decision making during the past two decades has been increasingly influenced by the information-processing paradigm developed within psychology since the early sixties. As a result, there has been a steady growth in research on descriptive aspects and an increasing interest in the strategies, mechanisms, and processes underlying judgment and choice (e.g., Einhorn, 1980; Einhorn & Hogarth, 1981; Kahneman, Slovic, & Tversky, 1982; Payne, 1976; Svenson, 1979).

How should one judge a decision according to the process by which it was reached? First, there are intricate problems involved in eliciting and identifying the different stages of the decision. Underlying most elicitation procedures are certain (at least implicit) assumptions that are not always justified. For instance, most analyses of the decision process (such as the use of a decision tree) assume that the decision process is serial, an assumption for which there is relatively little evidence (in most laboratory experiments such a serial order is imposed by the task, but the question as to how it occurs in real life remains open). A related problem is based on the observation that a decision may take place at a certain point in time, yet is usually preceded by several predecisional stages (Payne et al., 1978) that are as important as the final stage. The question is how to uncover these predecisional stages and their contribution to the final decision.

Another important underlying assumption concerns the principle of invariance (Tversky & Kahneman, 1986). Being normative in nature, this principle asserts that choices ought to depend solely on the situation itself, and not the way it is described and presented. In contrast to this assumption, there is ample research suggesting that people are highly vulnerable to framing effects (i.e., the way by which a problem is presented and consequently perceived) in violation of this assumption (e.g., Slovic, Fischhoff, & Lichtenstein, 1982; Tversky & Kahneman, 1986). Indeed, some suggest that preferences and choices are constructed during the elicitation process, and often may be sensitive to both framing effects and the elicitation method (e.g., Payne, 1982; Tversky & Kahneman, 1986).

Beside the problems involved in eliciting a person's decision or choice, there are intricate problems associated with eliciting the processes by which the decision was reached. Recently, there has been a growing trend to employ protocols and protocol analysis, a trend that has been stimulated by the work of Ericsson and Simon (1980). Despite the extensive use of this method, serious doubt remains with regard to its adequacy (e.g., Baron, 1988).

Disregarding the elicitation problem, for most complex decisions (e.g., What house to purchase? How to construct an investment portfolio?) we lack a normative or prescriptive theory of the decision process. There is thus rarely a yardstick to which an observed process can be compared. Formal normative models provide little help in this respect for several reasons: First, they are procedural in nature—offering a program or a computational strategy that should be followed. Such procedures usually provide only essential principles and guidelines but not the details, and may thus not be sufficient for guiding behavior. Moreover, normative models (e.g., utility theory) need inputs that in fact require subjective judgments and choices. Finally, for the more complex decisions of real life, normative models rarely exist.

A nice anecdotal example of the perils involved in assessing a decision by outcomes is provided by Vandenbroucke (1989). He reviewed the efforts of three scientists (Berkson, Eysneck, and Fisher), who were undoubtedly experts in their fields, to refute the belief that cigarette smoking may be a major cause of cancer. The arguments raised by these three scientists were certainly sound, and as noted by Vandenbroucke: "In themselves, the papers look so convincing that I wonder whether I would not belong to the skeptics (who questioned whether there is any causal relation between smoking and cancer) if this were the 1950s or early 1960s" (p. 5). Vandenbroucke thus concluded that assessment of scientific decisions may differ at different points in time, and that "what we decide to believe or not to believe, and why, will be largely subjective" (p. 5). This last statement is certainly not restricted to scientific decisions.

The major conclusion from this brief discussion is that even when normative guidelines exist, most decisions (except the simplest ones) are associated with a large subjective component. It is this subjective component that in turn can only be evaluated subjectively. In other words, judging decision by process, like much of decision analysis in general, remains to be to a large extent a "clinical" art (Fischhoff, 1983; von Winterfeldt, 1980). Despite the lack of rigorous criteria for evaluating decision processes, there are nevertheless some desirable defining characteristics of appropriate decision processes. While some of these characteristics are substantiated empirically, most are warranted by face validity.

DECISIONS AND JUDGMENTS: SKILL OR ART?

Related to the distinction of outcome-process is that between performance and competence (Kahneman & Tversky, 1982). The emphasis in judging decisions by performance is on observable behavior and in particular on outcomes. Judging competence entails an inference about capability (like latent traits), and goes beyond a particular observable event or outcome. The purpose of assessing competence is often part of an attempt to predict future performance.

Despite the apparent similarity, competence and performance judgment are not the same. Kahneman and Tversky (1982) distinguish in this regard between two basic types of judgmental errors: in one, which they label comprehension error, people fail to understand or recognize the (normative or, better, prescriptive) appropriate rule, indicating lack of competence. The other type is applications error, where it is assumed that comprehension exists and the failure is limited to a particular instance, a performance failure. Often, however, it is methodologically difficult, if not impossible, to determine the nature of an error. For instance, a reliable and robust finding in the problem-solving literature is the failure of subjects to respond correctly to Wason's (1968) verification task. Several subsequent studies (reviewed by Griggs, 1983), however, have shown that the same formal problem, framed in a more realistic and concrete manner, is correctly solved by a large proportion of the subjects. The debate concerning the nature of the processes underlying the verification task is not yet resolved, and the question whether it is a comprehension or an application error remains open.

The notion of competence implicitly assumes the existence of some skills, though it does not explicitly state how potential skills may be acquired. The question of main interest in the present context concerns competence in making decisions and judgments. What are the characteristics of such competence? Is it general, or is it task-specific? Regardless of whether the involved skills are specific or general, to what extent can they be learned? In what respects are decision experts better than laypeople in making decisions?

There is little research reported in the decision literature that has addressed these issues directly. Studies pertaining to these questions suggest that both experts and laypeople often perform poorly in different decision and judgmental tasks. Despite the evidence that decision makers often lack validity, reliability, use only very few cues, are poorly calibrated, and often rely on unwarranted heuristics (Shanteau, Chapter 5), many of the questions raised above still remain open for several reasons:

1. Many of the relevant studies have been conducted in the artificial laboratory, with a limited repertoire of tasks and a population restricted to undergraduates. Whether the results from these simple and artificial laboratory experiments can be generalized to the real world remains an open question (e.g., Winkler & Murphy, 1973).

2. Empirical results are often conflicting. For instance, there are several studies in the area of calibration and probability assessments that investigated potential differences in calibration between experts and laypeople. Are probability assessments of experts better calibrated than those of laypeople? The answer to this question is not unequivocal: Some researchers reported poor calibration (overconfidence), especially for different types of medical diagnosis (e.g., Lichtenstein et al., 1982). Chan (1982) reviewed various studies with experts and suggested that in several cases experts' probability assessments were not better than those of laypersons. In contrast, other studies of experts, in different fields, portray a different picture: weather forecasters (Murphy & Winkler, 1977), accountants (Tomassini, Solomon, Romney, & Krogstad, 1982), and professional bridge players (Keren, 1987) all were very well calibrated.

3. Many of the studies have used performance as their ultimate criterion. As mentioned, the inference from performance measures to competence is not always reliable.

Notwithstanding the above reservations, there is a growing body of literature (e.g., Kahneman, Slovic, & Tversky, 1982) suggesting that decision processes (or at least some components of these processes) often contain erroneous lines of reasoning, and reliance on heuristics that may result in unwarranted and unwanted decisions. Though recent research on judgmental heuristics and biases has certainly provided some initial insight into potential deficiencies of decision processes, it has remained fragmental. Perhaps the most disturbing fact concerning the existing research is that most of it has focused on relatively simple decision problems or only on fractions of the decision process. We still know very little about the processes underlying complex decisions which are multidimensional and often require several stages. It is in particular in those situations where one may question the existence of a systematic and robust decision process, and where it is not clear by which (if any), and to what extent is the decision process governed by specific identifiable skills.

The picture that emerges from the above brief review suggests that decision making, especially in complex situations, can be viewed to a large extent as an art. Note, however, that any art contains certain skills that can be identified and eventually learned. For instance, there are well-defined guidelines as to how to play a musical instrument. In learning to play the piano, for example, one may identify certain general necessary conditions that are conducive to good playing: it is possible to identify and describe the appropriate posture, manner of holding the hands over the keys, certain techniques of pressing the keys, efficient ways of reading notes (learn to read musical phrases [chunks], rather than single notes), and so forth.

However difficult these required skills may be, in principle they can accurately be described and eventually be learned. There will certainly be differences between individuals as to how well they may acquire these particular skills. We often account for these differences by referring to what is termed individual differences, but in fact the term often implies our lack of knowledge. In any event, even with those skills that can be identified and described, there is a certain component of art or intuition that apparently cannot be identified, and thus cannot be learned. More important, other facets of piano playing cannot be acquired in a systematic way. For instance, a piece can be played more or less musically. Although the ratings of different judges regarding the extent to which a piece was played musically may be highly correlated, the judgments remain subjective. The main reason is the lack of an unambiguous definition or description of what it means to play musically. As a consequence, little is also known regarding the component of musical talent that is innate as compared with what is or can be learned.

Decision making, in general, contains both components of skill and art. To be certain, decision sciences (and related areas such as operations research) have made remarkable strides in developing sophisticated models that may serve as efficient guidelines in order to attain certain goals, and solve a variety of complex problems. The development as well as the use of these normative tools clearly suggest the existence of some skill. Notwithstanding, all the normative models and sophisticated tools require a certain subjective input, and it is just that particular subjective input that is based on art rather then on skill.

I have elaborated on the distinction between art and skill because it has a direct bearing on the central question addressed in this chapter: Can judgments and decision processes be modified, and, in particular, can they be improved by learning? The answer, in my opinion, is a constrained and conditional yes. There are several sorts of qualifications: First, even if successful, the improvements that can be obtained via learning and the use of decision aids is modest and limited. Second, almost any decision (and certainly the more complex ones) require some *subjective* judgments for which one cannot specify an optimal algorithm. Apparently, a large component of decision making still relies on perceptive observations and good intuitions that at our current state of knowledge cannot be described accurately. Finally, decisions often rely on insights and creativity (in particular with regard to identifying alternative solutions) that cannot be prescribed.

LEVELS OF SUPPORT FOR IMPROVING DECISIONS AND JUDGMENTS

Attempts at improving decisions can be made at different levels. At the most general level one can provide global guidelines for improving decisions. For instance, people can be advised that structuring the decision problem is one of the most essential steps in the decision process (e.g., Pitz & Sachs, 1984). A useful tool to assist the decision maker in structuring the decision problem and providing a procedural framework for its solution is the method of *decision analysis* (e.g., Fischhoff, 1983; Hogarth, 1980). The structuring process should include a careful assessment of the structural interrelationships between different elements of the problem, an appraisal of all possible consequences and the corresponding uncertainties involved, a listing of alternative actions and their evaluation, and a planned search for information when needed (Hogarth, 1980). Decision analysis outlines the key questions that should be answered before the final decision should be made: Who is the decision maker and what are the goals to be attained? What are the relevant dimensions to be considered and their relative importance? What are the alternatives open for the decision maker? What constraints are imposed on each alternative? What are the uncertainties associated with each alternative?

To further assist the decision maker in structuring the problem in a systematic manner, one may suggest the use of a decision tree or a fault tree. Fischhoff, Slovic, and Lichtenstein (1978) have, however, pointed out several problems involved in the use of such trees. They suggest that people are quite insensitive to what has been left out of a tree, and that perceived importance depends on the particular way by which branches are constructed.

As another example of a general guideline, Einhorn and Hogarth (1987) proposed distinguishing between what they termed backward and forward reasoning in decision making. Thinking backward implies an intuitive assessment of the past searching for patterns, making links between different events (or variables), and tends to be diagnostic in nature (as was pointed out, however, such backward reasoning is vulnerable to the hindsight bias). Thinking forward implies a more quantitative mode of reasoning, in which different variables have to be weighed and integrated in order to yield a prediction. Einhorn and Hogarth claim that decision makers are often unaware of the differences between these two modes, and suggest that "this lack of unawareness makes decision makers stumble into mental traps that yield bad decisions" (p. 6). Unfortunately, it is often difficult, if not impossible, to prescribe exactly how backward and forward reasoning should be conducted. The best we can currently do is provide some general guidelines.

Although general guidelines, as in the examples mentioned above, may be helpful in assisting the decision maker in developing a systematic and analytic decision process, they have two related drawbacks. First, they still require a large amount of *subjective* input that may be crucial for the final decision. Nothing is said as to how to obtain these inputs, how to evaluate different inputs, and how to process them before inserting the different components into a more global process. For example, in the case of sensitivity analysis, how should one determine the relevant dimensions? Their relative importance? How should one estimate the corresponding uncertainties? The second, and related drawback is that general guidelines are procedural by nature. They specify a certain procedure that is often both inflexible and not sufficiently detailed. The final implementation of a method like decision analysis is highly dependent on the particular individual who performs it, and is based to a large extent on clinical judgments (Fischhoff, 1983). Neither the reliability or validity of the method have been submitted to serious scientific tests.

Attempts to improve decisions can also be made at a more specific (and less general) level, designed for a particular task (or class of tasks). The analysis of multi-attribute utility (Keeney & Raiffa, 1976), designed to help decision makers to assess their relative preferences for possible outcomes, is a good example. The strength of multi-attribute utility methods lies in the fact that they are based on a sound normative theory. As was mentioned, however, there is often a gap between normative theories and their potential application. Multi-attribute utility methods offer a relatively detailed description of how the method should be applied (e.g., Edwards, 1977). Notwithstanding, many improvisations may be required in the process of applying the methods that would depend on the "clinical" skills of the particular user. A more detailed discussion of the difficulties involved in applying those methods can be found in Beach and Barnes (1983), Keeney (1977), and Keeney and Raiffa (1976).

As another example of methods designed to assist the decision maker in a more defined and specific area, consider the statistical tools (mainly based on multiple regression) that may assist decision makers in better diagnosing (and thus using optimal treatment) and predicting human behavior (e.g., for personnel selection). There is by now a large literature and sufficient evidence to indicate that statistical judgments yield much better results compared with clinical methods[3] (e.g., Dawes, Fause, & Meehl, 1988). Apparently, despite the accumulating evidence, it seems that the majority of practitioners still rely on clinical or quasiclinical techniques.

Notwithstanding the superiority of the statistical methods, several points should be mentioned: First, statistical methods are far from providing perfect predictions and are certainly error-prone. Second, the use of statistical tools requires expertise and may often be quite expensive. Third, actuarial procedures are not available for many important decisions that are currently made in the clinical mode. Fourth, it may often be difficult, if not impossible, to obtain the data that are necessary as input to the statistical tools. Finally, and most important in the present context, the statistical tools do not identify the relevant variables that should be employed. Dawes and Corrigan (1974) proposed that for statistical decisions "the whole trick is to decide what variables to look at, and then know how to add" (p. 95). While the point they want to make, namely, that equal weighing of the variables is in most cases sufficiently good, to identify the relevant variables is the more serious problem for which there are no clear guidelines. Again, it is at that point (of identifying the relevant variables) that the process is often dependent on subjective inputs in which the "art" component is dominant.

For an even more task-specific example of attempts to improve the decision process, consider the efforts that were made to improve calibration of probability assessments. Calibration studies evaluate the appropriateness of assessors' subjective probability estimates, or confidence in their judgment. There is ample evidence to suggest that people's probability estimates are poorly calibrated; that is, there is a large discrepancy between their probabilistic assessments and the true probabilities. A pervasive and robust finding in the calibration literature is a strong tendency of overestimation of probabilities usually referred to as overconfidence (i.e., Lichtenstein, Fischhoff, & Phillips, 1982). Several attempts have been made to develop tools that may assist people in improving probabilistic assessments and reduce the overconfidence bias (for summaries, see Fischhoff, 1982; Keren, 1990).

Lichtenstein and Fischhoff (1980) exposed their subjects to detailed instructions (including examples of good and poor calibration) and then had several sessions of training with feedback. They reported a modest improvement, most of which was achieved in the first session. Arkes, Christensen, Lai, and Blumer (1987) also attempted to use initial training as a debiasing device. In their study, one group of subjects received several practice questions that appeared to be easy

---

[3]A major difference between clinical and statistical techniques, related to the earlier discussion, is that while the former relies much on intuitions and thus may be considered an art, the use of the latter is mainly based on the use of skills.

but were in fact quite difficult, and then received feedback on their answers prior to the experimental test. These subjects were less confident in the experimental session (in fact, they exhibited underconfidence) than several underconfidence groups. Keren (1985) had two identical groups with the exception that one group was instructed explicitly not to use ratings of 100% frequently, but reserve it for cases where "you are *absolutely sure* and you don't have the slightest doubt." As expected, the result of the instructions was to reduce the frequency of 100% estimates, and calibration (as assessed by traditional measures) has modestly improved. As Keren argued, however, the pattern of the calibration curve (except for ratings of 100%) was little affected by the instructions. The improvement, as was indicated by the formal measures, was more apparent than real.

The three studies briefly described above have several common attributes. All three studies were designed to achieve modifications for a rather specific task. All yield some modest improvements, but whether these can be generalized to other tasks is highly questionable. The improvement has been obtained by what can be termed "mechanical" means, which did not provide the subjects with a real understanding of how to achieve better calibration. In the Lichtenstein and Fischhoff (1980) study and the one by Arkes et al. (1987), subjects simply learned during the training sessions (through the feedback) that their probability estimates were too high, and lowered it accordingly. But the inference that they indeed became better calibrated is certainly unwarranted. In fact, in Arkes et al., the subjects became underconfident, which is not a desired outcome. Mere training on a task with feedback apparently has limited effect. Keren (1987) has shown that amateur bridge players, who were previously exposed to thousands of games and thus had ample experience and training with feedback, were very poorly calibrated in predicting game outcomes. As summarized by Fischhoff (1982), the methodological manipulations "have so far proven relatively ineffective and their results difficult to generalize" (p. 440).

Several points can be made with regard to this brief survey of some selected attempts for improving and aiding the decision process. At the more general level, it is possible to offer a general framework for the decision process and to present guidelines that may assist the decision maker in structuring the decision problem. However, such guidelines are open to many different interpretations and require a large amount of subjective inputs. Even a comprehensive method like decision analysis offers little help regarding judgments of what is relevant and important, appropriate interpretations of the circumstances under which a decision is taking place, correctly identifying potential constraints, and generating optimal and sensible alternative solutions. Apparently, good intuitions and a large amount of creativity are necessary conditions for which there is no substitute.

Cognitive tools that are designed for a restricted task (or class of tasks) usually contain more specific instructions, but those are often mechanical and inflexible. In addition, these also require some subjective input that may be crucial to the final outcome. Finally, and perhaps most importantly, many of the more specific aids are designed so as to alter and improve outcomes as indicated by certain formal measures. The question, however, remains whether these measures are indeed the most adequate ones for assessing the decision process. As pointed out by Lopes (1987), focusing entirely on quantitative measures may be misleading since it does not guarantee a qualitative improvement.

This last point deserves a further comment. Most of the methods that were designed to assist and improve decision making ultimately use the decision outcome as their main evaluation criterion. As mentioned in the introduction, whether these criteria are indeed valid may often be questionable. In addition, the use of outcome as a criterion, especially in unique decisions that are made only once, may be subject to chance factors and say little about the process. Finally, and most important, reliance on outcome may indeed suggest improvement in performance (as assessed by some formal measures) but little can be inferred about qualitative changes (i.e., competence).

The relatively modest success of methods for improving decisions and judgments reflects,[4] among other things, our insufficient knowledge of the mechanisms underlying decision processes. Research in decision making, which until recently was dominated by a normative approach, has gradually changed by shifting attention to behavioral aspects. During the last two decades psychologists have identified deeply rooted cognitive biases and unwarranted heuristics that may often hamper the decision process (Kahneman, Slovic, & Tversky, 1982). Despite this progress, we still lack a comprehensive and rigorous theory of judgmental heuristics and biases (Wallsten, 1983). Further advancement in developing methods for aiding and improving decisions, will require a better descriptive theory of decision making.

CLASSIFYING METHODS FOR IMPROVING DECISIONS: PROCEDURAL VERSUS STRUCTURE-MODIFYING TECHNIQUES

Several classifications of cognitive aids that are supposed to reduce potential biases and improve the decision process have been proposed. Fischhoff (1982), while discussing methods for reducing and eliminating cognitive biases, proposed to distinguish between three sorts of biases: *faulty tasks,* in which the source of the bias supposedly lies in the nature of the task. These include tasks

---

[4]It is of course difficult to assess the success of such methods, and as I have argued myself, they should certainly not be assessed against an absolute normative criterion. The assessment that the achievements of current methods is rather modest is thus based on a purely subjective judgment.

that are misunderstood or can be interpreted in different ways, or unfair tasks that contain some misleading elements (these are often tasks that occur in the experimental laboratory, and are not necessarily representative of real life), or artifacts. In such cases, the emphasis of corrective procedures should be on altering the nature of the task and enhancing the quality of instructions. In the case of *faulty judges,* the bias is supposed to lie mainly in the requisite cognitive skills of the judge. It is for this class of cases that psychological theory is most needed. Often, however, the distinction between the first two classes is not clear-cut, and we may then talk about a third category of biases due to *mismatch between judges and tasks.*

An alternative classification that is based primarily on the nature of the cognitive aid has been proposed by Arkes, Christensen, Lai, and Blumer (1987). While discussing methods for reducing overconfidence in probability assessments, they suggest distinguishing between *direct* and *indirect* approaches. In a direct approach, a person is explicitly presented with the alleged bias and is instructed to make an attempt to overcome it. In contrast, indirect methods are aimed at reducing the bias in a subtle implicit way, manipulating the variables that are supposedly closely related to the bias.

Recently, I have proposed another classification (Keren, 1990), between what I term *procedural* (or mechanical) methods, contrasted with *structure-modifying* techniques. Procedural methods supply the user with certain instructions or algorithms that attempt to manipulate certain variables relevant to the decision process or to a certain bias (in order to reduce it). The instructions in such cases may be directly related to the task, such as explicit warning of potential biases, telling a person to avoid certain operations (e.g., avoid using too-high estimates), explicitly stating a step-by-step procedure that the decision maker should follow. Indirect procedures may discourage guessing, offer higher incentives (a procedure that has relatively little effect, especially when monetary benefits are concerned), or propose a different response mode that may eventually reduce a certain bias. The common characteristics of such procedural methods is that the user is not necessarily forced to understand the internal structure of the problem or the task, nor is he or she required to comprehend the logic and design underlying the particular method. In certain respects the user is asked to follow the procedure blindly, in which case the method may cause some "technical" correction resulting in an improved performance as assessed by some quantitative measures. An essential issue, however, is that such procedural methods, by their nature, are not applicable to changing environmental conditions, and cannot be generalized to similar relevant tasks or decision problems.

Structure-modifying methods are those that lead to modifications of the internal representation of the task or decision problem. Such methods may provide a different perspective of the relevant "problem space" and provide new insights into relationships between different components of the decision problem. It is those types of methods that are still scarce, and require as a prerequisite an adequate cognitive theory.

The distinction between procedural and structure-modifying methods is similar, and closely related, to the classification of reasoning modes introduced in Wertheimer's (1959) seminal work on productive thinking. Wertheimer describes the manner by which children solve simple geometrical problems, such as calculating the area of a parallelogram. He differentiates between what he called blind solutions and genuine constructive solutions. Some of the children he observed followed blindly the procedure they were taught by their teacher and were successful in computing the area of a parallelogram as long as it was presented in the same way, namely in the same orientation. Once the parallelogram was rotated so that its base was the short side, they continued to apply the same procedure they memorized by rote learning and failed. In contrast, children who demonstrated structural understanding of the problem were quick to modify the procedure to the new circumstances, and applied it appropriately to obtain the correct answer. While Wertheimer's focus is on the child's cognitive processing (of the teacher's instructions), the emphasis in the present context is on the nature of the instructions and the training method: procedural methods lend themselves to blind processing, whereas structure-modifying methods lend themselves to genuine creative (and flexible) processing.

It should be emphasized that the distinction proposed here between procedural and structure-modifying methods is not dichotomous and should be viewed as two extremes on a continuum. Although most current techniques for improving decisions lie somewhere between these two extremes, most are more procedural methods.

A COMMENT ON EXPERTS

The question what is an expert and how expertise is acquired is closely related to several issues raised in this chapter. I will not dwell on the different definitions and characteristics of experts since these have been covered in length in other chapters. Regardless of the exact definition, a common underlying assumption regarding experts is that they perform better than nonexperts (and supposedly are more competent). What are decision experts, and what dimensions reflect their expertise?

Casual real-life observations as well as the existing decision literature suggest that expertise in decision making, if it exists at all, is task-specific. Although one can describe some very general attributes of a good decision process, it is knowledge or expertise in a particular domain that is a necessary requirement for making good decisions in that domain.

Current research portrays a mixed picture regarding experts' abilities: Some studies have shown that experts (in some areas) are often vulnerable to the same shortcomings as novices, whereas other studies have demonstrated the clear advantages of experts. Here I will only consider a few of the latter studies, and assess their implications for issues raised in the present chapter.

One area in which experts have a clear advantage, and which has been studied quite extensively, is the game of chess (De Groot, 1965; Simon, 1973). Apparently, skilled chess players encode the chess positions in chunks, and are able to identify quickly what are possible good moves. Simon (1973) suggested that the selection of moves is based, at least partly, on a set of rules that have been accumulated during years of experience. Two points are to be emphasized in relation to the previous discussion: One is that the main advantage of chess experts is in the structural representation of the problem. One may learn different strategies (i.e., openings, endgames, etc.), which are necessary but not sufficient requirements for expertise. What is important is whether these strategies are treated on the procedural level or are accommodated and used as structure-modifying methods. Second, training and experience, though important, are not sufficient for establishing expertise. While chess can be learned up to a certain level, further improvement requires certain cognitive modifications that we can still not specify. Chess experts can specify only portions of their expertise. The rest remains an art, a conclusion that is true for most complex decision tasks.

A second example of superb performance by experts concerns bridge players. Keren (1987) has shown that expert bridge players were extremely well calibrated in their probabilistic assessments of outcomes. A second group of lay bridge players showed poor calibration. It is important to emphasize that there was no difference between the two groups with regard to formal education in probability theory. Probabilistic assessments, however, are an inherent part of good bridge playing and the expert bridge players have acquired it through experience. It is important to emphasize that the second group of amateur players was composed of persons who played the game for many years and thus had a lot of experience, too. The difference between the two groups is probably due to the way in which this experience is processed and assimilated. For instance, every bridge player has experienced occasions in which the final outcome was against the odds. Bridge is a game with partial information and, consequently, uncertainty is always involved (even when one has an outstanding hand, things may go wrong, depending on how the rest of the cards are distributed among the remaining players). Apparently, the expert bridge players were able to incorporate this observation into their probability estimates: they very rarely used a probability of 1.0 (certainty), and whenever they did so they were right. In contrast, the amateur players were frequently certain (i.e., assigned a probability of 1.0), and were quite often wrong.

Experts in any specific domain have certainly a lot of experience which is consequently translated into knowledge. Experience and training, however, are at best necessary but not sufficient prerequisites for becoming an expert. It is the way by which the experience and training are absorbed, processed, accommodated, and structured that would determine its final use and the level of expertise. In a similar way, the success and effectiveness of methods and aids for improving decisions would largely depend on how the information and knowledge contained in such techniques is processed, assimilated, encoded, and applied. In that context, the claim was made earlier that structure-modifying methods would be more effective in securing such a productive process that would lead to a higher level of expertise.

REFERENCES

Arkes, H. R., Christensen, C., Lai, C., & Blumer, C. (1987). Two methods of reducing overconfidence. *Organizational Behavior and Human Decision Processes, 39,* 133–144.
Baron, J. (1988). *Thinking and deciding.* Cambridge: Cambridge University Press.
Beach, L. R., & Barens, V. (1983). Approximate measurement in a multi-attribute utility context. *Organizational Behavior and Human Performance, 32* 417–424.
Chan, S. (1982). Experts' judgments under uncertainty: Some evidence and suggestions. *Social Science Quarterly, 63,* 428–444.
Christensen-Szalanski, J. J. J. (1980). A further examination of the selection of problem solving strategies: The effects of deadlines and analytic aptitudes. *Organizational Behavior and Human Performance, 25,* 107–122.
Coombs, C. H., Dawes, R. M., & Tversky, A. (1970). *Mathematical psychology.* Englewood Cliffs, N.J.: Prentice-Hall.
Dawes and Corrigan (1974). Linear models in decision making. *Psychological Bulletin, B1,* 96–105.
Dawes, R. M., Faust, D., & Meehl, P. E. (1988). Clinical vs. actuarial judgment. *Science, 243,* 1668–1673.
De Groot, A. D. (1965). *Thought and choice in chess.* The Hague: Mouton.
Edwards, W. (1977). Use of multiattribute utility measurement for social decision making. In D. Bell, R. L. Keeny, & H. Raiffa (Eds.), *Conflicting objectives in decisions.* Chichester: Wiley.
Einhorn, H. J. (1980). Learning from experience and suboptimal rules in decision making. In T. S. Wallsten (Ed.), *Cognitive processes in choice and decision behavior.* Hillsdale, N.J.: Erlbaum.
Einhorn, H., & Hogarth, R. M. (1981). Behavioral decision theory: Processes of judgment and choice. *Annual Review of Psychology, 32,* 53–88.
Einhorn, H. J., & Hogarth, R. M. (1987). Decision making: Going forward in reverse. *Harvard Business Review, 65,* 66–71.
Ericsson, K. A., & Simon, H. A. (1980). Verbal reports as data. *Psychological Review, 87,* 215–251.
Fischhoff, B. (1982). For those condemned to study the past: Heuristics and biases in hindsight. In D. Kahneman, P. Slovic, & A. Tversky (Eds.), *Judgment under uncertainty: Heuristics and biases.* Cambridge: Cambridge University Press.
Fischhoff, B. (1982). Debiasing. In D. Kahneman, P. Slovic, & A. Tversky (Eds.) *Judgment under uncertainty: Heuristics and biases.* Cambridge: Cambridge University Press.
Fischhoff, B. (1983). Decision analysis: Clinical art or clinical science? L. Sjöberg, T. Tyszka, & J. Wise (Eds.), *Human decision making.* Bodafors: Doxa.

Fischhoff, B., Slovic, P., & Lichtenstein, S. (1978). Fault trees: Sensitivity of estimated failure probabilities to problem representation. *Journal of Experimental Psychology: Human Perception and Performance, 4,* 330–334.

Fischhoff, B., Slovic, P., & Lichtenstein, S. (1979). Subjective sensitivity analysis. *Organizational Behavior and Human Performance, 23,* 339–359.

Genther, D., & Stevens, A. (1983). *Mental models.* Hillsdale, N.J.: Erlbaum.

Goldsmith, R. W., & Sahlin, N. E. (1983). The role of second-order probabilities in decision making. In P. C. Humphreys, O. Svenson, & A. Vari (Eds.), *Analysing and aiding decision processes.* Amsterdam: North Holland.

Griggs, R. A. (1983). The role of problem content in the selection task and the THOG problem. In J. St. B. T. Evans (Ed.), *Thinking and reasoning: Psychological approaches.* London: Routledge & Kegan Paul.

Hogarth, R. M. (1980). *Judgment and choice.* New York: Wiley.

Janis, I. L., & Mann, L. (1977). *Decision making.* New York: The Free Press.

Kahneman, D., Knetch, J. L., & Thaler, R. H. (1986). Fairness and the assumptions of economics. *The Journal of Business, 59,* 285–300.

Kahneman, D., Slovic, P., & Tversky, A. (Eds.) (1982). *Judgment under uncertainty: Heuristics and biases.* Cambridge: Cambridge University Press.

Keeney, R. L. (1977). The art of assessing multiattribute utility functions. *Organizational Behavior and Human Performance, 19,* 267–310.

Keeney, R. L., & Raiffa, H. (1976). *Decisions with multiple objectives: Preferences and values tradeoffs.* New York: Wiley.

Keren, G. (1985). On the calibration of lay people and experts. Paper presented at the Tenth Conference of Subjective Probability, Utility, and Decision Making. Helsinki, Finland.

Keren, G. (1987). Facing uncertainty in the game of bridge: A calibration study. *Organizational Behavior and Human Decision Processes, 39,* 98–114.

Keren, G. (1990). Cognitive aids and debiasing methods: Can cognitive pills cure cognitive ills? In J. P. Caverni, M. Fabre, & M. Gonzalez (Eds.), *Cognitive biases.* Amsterdam: Elsevier.

Keren, G., & Wagenaar, W. A. (1987). Violation of utility theory in unique and repeated gambles. *Journal of Experimental Psychology: Learning, Memory, and Cognition, 13,* 387–391.

Lichtenstein, S., & Fischhoff, B. (1980). Training for calibration. *Organizational Behavior and Human Performance, 20,* 159–183.

Lichtenstein, S., Fischhoff, B., & Phillips, L. (1982). Calibration of probabilities: The state of the art to 1980. In D. Kahneman, P. Slovic, & A. Tversky (Eds.), *Judgment under uncertainty: Heuristics and biases.* Cambridge: Cambridge University Press.

Lopes, L. (1981). Decision making in the short run. *Journal of Experimental Psychology: Human Learning and Memory, 7,* 377–385.

Lopes, L. (1987). Procedural debiasing. *Acta Psychologica, 64,* 167–185.

Majone, G. (1979). Process and outcome in regulatory decision-making. *American Behavioral Scientist, 22,* 561–583.

March, J. G. (1978). Bounded rationality, ambiguity, and the engineering of choice. *Bell Journal of Economics, 9,* 587–608.

Mitroff, I., & Betz, F. (1972). Dialectical decision theory: A meta-theory of decision making. *Management Science Theory, 19,* 11–24.

Murphy, A. H., & Winkler, R. L. (1977). Can weather forecasters formulate reliable probability forecasts of precipitation and temperature? *National Weather Digest, 2,* 2–9.

Payne, J. W. (1976). Task complexity and contingent processing in decision making: An information search and protocol analysis. *Organizational Behavior and Human Performance, 22,* 17–44.

Payne, J. W. (1982). Contingent decision behavior. *Psychological Bulletin, 92,* 382–401.

Perrow, C. (1984). *Normal accidents: Living with high-risk technologies.* New York: Basic Books.

Pitz, G. F., & Sachs, N. J. (1984). Judgment and decision: Theory and application. *Annual Review of Psychology, 35,* 139–163.

Rasmussen, J., & Rouse, W. B. (1981). *Human detection and diagnosis of system failures.* New York: Plenum.

Simon, H. A. (1973). The structure of ill-structured problems. *Artificial Intelligence, 4,* 181–201.

Simon, H. A. (1978). Rationality as process and as product of thought. *American Economic Review, 68,* 1–16.

Slovic, P., Fischhoff, B., & Lichtenstein, S. (1982). Response mode, framing, and information processing effects in risk assessments. In R. M. Hogarth (Ed.), *New directions for methodology of social and behavioral science: Question framing and response consistency.* San Francisco: Jossey-Bass.

Svenson, O. (1979). Process descriptions of decision making. *Organizational Behavior and Human Performance, 23,* 86–112.

Tomassini, L. A., Solomon, I., Romeney, M. B., & Krogstad, J. L. (1982). Calibration of editors' probabilistic judgments: Some empirical evidence. *Organizational Behavior and Human Performance, 30,* 391–406.

Tversky, A., & Kahneman, D. (1986). Rational choice and the framing of decisions. *The Journal of Business, 59,* 251–278.

Vandenbroucke, J. P. (1989). Those who were wrong. *American Journal of Epidemiology, 130,* 3–5.

Von Winterfeldt, D. (1980). Structuring decision problems for decision analysis. *Acta Psychologica, 45,* 71–93.

Von Winterfeldt, D. (1983). Pitfalls of decision analysis. In P. Humphreys, O. Svenson, & A. Vari (Eds.), *Analyzing and aiding decision processes.* Amsterdam: North-Holland.

Vlek, C., Edwards, W., Kiss, I., Majone, G., & Toda, M. (1984). What constitutes a good decision? *Acta Psychologica, 56,* 5–27.

Wallsten (1983). The theoretical status of judgmental heuristics. In R. W. Scholtz (Ed.), *Decision making under uncertainty.* Amsterdam: Elsevier.

Wason, P. C. (1968). Reasoning about a rule. *Quarterly Journal of Experimental Psychology, 20,* 273–281.

Wertheimer, M. (1959). *Productive thinking.* New York: Harper & Row.

Wholstetter, R. (1962). *Pearl Harbor: Warning and decision.* Stanford, CA: Stanford University Press.

Winkler, R. L., & Murphy, A. H. (1973). Experiments in the laboratory and the real world. *Organizational Behavior and Human Performance, 10,* 252–270.

Wright, J. C., & Murphy, G. L. (1984). The utility of theories in intuitive statistics: The robustness of theory-based judgments. *Journal of Experimental Psychology: General, 113,* 301–322.

CHAPTER 3

Reliability and Validity in Expert Judgment

Fergus Bolger and George Wright

INTRODUCTION

As the world of human affairs becomes increasingly more complex, our reliance upon expert judgment grows correspondingly. Technological, economic, legal, and political developments—to name but a few—place ever-larger information-processing demands upon us, thereby forcing specialization. A single person can no longer be a master of his or her whole field and, consequently, knowledge becomes distributed among a number of specialist experts.

Against this background it is clear that the identification of factors contributing to expert judgment becomes a key issue. In other words, who is truly expert? How did they gain their expertise? And how accurate and reliable are their judgments?

Assessment of expertise is also becoming an increasingly important issue due to recent developments in information technology, arising out of research into artificial intelligence (AI). Expert systems (ES) and intelligent decision support systems (IDSS) are gradually finding favor in industry and commerce. Given that such systems model aspects of human judgment, it is evident that the quality of resulting systems depends on the quality of the information originally elicited. Accurate identification of high-quality expertise is therefore essential if

Fergus Bolger • Department of Psychology, University College London, Gower Street, London WC1E 6BT, England.   George Wright • Strathclyde Graduate Business School, 130 Rottenrow, Glasgow G4 0GE, Scotland.
Expertise and Decision Support, edited by George Wright and Fergus Bolger. Plenum Press, New York, 1992.

ES and IDSS are to become commercially viable propositions. Failure in the past to apply the fruits of AI research to commercial problems has been attributed to what Feigenbaum (1979) has termed the "knowledge acquisition bottleneck." Part of this bottleneck has largely been removed due to the development of some powerful techniques for eliciting knowledge from experts (see, for example, Wright & Ayton, 1987a, and Gammack, this volume). In our view, the only major obstacle now remaining to commercially viable ES and IDSS is locating *true* expertise in the domain of interest.

Judgment is also a prime input to decision analysis which is a major decision-aiding technique (see Watson & Buede, 1987; von Winterfeldt & Edwards, 1986), while in forecasting there are several purely judgmental techniques such as Delphi, Scenario Analysis, and Cross-Impact Analysis. In addition, the output of quantitative forecasting models is commonly adjusted by practitioner judgment by means of various "gateways" for the incorporation of judgment in decision analysis, forecasting tools, and knowledge-based systems (see, for example, Lawson, 1981; Soergel, 1983; Jenks, 1983; also Bunn, this volume). Such judgmental interventions are usually those of informed, expert opinion.

Thus expert judgment is essential input to both computer and noncomputer-based decision support. However, what do we know about the quality of expert judgment? If the assessments elicited from experts are poor in some way, then the results of any system of decision support will also be flawed (unless the assessments can be "debiased"). Can anything then be done to ensure the quality of expert judgment?

Various chapters in this volume address means for either selecting for expertise, or improving expert judgment if it is found to be lacking, but in order to be able to select and improve effectively it is first necessary to be able to assess the quality of judgment.

Ideally we would like to know if a judgment is correct or *valid*. In order to assess validity it is necessary to have an external, objective criterion (sometimes referred to as a "gold standard"). However, such a standard is not always available (especially in domains where expert judgment is most valued, i.e., where judgments must be made about variables whose behavior is uncertain because, for example, the behavior has yet to occur, is noisy, or is complex). When there is no gold standard it is usually possible to assess judgment in terms of its *reliability* which may be intrajudge reliability over time (consistency), interjudge reliability (consensus), or logical consistency (coherence).

In questionnaire design reliability is usually regarded as a necessary, but not sufficient prerequisite for validity. Put another way, valid judgments must be reliable, but reliable judgments are not necessarily valid (see Carmines & Zeller, 1979). For example, a meter rule which is actually 99cm long will reliably undermeasure (i.e., it is not a valid measure). However, an elastic rule which changes length from time to time is *both* unreliable and invalid.

In this chapter we shall:

- examine some of the methods used to assess the reliability and validity of expert judgment;
- review the results of some research using these methods;
- discuss some therapies which have been proposed as a consequence of these research findings;
- consider influences on judgment and its assessment which suggest that both the research findings and the consequent therapies may be questionable; and
- propose possible strategies for improving the reliability and validity of expert judgment.

We shall divide this discussion into two parts. In Part 1 we shall consider judgments about the likelihood of events (subjective probability estimates) since this type of judgment is the focus of much of the decision-making literature. In Part 2 we shall turn to other, nonprobabilistic judgments in order to see if the research conclusions regarding the quality of likelihood estimation generalize to judgments which do not require the expression of feelings of uncertainty.

PART 1: EXPERT PROBABILITY JUDGMENT

Expert probability judgment is essential input to many decision-aiding technologies including decision analysis (see Watson & Buede, 1987; von Winterfeldt & Edwards, 1986) and expert systems (see Kanal & Lemmer, 1986; Shafer, 1987; Lemmer & Kanal, 1988).

Calibration and Coherence

The two most frequently used approaches to the assessment of the quality of probability judgment are calibration and coherence. In studies of calibration, probability judgments are validated against an external objective standard. For perfect calibration, a set of test items all allocated a probability .X by a judge should also have a true base-rate probability of .X. For example, if one looked at all the days where a perfectly calibrated weather forecaster assessed the probability of rain to be .7, one would find that the true proportion of rain-days was also .7 (see Lichtenstein, Fischhoff, & Phillips, 1982, and Yates, 1990, for reviews). In studies of coherence, probability judgments are assessed in terms of the extent to which they conform to the axioms of probability theory. For example, a weather forecaster who assigns probabilities of .7 to both rain and no rain tomorrow is incoherent because his probabilities sum to more than unity. This contravenes the additivity axiom (i.e., for mutually exclusive and exhaustive events such as "rain"/"no rain," it is certain that either one or the other will occur thus formally: p(rain) and p(no rain) = p(rain or no rain) = 1).

Another axiom is the intersection law which states that the probability of event A and event B both happening is the product of the probability of event A multiplied by event B given that event A has occurred. Again, a judge who assessed the probability of the two events occurring together to be greater than the probability of either of the component events happening would be regarded as incoherent (see Brown, Kahr, & Peterson, 1974; Yates, 1990).

It has been argued that coherence and calibration are logically interrelated in the same manner as reliability and validity described above (see Wallesten & Budescu, 1983; Wright & Ayton, 1987b).

Laboratory studies of calibration have generally found judgment to be sub-optimal with two similar sorts of bias—overestimation and overconfidence—frequently being observed (see Lichtenstein et al., 1982; Yates, 1990, for reviews). Overestimation occurs when judges consistently give probability estimates to a set of test items which are larger than the true probabilities for that set of items. Overconfidence occurs when the assessments for high-probability items are too high but the assessments for low-probability items are too low. The overall quality of calibration performance can be measured in a variety of ways, but one of the most commonly used measures is the Brier (1950) score (also known as the probability score or quadratic score).

The Brier score is simply the squared difference between a judge's probability response (between 0 and 1) and the relevant standard or outcome index (e.g., 1 event happens, 0 event doesn't happen, or 1 statement is true, 0 statement is false). Of course, judges are usually asked to make more than one probability assessment, and their overall performance is expressed as the mean of Brier scores for individual items.

Perfect judgment on this measure results in a score of 0 and counter-perfect judgment a score of 1. However, in practice, most judges should attain Brier scores in the range of 0 to .25 because a score of .25 can be achieved by a judge with no knowledge about the test items. If this naive judge assumes that all events in the given situation are equally likely and therefore uniformly responds .5 s/he attains a mean Brier score of .25. If the judge can estimate the overall base rate (e.g., from historical data) then, by responding uniformly with this base rate, a Brier score somewhat better than .25 can usually be achieved. Strictly speaking, if expertise is to be attributed on the basis of a Brier score, then this score should be at least as good as that which could have been achieved by a judge uniformly responding with a historical base rate (see Yates, 1990, for a more complete discussion of these issues).

Calibration and Coherence Research with Expert Judges

We have reviewed 20 studies of expert calibration performance from four different task domains—weather forecasting, medical diagnosis, business, and sports—in terms of the standards and biases described above. These studies by no means exhaust the research literature; but we feel that they are representative with respect to the task domains considered and the spread of their conclusions. The studies and their findings are summarized in Table 1.

From this research, expert calibration performance appears to be quite variable, but in many cases less accurate than is possible on the basis of historical base-rate information. The same overestimation and overconfidence biases detected by the laboratory studies are manifest in several of the expert studies. On the other hand, in several instances, experts have been found to be very well-calibrated (e.g., Murphy & Brown, 1985 [weather]; Levi, 1986 [medical]; Balthasar et al., 1978 [business]; and Keren, 1987 [sports]). This provides what Wallesten and Budescu (1983) term an "existence demonstration," i.e., experts can make valid probability judgments under certain situations.

One explanation for poor calibration performance, where it has been found, might be lack of knowledge of the probability laws, leading to incoherence (remember the argument regarding the relationship between reliability and validity). A number of studies have demonstrated incoherence in students' probability judgment in the laboratory (e.g., Yates, 1990; Kahneman, Slovic, & Tversky, 1982, for reviews) although we have found few studies of coherence in experts. However, Eddy (1982) reviewing medical literature on the diagnosis of breast cancer from X rays found that physicians misunderstood the relationship between marginal probabilities (e.g., the probability of cancer, the probability of a positive test, etc.) and conditional probabilities (e.g., the probability of a positive test, given cancer). Schaefer, Borcherding, and Laemmerhold (1977) found that in 2 out of 3 tests, self-rated experts in soccer and statistics were slightly more coherent than nonexperts. In a similar study of coherence in self-rated experts in snooker we found experts to be significantly worse than nonexperts on conditional probability questions, but significantly more coherent on transitivity questions (Wright, Rowe, Bolger, & Gammack, in press). In a study of professional restaurant managers, Dube-Rioux and Russo (1988) found failure to conform to the additivity axiom with respect to the disjunction and conjunction of probable causes of restaurant failure.

Finally, DuCharme and Peterson (1968) and Youssef and Peterson (1973) found that the failure to revise probabilities in the light of new information to the extent required by Bayes' theorem was less marked in "ecologically valid tasks" than had previously been found in the laboratory (e.g., Phillips & Edwards, 1966; Phillips et al., 1966). Although the judges were not "experts" it can be argued that incoherence is reduced where judges can bring more knowledge to bear upon the task—as one would expect to be the case for true experts.

Thus, as with calibration, the picture with respect to coherence is unclear. Obviously, experts can demonstrate incoherence of the sort found in naive judges; but there is a suggestion that knowledge/expertise may, in some cases, lead to a reduction in the extent of this incoherence. Given this tension in the literature it remains to be demonstrated that it is poor probabilistic reasoning manifest as

Table 1. Summary of Studies of Expert Probability Judgment

Study	Task	Performance	Comments
Weather			
Root, 1962 Sanders, 1963	Prediction of a variety of weather conditions	Better than historical base rate (but worse for forecasts extended from one to two days). (Equivocal)	Sanders found that teachers of meteorology did NOT perform significantly better than students.
Stael von Holstein, 1971	Prediction of temperature and precipitation	Only 7 out of 30 judges were better than historical base rate. Overconfidence main reason for miscalibration. (Bad)	Research assistants performed better than professional meteorologists and statisticians.
Murphy and Winkler, 1977 Murphy and Brown, 1985	Short-term forecasting of precipitation, max/min temperature, and cloud cover	The judges were very well-calibrated and in some cases better than statistical models. (Good)	In 1977 study the best judge was the least experienced! There was significant improvement in performance between the two studies. Practical context.
Medicine			
Centor, Dalton, and Yates, 1984	Probabilistic diagnosis of "strep throat"	Better than historical base rate but not statistical models. Overdiagnosis of target disease observed. (Good)	Diagnosis made on basis of a physical examination of the patient.
Christensen-Szalanski and Bushyhead, 1981	Probabilistic diagnosis of pneumonia	Worse than a uniform judge. Gross overestimation of incidence of pneumonia. (Bad)	Diagnoses carried out in actual practice setting.
Dolan, Bordley, and Mushlin, 1986	Probabilistic diagnosis of heart disease	Worse than a uniform judge. (Bad)	Laboratory study.
Hlatky, Botvinick, and Brundage, 1982 Levi, 1986	Probabilistic diagnosis of coronary heart disease	Better than historical base rate and sometimes better than a statistical model. (Good)	Both studies were conducted in the laboratory. Small overestimation bias in '82 study.
Tierny et al., 1986	Probabilistic diagnosis of heart attack	Better than historical base rate. No significant bias found. (Good)	Study carried out in practical context.

52

Business			
Balthasar et al., 1978	Forecasting the technical success of R&D projects	No significant deviation from perfect calibration. (Good)	Study carried out in practical context.
Stael von Holstein, 1972	Prediction of stock prices	Only 3 our of 72 judges performed better than a uniform judge. (Bad)	Stock market experts> statisticians>business students>business teachers>investment bankers.
Yates, McDaniel, and Brown, in press	Prediction of stock prices and stock earnings	No judges outperformed a uniform judge. Predictions of stock earnings significantly>stock prices. (Bad)	Business students.
Sports			
Keren, 1987	Forecasting the number of tricks to be made in bridge	Very good calibration was found with no evidence of bias. (Good)	Experts were significantly better than novices. Novices were overconfident.
Yates, 1982 Yates and Curley, 1985	Predicting the outcomes of college basketball games	40% of the judges were worse than uniform. Expert significantly better calibrated than the novices. (Bad)	Only one expert studied and he demonstrated substantial bias.
Wagenaar and Keren, 1986	Assessing the probability of card combinations in blackjack	Overall the judges were well-calibrated but demonstrated large biases. (Equivocal)	Expert dealers were not significantly better calibrated than naive controls or statisticians.
Hoerl and Fallin, 1974	Predicting the probability of horse-race winners	No significant differences between bettor's subjective probabilities of winning and actual frequencies. (Good)	Analysis of historic data. Experts were bettors, not professional oddsmakers.
Snyder, 1978	Predicting the subjective odds the public creates through parimutuel betting in horse racing	4 of 5 professional handicappers not significantly different from punters" betting pattern but overestimation bias. (Equivocal)	The correspondence between the handicappers and the public was greater with experience.

incoherence that is responsible for poor calibration and also that the relationship between coherence and calibration is analogous to that between reliability and validity, as has been suggested by Wallesten and Budescu (1983) and Wright and Ayton (1987b). We shall examine some other possible causes of apparent lack of validity in probabilistic judgment shortly. However, first we shall address ourselves to a particular technique which is an attempt to remedy problems of judgmental validity suggested by the research literature by resolving incoherence—thereby implicitly assuming that poor coherence is a cause of poor validity.

Removing Incoherence in Probability Judgment

Most procedures for producing coherent probability judgments involve a technique called decomposition-recomposition (or divide-and-conquer). On the basis of the observation that most incoherence is manifest when judges attempt to revise or combine probabilities, it has been assumed that it is difficulties in computation (not probabilistic estimation per se) that lead to errors. From this assumption it has been proposed that judgment problems should be broken up (decomposed) into small elements for which judges supply probability estimates. Probability assessments for the problem as a whole are then produced by mechanically combining the individual component judgments on the basis of the laws and axioms of probability theory (a process known as recomposition). For example, rather than holistically assessing the probability of a patient having both high blood pressure and chest pains, a physician could individually estimate the marginal probability of high blood pressure and the conditional probability of chest pains given high blood pressure. The probability of high blood pressure and chest pains could then be calculated according to the laws of probability theory from the product of the marginal and conditional assessments.

Decomposition-recomposition has been shown to produce more coherent complex probabilities than those assessed by judges holistically (e.g., Edwards et al., 1968) but are these probabilities more valid, for example, in terms of calibration? Unfortunately there is little empirical evidence available to answer this question; however, Wright, Saunders, and Ayton (1988) found that calibration for mechanically recomposed probabilities was no better than calibration for holistically judged probability estimates. Further, no significant correlation was found between coherence and calibration performance. Our snooker forecasting study mentioned earlier produced similar findings, thereby adding a little weight to the conclusion that improving coherence does not necessarily increase validity. Why should this be the case?

As has already been indicated, greater reliability doesn't necessarily imply greater validity, although greater validity does imply greater reliability. Thus, the reliability-validity analogy might still hold for coherence-calibration although factors other than lack of knowledge and/or misapplication of the probability laws (manifest as incoherence) may be the most significant causes of miscalibration. However, in our snooker study we found that self-rated experts could use their domain knowledge to assess compound probabilities more accurately than nonexperts. If judges can make good judgments despite poor probabilistic knowledge, as was the case in this study, then it seems that the psychometric interpretation of the relationship between calibration and coherence is incorrect. If this is so, then it may be that in *psychological* terms incoherence and miscalibration are both symptoms of other heuristics and biases in reasoning, or that coherence and calibration are completely unrelated. If either is the case, then it follows that decomposition-recomposition is at most a partial solution to lack of validity in probabilistic judgment.

We propose that a major problem with the decomposition-recomposition approach lies in the assumption that the simple probabilities elicited for recomposition are themselves free of bias. If error exists in these simple assessments, then, to use the computer adage, recomposition will be a case of garbage in, garbage out. In fact, recomposition will attenuate any bias due to the large number of simple assessments that need to be combined in order to attain the single complex assessment required. We will now discuss various ways in which bias may enter into judges' probability assessments of all types (i.e., both simple and complex) with the view to suggesting measures for reducing such bias.

Processes Involved in Making and Assessing Probability Judgments

Typically, lack of validity in human judgment has been attributed to failings on the part of the judge. We would like to argue that this is not necessarily the case—indeed, as we have already indicated, good calibration has been demonstrated in a number of instances—instead, we propose that a skilled judge can give valid probability estimates if the task, and elicitation and assessment procedures are amenable (see also Shanteau, this volume).

We shall address each of these points in turn shortly; but first it might be useful to consider briefly the process by which a numeric probability estimate is arrived at and assessed. A plausible account (see, for example, Keren, 1987) is that, when asked to make a likelihood judgment, a judge will make an estimate on his/her subjective scale (of course, assuming judgment under uncertainty not perfect knowledge). This subjective value has then to be mapped onto the scale tendered by the investigator. Finally, a number of probability estimates are assessed against some external standard. Thus assessment of probability judgment can be considered a three-stage process, each stage of which may be subject to error or distortion due to the various influences outlined above (namely, features of the judgment domain, the judge, the elicitation process, and the assessment procedure—see Figure 1). If a judge is inexperienced in a domain and/or the true

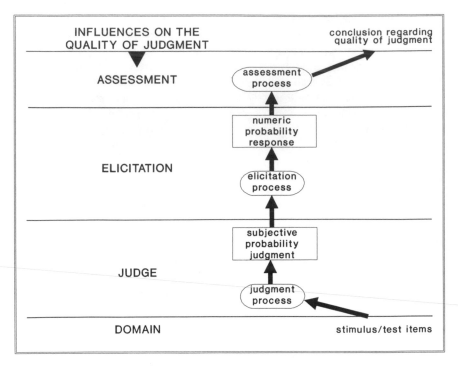

Figure 1. Some factors influencing the conclusion regarding the quality of expert probability judgment.

probability is difficult to assess (e.g., due to unreliable outcome feedback) then the initial subjective feeling will be liable to substantial error variance. However, a judge's feelings of subjective probability could covary perfectly with true probability in a domain, but this perfect correspondence might not be reflected in his or her numeric response used for calibration (e.g., if the judge was unfamiliar with the metric tendered by the investigator). Of course, usually there will be some error involved at each of the three stages.

It must be stressed here that the four types of influence indicated in Figure 1 are not strictly independent. For example, the elicitation and assessment processes can both be regarded as part of the judgment domain. However, we feel that it is useful for analytic purposes to differentiate general aspects of a judgment task related to domain knowledge (or the judge's "expertise") and those related to the specific contingencies of the "experimental" (elicitation and assessment) procedures. In practice, features of the judge are also likely to interact with features of the task to influence the final judgment. For example, the extent to which the outcome of a judgment lies in the future (e.g., as in the cases of forecasting versus almanac tasks) is likely to affect the perceived controllability of that event. This perceived controllability is also likely to be a function of locus of control, which can be regarded as a characteristic of the judge. Again, for analytic simplicity and clarity we shall, for the most part, treat aspects of judges and tasks separately, while acknowledging that an interactionist viewpoint is likely to be a more accurate reflection of reality. Accordingly, we shall proceed by examining in more detail some of these influences at each of the three levels of processing described.

Some Influences on the Reliability and Validity of Probability Judgments

Specifically, we propose that invalid probability judgments arise when:

- Features of the judgment domain are unfavorable, e.g., learnability is low, by which we mean that valid probability judgment cannot easily be learned due to the lack of relevant background data and/or outcome feedback upon which to base and revise domain models respectively (see Keren, this volume).
- The judge is unskilled due to, e.g.: lack of knowledge about the task domain; lack of knowledge about probabilities and/or how to manipulate them; cognitive characteristics such as the ability to integrate judgments and think probabilistically; and motivational factors such as preferred outcome in a forecasting scenario.
- Probability estimates are elicited in a manner which makes them unrepresentative of the judge's true feelings of subjective probability, e.g., by asking him or her to respond in an unfamiliar metric or by asking for probability estimates about inappropriate items or events.

Further, the conclusion regarding the quality of judgment can be biased when:

- The assessment method does not do justice to the probability estimates that have been elicited, e.g., by attempting to validate them against an inappropriate or faulty standard, or by imposing criteria that are too stringent (again, see Keren, this volume).

Evidence for the Proposed Influences on Probability Judgment

Our proposition—that the factors described above influence the validity and reliability of expert probability judgment, and the conclusion regarding the quality of expert judgment—is a hypothesis that remains to be formally tested. However, there is some evidence to support our claims. For example, calibration for future events has generally been found to be better than for past (see Wright & Ayton, 1986)—thus features associated with the task can influence the validity of probability judgment. Also, Wright and Ayton (1984, 1987b) have found that calibration performance is significantly influenced by factors such as perceived desirability and controllability of events—these can be regarded as being partly a function of the judge and partly a function of the task (see the discussion of person-situation interaction above).

Also, life underwriters may be considered to be experienced risk assessors (see Shanteau, 1978), but what sort of risk do they know about? We have found in an unpublished study that an overestimation bias in life underwriters' estimations of the marginal probability of death by various causes (e.g., what is the probability of dying from cancer?) was much reduced when the probabilities they were asked to judge were replaced by conditional questions (e.g., what is the probability of dying of cancer, once cancer has been diagnosed?). Although both questions entail risk assessment, only the conditional questions were encountered by the underwriters during everyday practice. This demonstrates that it is necessary to go beyond the superficial features of a task to establish whether expert subjects are indeed experienced with the test items presented. Lack of ecological validity of this sort (i.e., matching subjects to tasks) might be responsible for some of the other findings of poor calibration in experts (see Table 1), e.g., Yates, 1982; Yates and Curley, 1985; and Yates et al., in press—judges were not truly expert; Wagenaar and Keren, 1986—blackjack dealers do not need to make any probability assessments in their job; other studies may have similar problems, although it is difficulty to establish retrospectively due to lack of detail in the experimental reporting.

Further, judges' psychological and cognitive characteristics have been shown to influence the process of probability judgment. For example, Wright and Phillips (1984) proposed two alternative cognitive styles which they called probabilistic and nonprobabilistic thinking. In the former case, a judge would be inclined to take a probabilistic rather than a deterministic view when confronted with uncertainty, would revise probabilities in the light of new information, and would take uncertainties into account when making plans. Conversely, a nonprobabilistic thinker would think in terms of yes/no/don't know rather than probabilities, undervalue fallible information, and would not tend to revise his or her decisions. Phillips and Wright (1977) and Wright et al. (1978) found cross-cultural differences in calibration which seem to support these alternative cognitive styles.

Motivational factors may also influence the judgment of probabilities. For example, a number of studies have shown that desirable events are perceived as having a greater probability of occurring than undesirable events which are matched in terms of their true probability of occurrence (e.g., Zakay, 1983; Milburn, 1978).

It has been shown in a number of studies that the overconfidence bias in calibration is largely dependent on task difficulty—the harder the task, the greater the overconfidence (e.g., Clarke, 1960; Nickerson & McGoldrick, 1965; Pitz, 1974; Lichtenstein & Fischhoff, 1977). Ferrell and McGoey (1980) and Smith and Ferrell (1983) present a mathematical model based on signal detection theory which predicts patterns of calibration performance. They propose that a judge transforms his or her subjective feelings regarding probability into a decision variable which is partitioned according to fixed cut-off values. Each partition of the decision variable is mapped onto a particular probability response. If task difficulty changes, but the cut-off values are held constant (as would be the case for judges receiving no feedback regarding their calibration performance) then the hard-easy effect is observed. In other words, overconfidence in calibration can largely be regarded as a problem of transforming subjective feelings of likelihood (changing cut-offs) into the experimenters' metric (for a similar account see Poulton, 1989, under response contraction bias).

The metric in which probability responses are elicited can take a number of different forms (e.g., percentages, point probability estimates, odds, relative frequencies, etc.). Depending on which metric is used the judge's task of turning subjective feelings of uncertainty into measurable/usable numeric estimates can be either helped or hindered. For example, judgments can appear biased when ratio responses are asked for (e.g., how many times more likely are the Japanese to have put a man into space in the next decade than the U.K.?). According to Poulton (1989), judgments become distorted because judges' subjective scales are naturally equal-interval linear scales, not a log scale, as is required for ratio judgments. In a ratio judgment task, judges typically fail to adjust their inner subjective units adequately to the new scale, if they adjust at all. Accurate conversion of subjective units onto a ratio/log scale is impossible, claims Poulton, because subjective scales are not anchored at zero. Imagine two straws A and B protruding from someone's fist. You are told that the concealed ends of the two straws are level, and you can see that B protrudes farther than A. You therefore know that B is longer than A, but not by how may times, as you do not know how far the ends of the straws extend into the fist. Poulton (1989) presents a large number of examples from experimental work in a variety of domains to support his claims.

Ratio judgments are frequently elicited in research into the quality of judgment, especially when it is thought that the judges will not be familiar with making judgments in the conventional objective metric (e.g., mortality rate per 100,000). For this reason probability judgments are often elicited in the form of odds. Poulton shows that overconfidence in odds judgment found by, among others, Fischhoff, Slovic, and Lichtenstein (1978) can be attributed to the logarithmic response bias (pp. 153–154). Odds judgments have been elicited because untrained judges have been shown to misunderstand probabilities (see, e.g., Kahneman, Slovic, & Tversky, 1982).

So far, in this discussion of elicitation and assessment effects, we have not differentiated between the sorts of probability estimates that are being elicited (e.g., marginal or conditional? simple or complex? intersections or disjunctions?); this is because calibration studies have not tended to differentiate either.

However, it seems to us that an important question must be: is it easier to make some sorts of probability assessments than others?

Decomposition-recomposition implies that simple probabilities, such as marginals and conditionals, are easier for judges to assess than complex probabilities, such as intersections, disjunctions, and unions. However, what little empirical evidence we have suggests that if simple probability assessments are easier than complex, then this has little or no consequence in terms of calibration performance. One possible reason for this rather surprising finding (given what we said earlier regarding the relationship between calibration and task difficulty) is that the problem decompositions used may not have been appropriate for the judges. In other words, the judges may have been framing the problem differently to the experimenter so that neither the complex nor the simple probabilities elicited were calibrated by the experimenter against an appropriate standard.

Problems associated with framing have been extensively demonstrated with regard to probability judgment (see Tversky & Kahneman, 1981). For example, Barnes (1984) presented judges with a variety of word problems which had previously been framed by experimenters as sample-size problems, conjunction problems, and prior-probability problems. However, when allowed to categorize the problems in their own way, judges framed the questions quite differently, for example: maths problems, problems about people, and so on. Further, the process by which the judges solved the problems—and consequently their answers—were found to be quite consistent with their own framing, but incorrect in terms of the experimenters' frame. Thus seemingly low validity might arise during elicitation through judges answering different questions from the ones the investigator thought s/he was asking, thereby leading to validity of judgment to be assessed against an inappropriate standard. The judges' framing is likely to be the one in which they are skilled, thus it is the experimenters' understanding of the problem which may be incorrect.

This conflict in framing between judge and experimenter may result in problems being decomposed into the wrong primitives, in other words, ones that are inappropriate to the problem and/or that the judge knows nothing about. This relates back to the point we made earlier regarding the life underwriters. If the experimenters' framing of underwriting was one of marginal risk assessment and underwriters were asked to make judgments of this type, then they will be (were) inaccurate. This is either because the underwriters were attempting to do something unfamiliar, or because they incorrectly thought that the question was about conditional risk assessment. Of course, a characteristic of expertise is surely that an expert can discriminate questions of a type s/he can answer from those s/he cannot (see Shanteau, this volume). However, in an experimental setting the demand characteristics are usually such that judges have little recourse to complaint, and thus may feel obliged to accept the experimenters' framing of the problem.

PART 2: RELIABILITY AND VALIDITY
IN NONPROBABILISTIC JUDGMENT

Probability judgment is of great relevance to the concerns of this book because it is usually in decision making under *uncertainty* where expertise is most valued, and where decision support is most needed. However, probabilistic judgment is not the only area to which expertise is attributed, nor where decision support is sought. In many cases it is the ability to judge the occurrence of an event or the size of a quantity itself that is of central interest and *not* the subjective feeling of (un)certainty associated with that judgment. Of course there has to be some uncertainty associated with the event or quantity, or else there would be no need for judgment, expertise, nor decision support. Uncertainty arises because of the inadequacy of domain models as a result of lack of knowledge regarding the factors that will determine the target quantity or event. This may come about, for example, due to domain complexity, measurement difficulties, lack of usable outcome feedback, or unreliable source information.

Multidimensional Judgment Tasks

Many of the domains where nonprobabilistic judgment has been tested derive uncertainty principally from complexity—judges are required to integrate many disparate pieces of information (or cues) into a single global judgment. Einhorn (1974) proposes that there are several stages in such a "multidimensional" judgment task. First, a judge must be able to identify the relevant cues to be considered, then these cues must be assessed in some manner in order for them to be categorized (i.e., how do the cues covary?). Next, it is necessary to assess the relative weightings of various cues in order that one can combine individual cues into global judgments. In Einhorn's (1974) example, three medical pathologists assessed histological information presented as biopsy slides (there were 10 cues, the extent of each being coded by the judges on a 6-point scale). On the basis of this information the judges had to make global judgments regarding disease classification.

Each stage of this multidimensional judgment process is dependent on domain knowledge which may be subject to bias. In other words, you need to be experienced in a domain in order to make valid decisions of this type, but this knowledge might be incorrect (or be applied inappropriately), thereby leading to lack of validity. For example, Einhorn's pathologists might make mistakes determining the relevant cues to assess (although in the experiment the 10 cues were predetermined), perceptual errors in assessing the extent of particular cues, mistakes in weighting the cues, or errors in combining the weighted cues into global judgments. In actual fact, the most variation occurred with respect to the weighting process.

Research Findings

Both the reliability and validity of expert judgment have been assessed for multidimensional decision tasks. For example, with respect to reliability, Einhorn's three pathologists were found to agree on how cues clustered, but not on how to weight them—test-retest reliability was fair. Sixty-three independent auditors (Ashton, 1974) were found to agree moderately well and were highly consistent regarding their evaluations of clients' systems of "internal control." However, 40 grain inspectors (Trumbo, Adams, Milner, & Schipper, 1962) showed very poor levels of agreement and consistency in their codings of percentage foreign material and damaged ears in wheat samples. More positively, though, 12 maize judges agreed fairly well on their forecasts of yield from perceptual analyses of ears (Hughes, 1917; Wallace, 1923). Also, seven banking executives (Kabus, 1976) showed considerable consensus and consistency in their assessment of the value of future interest rates. Further, 21 community health workers agreed highly on their estimates of postaccident incapacity time (Hindle & Torkzadeh, 1985).

In the same studies (and a few others) expert judgment has also been validated against some external "objective" standard. For example, the pathologists (Einhorn, 1974) were found to be reasonably accurate in their diagnoses as compared to the "true" state of the patients as determined by autopsy . . . and Ashton's (1974) auditors agreed .89 with statistically derived estimates. However, the grain inspectors (Trumbo et al., 1962) made poor estimates in comparison with laboratory analyses demonstrating consistent overestimation biases . . . while the maize judges' (Hughes, 1917; Wallace, 1923) forecasts of yield only correlated .2 with actual yield. More positively again, the bankers' (Kabus, 1976) forecasts of interest rates corresponded well with actual movements and, likewise, the estimates of incapacity time made by the community health workers also corresponded well with reality (Hindle & Torkzadeh, 1985).

The other studies we have found of the validity of expert non-probabilistic judgment, where reliability has not been measured, all demonstrate poor accuracy and/or biases. For example, a number of studies have demonstrated that professionals do not always select the most appropriate information as the basis of their decisions. A study by Ebbesen and Konecni (1975) of court judges' sentencing decisions found that judges used only a very restricted subset of available dimensions when making their decisions. Further, Gaeth and Shanteau (1984) found that expert soil judges referred to soil materials when categorizing samples which were irrelevant to the discriminations they were trying to make. Similar findings come from studies of State Registered Nurses (Shanteau, Grier, Johnson, & Berner, 1981), of audit managers (Bamber, 1983), and of personnel selectors (Nagy, 1981).

A common finding in laboratory studies is that subjects tend to overestimate quantities that they are asked to judge (e.g., Lichtenstein, Slovic, Fischhoff, Layman, & Coombs, 1978)—although sometimes very large quantities are underestimated. This effect has been found in 236 physicians' estimates of percentage mortality and nonfatal complications after invasive diagnostic procedures (Manu, Runge, Lee, & Oppenheim, 1984). Also, eight clinical psychologists' predictions of behavior from case studies (Oskamp, 1965) and 88 security analysis firms' estimates of share earnings (Basi, Carey, & Twark, 1976) manifest overestimation biases.

Several other judgmental biases have been demonstrated in professionals. For example, in a study of estate agents, Northcraft and Neale (1987) found that the arbitrary valuations tendered by property owners influenced both estate agents' and students' subsequent property valuations, thereby demonstrating the *anchoring and adjustment* heuristic (estimates are insufficiently adjusted away from an initial—and possibly arbitrary—baseline "anchor"; see Tversky & Kahneman, 1974). *Availability* of information (either physically, or how easily it comes to mind, op. cit.) has also been shown to affect the judgments of experts in the same way as nonexperts. For example, research by Christensen-Szalanski, Beck, Christensen-Szalanski, and Koepsell (1983) found that expert physicians overestimated the risk of certain diseases in a similar manner to that of a comparison group of students. The source of this particular bias was identified as being the physicians' exposure to patients suffering from the diseases in question. Further, from our own investigation of judgment by life underwriters we have anecdotal evidence to suggest that underwriting decisions are often subject to the *representativeness* bias (a form of stereotyping; see Tversky & Kahneman, 1974)—relatively "poor" predictors of risk, such as the applicant's name, sex, and occupation seem often to be given greater weight in risk assessment than "good" predictors, such as age and medical history.

Although the above review of the literature is not exhaustive, we believe it to be representative of the research into expert nonprobabilistic judgment. In general, it seems that expert judgment is more likely to be reliable than it is valid—and that where judgment is accurate it is usually reliable too, but not vice versa. It thus seems that the relationship between reliability and validity assumed in psychometrics (reliability is a necessary but not sufficient prerequisite of validity) holds better for nonprobabilistic judgment than it does for calibration and coherence.

Bootstrapping

Another method of validating judgments is against some normative model. Whereas probability judgment is validated against the axioms of Bayes' theorem, multidimensional judgments have been validated against least-squares regression models (e.g., Frenkel-Brunswik, 1943; Kelly & Fiske, 1951; Hammond, 1955; Hoffman, 1960; see also Clark, this volume). Typically this sort of approach has been taken for the assessment of medical decision making and, overwhelmingly, the earlier studies—including those cited above—showed that judgment is inaccurate in comparison to a few fairly simple mathematical formulae.

The linear models against which judgment is validated are essentially models of the multidimensional decision process described above. The experts themselves are required to specify the cues (predictor variables) and the weights, while the rest of the process is carried out mechanically. In the majority of cases where this "policy capturing" procedure has been used (the selected cues and weights are said to represent the experts' preferred diagnostic policy) the model of the judges' behavior outperformed the judges themselves. Dawes noted:

> I know of no studies in which human judges have been able to improve upon optimal statistical prediction. . . . A mathematical model by its very nature is an abstraction of the process it models; hence if the decision-maker's behaviour involves following valid principles but following them poorly these valid principles will be abstracted by the model.

Dawes and Corrigan (1974) have called the replacement of the decision maker by his/her model "bootstrapping" because although the model is based on the decision maker's input it allows him/her to "pull him/herself up by his/her own bootstraps" and thereby perform better than s/he would have done unaided.

The underlying rationale of linear models as decision support is therefore similar to the decompose-recompose procedure for probability judgment. In other words, primitive judgments are considered to be fine, but the computational errors by judges—which lead global judgments based on these primitives to be invalid—can be eliminated by mechanical means. However, this account does not strictly run true, given the experimental findings that expert judgment is more often reliable than not although rarely valid. In other words, one would expect computational deficiencies to show up as poor reliability in the same way that difficulties in combining probabilities are manifest as incoherence. Thus it appears that lack of validity in experts' nonprobabilistic judgment might—like probabilistic judgment—also be largely a product of other factors such as task variables, heuristics and biases of the judges, and elicitation and measurement techniques.

Conflicting Findings

Before we go on to discuss the various influences on the reliability and validity of nonprobabilistic judgment, we would like first to refer to a research tradition which suggests that expert judgment may not be as poor with respect to validity as so far suggested. In addition we would also like to discuss some recent research which shows that in certain situations expert judges can outperform linear models.

In the first instance, various studies by Shanteau and his colleagues have found many qualities to admire in expert judges. For example, expert livestock judges were found to be "careful, skilled, and knowledgeable decision makers" (Phelps & Shanteau, 1978). In another study (Shanteau & Phelps, 1977) live-stock judges were found to be better able to recognize situations that could not be tackled by routine methods than were novices. Also, Ettenson, Krogstad, and Shanteau (1985) found that expert auditors have "an enhanced capacity to get to the crux of the problem" in comparison to novices. Shanteau (1987, and this volume) claims that their positive results regarding expert judgment are a conse-quence of focusing on factors which lead to *competence* in experts (in contrast to most studies, which attempt to identify lack of competence relative to some gold standard or normative model). By comparing experts with novices, Shanteau and his colleagues have been able to demonstrate performance advantages for experts and also identify particular characteristics of experts which leads to this im-proved performance (see Shanteau, this volume, for details of these charac-teristics). He concludes (Shanteau, 1987) that the poor showing of experts in much of the judgment and decision-making literature can be attributed to the use of inappropriate criteria for the assessment of expertise.

Implicit in Shanteau's (1987) account is the suggestion that normative mod-els may be inappropriate *psychological* models. In other words, experts have many skills in their repertoire which are not captured by normative models—the corollary of this being that normative models will not be able to perform as well as experts in situations where the (unmodeled) skills of the human experts come into their own. This view has gained some support from recent research which shows that experts can indeed outperform such models in certain situations.

Studies of bankruptcy prediction and credit-worthiness assessment by loan officers (see Libby, 1975; Shepanski, 1983) found overall accuracy to be high, while a number of their expert subjects outperformed linear models utilizing the same data sources. Whitred and Zimmer (1985) suggest that these findings are due to loan officers exploiting valid nonlinear relationships in the data which are not captured by the regression models. Shepanski (1983) comes to the same conclusions and also proposes that, due to the cost and difficulty of gathering the relevant data in this domain, in real-world credit valuations the composition and size of information employed in decisions will change frequently. Such flexibil-ity in data search cannot be captured easily by statistical modeling, which is better suited to repetitive forecasts with a static number of predictor variables.

Thus, in domains where linearity is not an appropriate assumption and/or constant data sources are not available, expert judgment may prevail over statis-tical techniques. However, linear models are extremely robust to violations of linearity, so it is unlikely that many situations will occur where experts can win out with regard to this task feature. With regard to data flexibility, as Dawes, Faust, and Meehl (1989) have pointed out, the small number of studies that have provided clinicians with access to preferred sources of information have generally shown the superiority of the statistical model. But, as these authors note, human judgment can theoretically improve on statistical modeling by recognizing events which are not included in the model's formula, and that countervail the actuarial conclusion. Dawes et al. argue that such events are rare but this is the exact situation where forecasting practitioners advocate the need for judgment.

Indeed, recent studies by Johnson (1988) and Blattberg and Hoch (1989)—not cited in Dawes et al. (1989)—provide evidence of the quality of human judgment compared to statistical models when "broken leg" cues are part of the data available for decision making. The term broken leg cue is from Meehl (1954). He noted that the knowledge that a certain person had just broken his or her leg would invalidate any predictions of a person's movements (e.g., to the theater, particular restaurants, etc.) based on historical statistical data. To illustrate, Chalos (1985) investigated the ability of an outcome-based credit-scoring model to assess financial distress and compared the performance of the model with that of loan review committees and individual loan officers. The major finding was that the loan review committees significantly outperformed the model and the individual loan officers. The model was a stepwise discriminant model built using eight financial ratios as cue variables. The loan review officers/committees had additional information for each judgment in the previous three years' financial statements. Chalos's results indicated that loan committees may be beneficial, and that the additional time required may be more than offset by the reduction in loan cost errors. In a related study, Casey and Selling (1986) used MBA students as subjects in a bankruptcy-prediction task and noted that if a firm's specific financial data do not provide a clear-cut signal of its financial viability, then subjects would be expected to incorporate available prior probability information into their judgment processes. Such additional information is, of course, likely to be available in the workaday situations to loan officers.

Some Reasons for the Findings of Poor Expert Judgment

The work of Shanteau and his colleagues, and the recent findings regarding the applicability of linear models, both show—as we have already seen for probability assessments—that reliable and valid judgments are a function of an interaction between features of the task domain and characteristics of the judge. In fact, many of the same person and task variables influence nonprobabilistic judgment and probabilistic judgment. However, we would like to make some

ments are much more open to specific methodological criticisms than research into nonprobabilistic judgment.

CONCLUSIONS

In the preceding sections we identified features of judges and tasks and also aspects of the elicitation and assessment processes, all of which could influence the validity (or perceived validity) of expert judgment.

Given these various sources of potential error, what is the best strategy for eliciting reliable and valid judgments? In order to reduce potential error due to task features, we propose that before attempting to elicit probability judgments a thorough task analysis should be performed: Can the judge attain good probability performance through experience? Is the feedback loop subject to treatment effects? Is it possible to validate judgment against some external standard? What sort of judgments are required?

If the conclusion of the task analysis is that good judgmental performance cannot be attained in the task domain in question and/or there are no available objective criteria for validating judgment, then the best strategy is to ensure judgments are reliable (consistent, coherent, and demonstrate consensus).

A judge should also be assessed to determine how experienced s/he is in the task domain, how familiar s/he is with the response metric, and what his or her stake is in the outcome of the judgment—many motivational biases can be reduced if the relevant assessment procedures are used (see Stael von Holstein & Matheson, 1979). If appropriate, each judge could also be assessed to determine whether s/he is a probabilistic thinker, and whether s/he demonstrates incoherence.

Judges lacking in domain experience should obviously be passed over for the elicitation process. Judges will more often than not be lacking in probabilistic knowledge. As we have pointed out, this seems not necessarily to preclude the ability to make valid probability estimates. However, training in the concepts and laws of probability should still help to remove incoherence which may, in some situations, act as a barrier to valid probability judgment. Having a naturally probabilistic thinker as a judge should make this training significantly easier. Despite the above doubts decomposition-recomposition can still usefully be applied to remove any remaining incoherence, while in nonprobabilistic contexts bootstrapping can often be used to remove computational inconsistencies, thereby potentially leading to an improvement in validity.

From the practical standpoint of providing decision support it is worth noting that expert systems can provide means for modeling contextual information—such as broken leg cues—which is not represented in statistical models

specific comments on the conclusion of poor validity of expert nonp
judgment.

In some instances expert performance has been tested outside the c
the professional experience of the experts in question. For example, c
have been asked to make predictions rather than the diagnoses normally
of them (e.g., Oskamp, 1962; Christensen-Szalanski et al., 1983; Man
1984). Also, corn judges have been required to predict yield on the bas
examination of ears of maize, whereas their usual task is to judge the ae
qualities of ears presented at shows (Hughes, 1917; Wallace, 1923). It
argued that in these cases the expert is at no particular advantage over
subjects and, therefore, it is unsurprising that they demonstrate the same
ciencies in judgment.

In other studies experts have been required to express judgments in
familiar metrics. For example, grain inspectors have been asked to idei
percentages of foreign material in samples, whereas they are used to estima
the weight of these materials (Trumbo et al., 1962). Assuming that skil
expressing subjective judgmental feelings in conventional metrics comes larg
from practice at doing so, and allowing that there may be only a limited degree
transfer between different conventional metrics, then many of the findings
poor judgment among experts may be the consequence of their inexperience wit
the mode of responding required by the experimenters.

A third reason to question the findings of some of the expertise research is
that the subjects studied may not have been sufficiently experienced to qualify as
"experts." The authors of the majority of papers we have reviewed do not specify
the professional qualifications of their chosen experts, nor do they indicate the
length of time spent "on the job," or describe the nature of the subjects' work
duties in any detail. It therefore seems likely that in most cases expertise is
attributed on the basis of role rather than proven performance. In some other
studies it is clear the "experts" were *not* highly experienced in the domain in
question as, for example, is the case with the student soil judges used by Gaeth
and Shanteau (1984) and the trainee independent auditors studied by Ashton
(1974).

Most of the measurement/elicitation issues described in the first section are
also relevant here. The points regarding probability response formats and assessment criteria are obviously specific to calibration experiments but the general
message—that the way judgments are elicited and validated influences the conclusions reached regarding the quality of these judgments—still holds true (see
also Keren, this volume, for a general discussion of measurement issues). It
should be noted that assessment of probability judgment has become much more
"paradigm-bound" (i.e., tied to particular methods) than is the case for research
into other kinds of judgment. The consequence of this is that calibration experi-

(see Gammack, and also Clark, this volume). Expert systems also have an advantage over linear models due to their having greater psychological plausibility—i.e., they are not "black boxes" whose workings are opaque to users—expert systems can therefore provide justifications for decisions which statistical systems cannot (see Bunn, this volume, on the necessity of providing "audit trails" in decision support).

The elicitation process itself can be examined, for example: Is the response mode appropriate to the task and judge? How are you framing the problem? How is the judge framing the problem? What are the relevant primitives for decomposition-recomposition or bootstrapping? One possibility here is to allow the experts to select their own primitives, perhaps by means of knowledge elicitation techniques (see Gammack, this volume) or decision conferencing (see Reagan-Cirincione & Rohrbaugh, this volume) or by encouraging them to interact with one of the many computer-based decision aids now available implementing, among other things, decision trees (e.g., SUPERTREE); systems dynamics (e.g., DYNAMO); or influence diagrams (e.g., DAVID). All of these allow the user to interactively create probabilistic or nonprobabilistic domain models on the basis of his/her experience then test out their models on real or fictitious data (see Bunn, this volume, for a discussion of the pros and cons of such aids).

Two practical steps that can be taken to ensure that the elicitation process influences the validity of probabilistic judgment as little as possible include using percentages rather than odds or probabilities, and encouraging judges to decompose the problem in their own way—probability estimates for primitives thus derived can then be combined mechanically if incoherence is suspected.

Finally, with respect to the method of assessment one should ask: How discriminable are the test alternatives? Who controls the task difficulty? What alternative outcome indices are available for validation? Which is the most appropriate?

Suggested solutions here are to only use outcome indices which are based on an external gold standard (i.e., not those based on a judge's own performance, such as proportion correct selections), and to attempt to assess task difficulty independently of the test instrument itself.

The above solutions to problems of lack of reliability and/or validity in expert judgment can only be tentative because there is still much we don't understand about the factors influencing judgmental performance, and how they interact. Since, as we have suggested, the experimental assessment and elicitation techniques themselves constitute factors influencing the quality of judgment, progress toward a complete understanding of such factors is likely to be slow.

The contradictory research findings which we have reported here regarding the reliability and validity of expert judgment are testament to the many problems associated with experiments in this area. We have suggested that much of the variability in the conclusions regarding expert judgment is due to the failure of experimenters to systematically control for the factors (task, person, elicitation, and assessment) which moderate performance.

Put another way, the "ecological validity" of expert judgment research has not been constant across the board. For example, tasks have not been equated in terms of difficulty, judges in terms of their levels of experience, nor assessment methods in terms of their fidelity. Thus knowledgeable judges on easy tasks assessed by measures which truly reflect their skills have led to good performance being manifest, whereas inexperienced judges on difficult tasks and/or assessed by "unfair" measures have manifest poor performance. Without a systematic manipulation of person and situation variables, we shall never discover how experts and tasks interact to produce reliable and valid judgments . . . and therefore we shall be largely guessing when it comes to the design and implementation of decision support.

Unfortunately there are several problems in implementing the research strategy we are proposing:

- finding a sufficient number of experts
- finding experts who have homogeneous experience both in terms of quantity and quality
- understanding the nature of the expert's task in sufficient detail to enable the effect of task factors to be explored
- controlling in naturalistic settings aspects of the task such as the feedback loop, degree of probabilistic reasoning required, and the desirability of the outcome
- eliciting and measuring performance without distorting it (especially given constraints on experts' time).

The easy answer is to return to the laboratory, but then we are no longer dealing with people who have any experience or stake in the judgment tasks; therefore generalizability to real experts is questionable. We suggest that there is a need to progress along both paths to make headway (i.e., research both in the laboratory and the real world) and also believe it could be profitable to attempt more naturalistic laboratory experiments (e.g., train subjects on more realistic tasks—i.e., in terms of complexity, different types of reasoning involved, etc.).

To conclude, we shall return to the questions raised in the introduction to this chapter. First, who is truly expert? In objective terms this must be anyone who demonstrates significantly more valid judgment than persons or systems not accredited with expertise. In some instances it may be necessary to settle for more reliable judgment (i.e., if no gold standard is available). Second, how accurate and reliable is expert judgment? We have indicated that while the majority of "experts" do not fulfill the above criterion for expertise, some do and many of the others might qualify if their performance had been tested in a more "ecologically valid" manner. We therefore conclude that expert judgment can be highly reliable and accurate; that high reliability is more common than high validity; that reliability and validity are often poorly related; that most studies of experts find judgment is neither reliable nor valid; that many more studies would find good expert judgment if conducted in a manner which allowed experts to demonstrate their skills; and that even so there will be many instances where expert judgment is suboptimal due to a variety of task and person factors influencing the decision-making process. In response to the third major question raised in the Introduction—can anything be done to ensure the quality of judgment? We have proposed a number practical steps that can be taken to reduce potential sources of poor reliability and validity. It must be stressed, however, that even by taking these steps, validity cannot be ensured in any domain where there is a degree of uncertainty (i.e., all those in which expert judgment is most useful). This said, the more we understand about the factors influencing judgmental performance—and how to measure this performance accurately—the more we can hope to know true expertise when we encounter it, and support expert decision making when it is lacking. With this in mind we have suggested that more research is still required in order to maximize the reliability and validity of expert judgment.

REFERENCES

Ashton, R. H. (1974). Cue utilization and expert judgments: A comparison of independent auditors with other judges. *Journal of Applied Psychology, 59*(4), 437–444.

Balthasar, H. U., Boschi, R. A. A., & Menke, M. M. (1978). Calling the shots in R and D, *Harvard Business Review,* May–June, 151–160.

Bamber, E. M. (1983). Expert judgment in the audit team: A source reliability approach, *Journal of Accounting Research, 21,* 396–412.

Barnes, V. E. (1984). *The quality of judgment: An alternative perspective.* Unpublished doctoral dissertation, University of Washington, Seattle, Wash.

Basi, B. A., Carey, K. J., & Twark, R. D. (1976). A comparison of the accuracy of corporate and security analysis forecasts of earnings. *The Accounting Review, 51,* 244–254.

Brier, G. W. (1950). Verification of forecasts expressed in terms of probability. *Monthly Weather Review, 78,* 1–3.

Brown, R. V., Kahr, A. S., & Peterson, C. (1974). *Decision analysis for the manager,* New York: Holt, Rinehart & Winston.

Blattberg, R. C., & Hoch, S. J. (1989). Database models and managerial intuition: 50% model and 50% manager. Report from the Center for Decision Research, Graduate School of Business, University of Chicago, May.

Centor, R. M., Dalton, H. P., & Yates, J. F. (1984). Are physicians' probability estimates better or worse than regression model estimates? Paper presented at the sixth Annual Meeting of the Society for Medical Decision Making, Bethesda, MD, November.

Carmines, E. G., & Zeller, R. A. (1979). *Reliability and validity assessment.* Sage University Papers Series, Beverly Hills, CA.

Casey, C., & Selling, T. I. (1986). The effect of task predictability and prior probability disclosure on judgement quality and confidence. *The Accounting Review, 61,* 302–317.

Chalos, P. (1985). The superior performance of loan review committee. *Journal of Commercial Bank Lending, 68,* 60–66.

Christensen-Szalanski, J. J. J., & Bushyhead, J. B. (1981). Physicians' use of probabilistic information in a real clinical setting. *Journal of Experimental Psychology: Human Perception and Performance, 7,* 928–935.

Christensen-Szalanski, J. J. J., Beck, D. E., Christensen-Szalanski, C. M., & Koepsell, T. D. (1983). Effects of expertise and experience on risk judgments. *Journal of Applied Psychology, 68,* 278–284.

Clarke, F. R. (1960). Confidence ratings, second-choice responses, and confusion matrices in intelligibility tests. *Journal of the Acoustical Society of America, 32,* 35–46.

Dawes, R. M., & Corrigan, B. (1974). Linear models in decision-making. *Psychological Bulletin, 81,* 95–106.

Dawes, R. M., Faust, D., & Meehl, P. (1989). Clinical versus actuarial judgement. *Science, 243,* 1668–1673.

Dolan, J. G., Bordley, D. R., & Mushlin, A. I. (1986). An evaluation of clinicians' subjective prior probability estimates. *Medical Decision Making, 6,* 216–223.

DuCharme, W. M., & Peterson, C. R. (1968). Intuitive inference about normally distributed populations. *Journal of Experimental Psychology, 78,* 269–275.

Dube-Rioux, L., & Russo, J. E. (1988). An availability bias in professional judgment. *Journal of Behavioral Decision Making, 1,* 223–237.

Ebbesen, E., & Konecni, V. (1975). Decision making and information integration in the courts: the setting of bail. *Journal of Personality and Social Psychology, 32,* 805–821.

Edwards, W., Phillips, L. D., Hays, W. L., & Goodman, B. C. (1968). Probabilistic information processing systems. *IEEE Transactions on Systems Science and Cybernetics, 4,* 248–265.

Eddy, D. M. (1982). Probabilistic reasoning in clinical medicine: problems and opportunities. In D. Kahneman, P. Slovic, & A. Tversky (Eds.), *Judgment under uncertainty: Heuristics and biases.* Cambridge: Cambridge University Press.

Einhorn, H. J. (1974). Expert judgment: Some necessary conditions and an example. *Journal of Applied Psychology, 59,* 562–571.

Ettenson, R., Krogstad, J., & Shanteau, J. (1985). Schema and strategy shifting in auditors' evidence gathering. In *Symposium on Audit Judgment and Evidence Evaluation,* USC School of Auditing.

Feigenbaum, E. A. (1979). Themes and case studies in knowledge engineering. In D. Michie (Ed.), *Expert systems in the microelectronic age.* Edinburgh: Edinburgh University Press.

Frenkel-Brunswik. (1943). Motivation and behaviour. *Genetic Psychology Monographs, 26,* 121–265.

Ferrell, W. R., & McGoey, P. J. (1980). A model of calibration for subjective probabilities. *Organizational Behaviour and Human Performance, 25,* 32–53.

Fischhoff, B., Slovic, P., & Lichtenstein, S. (1978). Fault trees: Sensitivity of estimated failure probabilities to problem representation. *Journal of Experimental Psychology: Human Perception and Performance, 4,* 330–334.

Gaeth, G. J., & Shanteau, J. (1984). Reducing the influence of irrelevant information on experienced decision makers. *Organizational Behaviour and Human Performance, 33,* 263–282.

Hammond, K. R. (1955). Probabilistic functioning and the clinical method. *Psychological Review, 62,* 255–262.

Hindle, T., & Torkzadeh, G. (1985). Estimating the incapacity time caused by home accidents, particularly using expert judgments. *Journal of the Operational Research Society, 35,* 193–201.

Hlatky, M., Botvinick, E., & Brundage, B. (1982). Diagnostic accuracy of cardiologists compared with probability calculations using Bayes' Rule. *American Journal of Cardiology, 49,* 1927–1931.

Hoerl, A., & Fallin, H. K. (1974). Reliability of subjective evaluation in a high incentive situation. *Journal of the Royal Statistical Society, 137,* 227–230.

Hoffman, P. J. (1960). The paramorphic representation of clinical judgment. *Psychological Bulletin, 57,* 116–131.

Hughes, H. D. (1917). An interesting seed corn experiment. *Iowa Agriculturalist, 17,* 424–425.

Jenks, J. M. (1983). Non-computer forecasts to use right now. *Business Marketing, 68,* 82–84.

Johnson, E. J. (1988). Expertise and decision under uncertainty: Performance and process. In Chi, M. T. H., Glaser, R. & Farr, M. J. (Eds.), *The nature of expertise,* Hillsdale, NJ: Erlbaum.

Kabus, I. (1976). You can bank on uncertainty. *Harvard Business Review,* May–June, 95–105.

Kahneman, D., Slovic, P., & Tversky, A. (1982). *Judgment under uncertainty: Heuristics and biases.* Cambridge: Cambridge University Press.

Kanal, L. N., & Lemmer, J. F. (Eds.) (1986). *Uncertainty and artificial intelligence.* Amsterdam: Elsevier.

Kelly, E. L., & Fiske, D. W. (1951). *The prediction of performance in clinical psychology.* Ann Arbor, Mich: University of Michigan Press.

Keren, G. (1987). Facing uncertainty in the game of bridge: a calibration study. *Organizational Behaviour and Human Decision Processes, 39,* 98–114.

Lawson, R. W. (1981). Traffic usage forecasting: is it an art or a science? *Telephony,* February, 19–24.

Lemmer, J. F., & Kanal, L. N. (1988). *Uncertainty and artificial intelligence 2.* Amsterdam: Elsevier.

Levi, K. R. (1986). *Numerical likelihood estimates from physicians and linear models.* Unpublished doctoral dissertation, University of Michigan, Ann Arbor.

Libby, R. (1975). Accounting rations and the prediction of failure: Some behavioral evidence. *Journal of Accounting Research,* Spring, 150–161.

Lichtenstein, S., & Fischhoff, B. (1977). Do those who know more also know more about how much they know? *Organizational Behavior and Human Performance, 20,* 159–183.

Lichtenstein, S., Slovic, P., Fischhoff, B., Layman, M., & Coombs, B. (1978). Judged frequency of lethal events. *Journal of Experimental Psychology: Human Learning and Memory, 4,* 551–78.

Lichtenstein, S., Fischhoff, B., & Phillips, L. D. (1982). Calibration of probabilities: The state of the art to 1980. In D. Kahneman, P. Slovic, & A. Tversky, (Eds.), *Judgment under uncertainty: Heuristics and biases,* New York: Cambridge, 1982.

Manu, P., Runge, L. A., Lee, J. Y., & Oppenheim, A. D. (1984). Judged frequency of complications after invasive diagnostic procedures: Systematic biases of a physician population. *Medical Care, 22,* 366–370.

Meehl, P. E. (1954). *Clinical versus Statistical Prediction: A Theoretical Analysis and Review of the Evidence,* Minneapolis, Minn: University of Minnesota Press.

Meehl, P. E. (1957). When shall we use our heads instead of the formula? *Journal of Counselling Psychology, 4,* 268–273.

Milburn, M. A. (1978). Sources of bias in the prediction of future events. *Organizational Behavior and Human Performance, 21,* 17–26.

Murphy, A. H., & Brown, B. G. (1985). A comparative evaluation of objective and subjective weather forecasts in the United States. In G. Wright (Ed.), *Behavioral decision making,* New York: Plenum.

Murphy, A. H., & Winkler, R. L. (1977). Reliability of subjective probability forecasts of precipitation and temperature. *Applied Statistics, 26,* 41–47.

Nagy, G. F. (1981). *How are personnel selection decisions made? An analysis of decision strategies in a simulated personnel selection task.* Unpublished doctoral dissertation, Kansas State University.

Nickerson, R. S., & McGoldrick, C. C. (1965). Confidence ratings and level of performance on a judgmental task. *Perceptual Motor Skills, 20,* 311–316.

Northcroft, M. A., & Neale, G. B. (1987). Experts, amateurs and real-estate: An anchoring and adjust perspective in property pricing decisions. *Organizational Behavior and Human Decision Processes, 39,* 84–97.

Oskamp, S. (1962). The relationship of clinical experience and training methods to several criteria of clinical prediction. *Psychological Monographs, 76.*

Oskamp, S. (1965). Overconfidence in case-study judgments. *Journal of Consulting Psychology, 29,* 261–265.

Phelps, R. H., & Shanteau, J. (1978). Livestock judges: how much information can an expert use? *Organizational Behavior and Human Performance, 21,* 209–219.

Phillips, L. D., Hays, W. L., & Edwards, W. (1966). Conservatism in complex-probabilistic inferences. *IEEE Transactions on Human Factors in Electronics, 7*–18.

Phillips, L. D., & Edwards, W. (1966). Conservatism in a simple probabilistic inference task. *Journal of Experimental Psychology, 72,* 346–354.

Phillips, L. D., & Wright, G. (1977). Cultural differences in viewing uncertainty and assessing probabilities. In H. Jungermann & G. de Zeeuw (Eds.), *Decision making and change in human affairs.* Dordecht, Holland: Reidel.

Pitz, G. F. (1974). Subjective probability distributions for imperfectly known quantities. In L. W. Gregg (Ed.), *Knowledge and cognition,* New York: Wiley.

Poulton, E. C. (1989). *Bias in quantifying judgments.* New York: LEA.

Root, H. E. (1962). Probability statements in weather forecasting. *Journal of Applied Meteorology, 2,* 163–167.

Sanders, F. (1963). On subjective probability forecasting. *Journal of Applied Meteorology, 2,* 191–201.

Schaefer, R. E., Borcherding, K., & Laemmerhold, C. (1977). Consistency of future event assessments. In H. Jungermann & G. de Zeeuw (Eds.), *Decision making and change in human affairs.* Dordecht, Holland: Reidel (pp. 331–345).

Shafer, G. (1987). Probability judgment in artificial intelligence and expert systems. *Statistical Science, 2,* 3–44.

Shanteau, J. (1978). When does a response error become a judgmental bias? *Journal of Experimental Psychology: Human Learning and Memory, 4,* 579–581.

Shanteau, J. (1987). Psychological characteristics of expert decision makers. In J. Mumpower, L. D. Phillips, O. Renn, & Y. R. R. Uppuluri (Eds.), *Expert judgment and expert systems* (pp. 289–304). Berlin: Springer-Verlag.

Shanteau, J., & Phelps, R. H. (1977). Judgment and swine: Approaches and issues in applied judgment analysis. In M. F. Kaplan & S. Schwartz (Eds.), *Human judgment and decision processes in applied settings.* New York: Academic Press.

Shanteau, J., Grier, M., Johnson, J., & Berner, E. (1981). "Improving decision making skills of nurses". In *ORSA-TIMS Proceedings,* Houston, Tex: ORSA-TIMS.

Shepanski, A. (1983). Tests of theories of information processing behaviour in credit judgment. *The Accounting Review, 58,* 581–599.

Smith, M., & Ferrell, W. R. (1983). The effect of base rate on calibration of subjective probability for true-false questions: model and experiment. In P. Humphreys, O. Svenson, & A. Vari (Eds.). *Analyzing and aiding decision processes,* Amsterdam: North Holland.

Snyder, W. W. (1978). Horse racing. *Journal of Finance, 33,* 1109–1118.

Soergel, R. F. (1983). Probing the past for the future. *Sales and Marketing Management, 130,* 39–43.

Stael von Holstein, C. S. (1971). An experiment in probabilistic weather forecasting. *Journal of Applied Meteorology, 10,* 635–645.

Stael von Holstein, C. S. (1972). Probabilistic forecasting: An experiment related to the stock market. *Organizational Behavior and Human Performance, 8,* 139–158.

Stael von Holstein, C. S., & Matheson, J. (1979). *A manual for encoding probability distributions,* Menlo Park, Cal: SRI International.

Tierney, W. M., et al. (1986). Physicians' estimates of probability of myocardial infarction in emergency room patients with chest pain. *Medical Decision Making, 6,* 12–17.

Trumbo, D. A., Adams, C. K., Milner, M., & Schipper, L. (1962). Reliability and accuracy in the inspection of hard red winter wheat. *Cereal Science Today, 7,* 62–71.

Tversky, A., & Kahneman, D. (1974). Judgment under uncertainty: Heuristics and biases. *Science, 185,* 1124–1131.

Tversky, A., & Kahneman, D. (1981). The framing of decisions and the psychology of choice. *Science, 211,* 453–458.

Von Winterfeldt, D., & Edwards, W. (1986). *Decision analysis and behavioral research,* Cambridge: Cambridge University Press.

Wagenaar, W. A., & Keren, G. B. (1986). Does the expert know? The reliability of predictions and confidence ratings of experts. In E. Hollnagel, G. Mancini, & D. D. Woods (Eds.), *Intelligent decision support in process environments.* Berlin: Springer-Verlag.

Wallace, H. A. (1923). What is in the corn judge's mind? *Journal of the American Society of Agronomy, 15,* 300–304.

Wallesten, T. S., & Budescu, D. V. (1983). Encoding subjective probabilities: A psychological and psychometric review. *Management Science, 29,* 151–173.

Watson, S. R., & Buede, D. M. (1987). *Decision synthesis.* Cambridge: Cambridge University Press.

Whitred, G., & Zimmer, I. (1985). The implications of distress prediction models for corporate lending. *Accounting and Finance, 25,* 1–13.

Wright, G., & Ayton, P. (1984). Judgmental forecasting: Personologism, situationism or interactionism? Paper presented to the *2nd European Conference on Personality,* Bielefeld, FRG.

Wright, G., & Ayton, P. (1986). Subjective confidence in forecasts: A response to Fischhoff and MacGregor. *Journal of Forecasting, 5,* 117–123.

Wright, G., & Ayton, P. (1987a). Eliciting and modelling expert knowledge. *Decision Support Systems, 3,* 13–26.

Wright, G., & Ayton, P. (1987b). The psychology of forecasting. In G. Wright & P. Ayton (Eds.), *Judgmental Forecasting,* Chichester, UK: Wiley.

Wright, G., & Phillips, L. D. (1984). Decision making: Cognitive style or task-related behaviour? In H. Bonarius, G. van Heck, & N. Smid (Eds.), *Personality psychology in Europe.* Lisse: Swets & Zeitlinger.

Wright, G., Saunders, C., & Ayton, P. (1988). The consistency, coherence and calibration of holistic, decomposed and recomposed judgmental probability forecasts. *Journal of Forecasting, 7,* 185–199.

Wright, G., Phillips, L. D., Whalley, P. C., Choo, G. T. G., Ng, K.-O., Tan, I., & Wishuda, A. (1978). Cultural differences in probabilistic thinking. *Journal of Cross-Cultural Psychology, 9,* 285–299.

Wright, G., Rowe, G., Bolger, F., & Gammack, J. (1991). Coherence, calibration and expertise in judgmental probability forecasting. *Organizational Behavior and Human Decision Processes.*

Yates, J. F. (1982). External correspondence: decompositions of the mean probability score. *Organizational Behaviour and Human Performance, 30,* 132–156.

Yates, J. F. (1990). *Judgment and decision making.* Englewood Cliffs, NJ: Prentice-Hall.

Yates, J. F., & Curley, S. P. (1985). Conditional distribution analyses of probabilistic forecasting. *Journal of Forecasting, 4,* 61–73.

Yates, J. F., McDaniel, L., & Brown, E. (1991). Probabilistic forecasts of stock prices and earnings: The hazards of nascent expertise. *Organizational Behaviour and Human Decision Processes.* (In press.).

Youssef, Z. I., & Peterson, C. R. (1973). Intuitive cascaded inferences. *Organizational Behavior and Human Performance, 10,* 349–58.

Zakay, D. (1983). "The relationship between the probability assessor and the outcomes of an event as a determiner of subjective probability. *Acta Psychologica, 53,* 271–280.

CHAPTER 4

On the Competence and Incompetence of Experts

Peter Ayton

INTRODUCTION

The widespread and unexceptional use of the term "expert" suggests that there is general public acceptance of the validity of the concept of an expert. For example, in news reports of particular "specialist" areas such as foreign politics, economics, and transport disasters, it is quite routine for particular individuals, presented as experts, to be explicitly consulted, and asked for their analyses, judgments, and opinions, which are quoted and duly accorded some weight and prominence.

In such contexts experts may well give quite uncontroversial factual explanations of arcane terminology and procedures in order to assist the layperson to comprehend some unfamiliar scenario. It is not unreasonable to expect that such terminology and procedures will reflect the operation of relatively sophisticated expert modes of analysis.

Experimental psychologists have provided some empirical corroboration of the notion that the superior knowledge of experts provides them with more adroit methods for understanding the circumstances within their domain of expertise. However, there is also evidence that expert modes of analysis are vulnerable to systematic and serious error. Within the psychological literature on human judgment and problem solving there are a number of studies that have scrutinized

Peter Ayton • Department of Psychology, City of London Polytechnic, Old Castle Street, London E1 7NT, England.

Expertise and Decision Support, edited by George Wright and Fergus Bolger. Plenum Press, New York, 1992.

expert reasoning, often by comparing experts with nonexperts, in order to identify mental processes and evaluate the nature of expertise. This chapter reviews this research and discusses the notion that while the possession of expert knowledge may be beneficial to, or even necessary for, optimal decision making, it is not always sufficient.

EXPERTISE AND PROBLEM SOLVING

There is considerable evidence that experts, compared to novices, invoke different, and indeed superior, strategies for approaching problems within their domain of expertise. For example, de Groot (1965, 1966) found that chess masters could, after viewing an authentic board position for 5–10 seconds, recall it much better than inexperienced players. It cannot be claimed that the chess masters simply have better memories though, because they were no better at recalling board positions which displayed chess pieces placed randomly.

This finding is easily interpreted as a reflection of the operation of different classes of perceptual analysis—expert and inexpert. With randomly distributed pieces, which will not reflect any plausible game positions, a superior knowledge of chess strategies would be less likely to afford the chess masters any particular advantage in representing the array. This interpretation has led to the hypothesis that chess players are readily able to segment the board into a number of chunks or configurations that correspond to already known patterns stored in long-term memory. Accordingly, the superior ability of expert chess players is assumed to derive not so much from their powers of calculation but from a perceptual-organizational ability specific to the game. Novice chess players sometimes naively assume that experts' ability in chess is strongly determined by the number of moves that they can compute ahead. However, de Groot has estimated that the average number of moves considered in each position by a chess master to be 1.48. Of course, expert chess players obviously do calculate, but their positional sense advises them when and what to calculate to best effect.

This superior strategic awareness of possibilities may well be a significant common characteristic of experts cross different domains. This notion is supported by Hunter's (1977) observations of Professor Aitken of Edinburgh University who was capable of tremendous feats of mental arithmetic. Hunter describes how Aitken's ability appeared to be based on two basic features, namely his large repertoire of number facts and his repertoire of calculative plans.

Most people have a limited repertoire of numerical questions that they can answer rapidly without any awareness of having to calculate (e.g., "What is twelve divided by two?"). For accountants, or people used to doing a lot of number work, the repertoire will be more extensive. Aitken's repertoire of number facts was vast; given any number up to 1,500 he could automatically say whether it was a prime number or not; if it was not, he could give its factors. However, Hunter argues that more important than this ability was Aitken's ability to decide a calculative plan:

> Ability to carry out the component steps is necessary for skill but is not sufficient. The expert typist requires more than the ability to strike any required key on the keyboard; the master violinist requires more than the ability to produce any required note from his violin; the fluent orator needs more than a large vocabulary. (p. 36)

According to Hunter, Aitken's first priority when tackling a problem was to decide on a calculative plan. The plan preselects what is to be done at each stage and ensures that each successive step follows smoothly. Aitken selected a plan that would achieve the best economy of effort; typically, he searched for the plan that would carry him to the solution in the shortest time and with the least difficulty.

Such observations accord well with Newell and Simon's (1972) theory of general problem solving. These authors have proposed that problem solving can be conceived of as taking place in a "problem space." The elements of this space consist of states of knowledge about the problem. Both the initial situation and the desired situation are represented as elements of this space. Problem solving involves moving around the space and is always a matter of search—of starting from some initial position (state of knowledge) and exploring until a position is attained that includes the solution—the desired state of knowledge. A problem space also has associated with it a set of operators, which, when applied to an element of the space, produces new elements. These operators are the means by which new information and insights about the problem can be obtained from old.

Newell and Simon's conception of problem solving provides a useful framework for discussing some of the possible differences between experts and nonexperts. Experts and nonexperts may be different in terms of their initial state of knowledge concerning a problem as well as *how* they navigate the problem space; experts may apply different operators on the same knowledge as is possessed by nonexperts. Also, it is plausible that for the kind of problems that have no obvious definite solution (e.g., determining the value of a house), they differ in terms of what information they consider to be necessary to obtain the desired state of knowledge.

A recently reported empirical study has explored the potential of this conception of problem solving for explaining the operation of expertise. Selnes and Troye (1989) found that experts and novices used different methods for analyzing problems. For subjects making purchasing decisions, experts (those with superior knowledge of the products being considered) sought out different types of information and also devoted more effort to identifying and defining the problem than did nonexperts. They claimed that experts were more likely to frame the problem so as to predefine their information needs, while the nonexperts would react to the information they happened upon as they examined the stimulus.

EXPERT STRATEGIES AND CONCEPTS

Chi, Feltovich, and Glaser (1981) and Chi, Glaser, and Rees (1982) studied the representation of physics problems by experts and novices and made quite specific distinctions between the mental strategies of experts and novices. They found that experts categorized the problems according to the relevant underlying principles of physics. This was in contrast to novices who categorized according to the mention of particular features in the statement of the problem. Therefore, experts might place several problems in the same category because they can be solved by the principle of conservation of energy, while the novices might place all the problems dealing with an inclined plane into the same category.

Chi et al. have claimed that a differential ability to categorize problems may be an important factor that distinguishes novice from expert problem solvers. They argue that the categorization of problems according to physics principles will prompt the activation of particular knowledge structures or schemata that, in turn, will determine which equations are to be used for the solution to be computed. Because the knowledge structures used by experts to select equations are not activated by reference to the problem goal, the strategy of experts is forward thinking—they tend to work forward from the given information towards the solution.

Physics novices, on the other hand, characteristically tended to use a "means-end" analysis; lacking the appropriate schemata, they could not work forward from the given information, and so they selected equations which contained the goal, and then worked backwards towards the given information by choosing new equations that might solve for unknowns in preceding equations. Once they had solved these equations, they then reversed the direction of the process and worked towards the goal. Such a strategy is relatively inefficient (and presumably makes greater demands on working memory) because it increases the number of inferences and amount of information required to obtain a solution. This same distinction between expert and novice problem-solving strategies has also been made by Larkin, McDermott, Simon, and Simon (1980a, 1980b) and Simon and Simon (1978).

As the means-end type of information processing can, by definition, operate without acquisition of the schemata held by experts, Sweller, Mawer, and Ward (1983) suggested that dependency on it may restrict the acquisition of information by problem solvers concerning generic problem structures. This led them to the slightly paradoxical suggestion that novices' problem-solving experience is unlikely to allow the rapid development of expertise. Using physics and geometry problems, Sweller et al. were able to confirm the existence of these two types of strategy and also showed that the means-end strategy favored by the novices inhibited the acquisition of the appropriate schema for forward thinking. These findings imply that amount of experience per se may not be a reliable indicator of the presence of expertise. Furthermore, for educational and training purposes, there may be benefits in encouraging novices to explore the problem space in an undirected fashion rather than pursue specific problem goals.

Murphy and Wright (1984) found evidence for structural differences between the concepts of experts and novices. Their subjects had varying degrees of experience in dealing with disturbed children, ranging from practicing clinical psychologists to introductory psychology students. Not surprisingly, the experts listed more attributes (e.g., "feels anxious") of three psychological categories (depressive, aggressive, disorganized) and exhibited greater consensus as to the attributes of each category, suggesting that the experts knew more about the categories. However, and to their surprise, Murphy and Wright found that the experts' concepts were *less* distinctive than the novices'. For example, novices listed "feels sad" only for the depressive category and "feels angry" only for the aggressive category. Experts, however, listed these features as attributes of all three categories. Furthermore, it was the additional features, those uniquely elicited from the experts, that were more likely to be listed under more than one category.

Murphy and Wright explain this as being due to an increasing recognition that the categories have more in common than might at first be appreciated. When people learn a new concept they probably focus on its distinctive features in order to distinguish it from other concepts, but, with experience, the clinical psychologists had noticed the regularities found in all disturbed children and realized that the diagnostic categories are less clear-cut. Murphy and Wright note that experts' taxonomies often group together objects that, to the layperson, seem quite disparate. Biologists group together shrimp, spiders, and crabs as they are all members of the arthropod phylum, while the layperson, less aware of genetic and anatomical similarities and more conscious of perceptual or functional properties, may not notice their overlapping features. Because of their theories of underlying molecular structure, chemists group together substances that may appear, to the uninitiated, quite different. For an expert, such recognition of similarity may be crucial. For example, the treatment plans for two disturbed children may be similar, even where the children appear to behave quite differently, because of expert theories as to the similarity of underlying causes.

EXPERIENCE AND DEDUCTIVE REASONING

Studies of deductive reasoning also provide evidence that expertise may improve problem-solving strategy. One of the major tasks that has been used to study deductive reasoning is the selection task (Wason, 1966). In the original version of this task, subjects are presented with an array of four cards and told that each card has a letter on one side and a number on the other. The subjects are asked to select the cards they need to turn over in order to determine whether a given rule concerning the cards is true or false. For example, the rule might be "If there is an A on one side then there is a 4 on the other side," and the cards A, B, 4, and 7.

Only the cards that can potentially falsify the rule should be selected, A and 7 in the example. A number other than 4 on the other side of the A or an A on the other side of the 7 would falsify the rule. The overwhelming majority of subjects fail to solve the problem correctly, however, and, while usually selecting A, typically fail to select 7 and frequently incorrectly select 4 which, while it might reveal evidence consistent with the rule (A) or irrelevant to the rule (a letter other than A) cannot falsify the rule.

The early interpretation of performance with this task was that human reasoning was seriously flawed by a bias to seek confirming rather than falsifying evidence. Although it is now clear that this explanation is insufficient to account for the observed variations in performance across different versions of the task, it does seem that people fail to consider falsifying evidence because they focus on the cards referred to in the statement of the rule (see Evans, 1989a). Poor performance has been observed in well-educated subjects, such as Ph.D. scientists (Griggs & Ransdell, 1986), which suggests that experts may not be immune to the fallacy. Nevertheless, there are versions of the problem, expressed using familiar knowledge-related content terms, that are easier for subjects to solve. For example, Griggs and Cox (1982) developed a version of the problem that directly related to their subjects' experience. The four cards each represented a person drinking in a bar, with a drink written on one side and their age on the other. The rule "If a person is drinking beer, then that person must be over 19 years of age" was based on the actual drinking law in the state of Florida where the experiment was conducted. Even though the logical structure of this problem is identical to Wason's original task, the majority of subjects correctly solved this problem selecting the card marked "beer" rather than "coke" and those marked with ages under 19 rather than over 19.

Johnson-Laird, Legrenzi, and Legrenzi (1972) also found good performance on a version of the selection task that referred to a now-obsolete postal rule. They presented subjects with envelopes that were either face-up, revealing the postage stamp, or face-down, revealing whether the letter was sealed or not. Their subjects were English students who were familiar with an old postal rule that used to allow unsealed letters to be sent at a cheaper rate and were, in general, able to select the envelopes required to evaluate the rule "A letter is sealed only if it has a 5d stamp on it." Significantly, Griggs and Cox's (1982) American subjects, lacking any experience with such a rule, did not show enhanced performance—as they did with the drinking problem. In similar vein, Golding (1981) reports in a study of British subjects that only the older ones showed enhanced levels of performance with the postal rule—plausibly because they were the only ones who had had experience of the application of the rule.

The precise reason why performance on the selection task benefits from familiarity with a given domain continues to be discussed (e.g., Evans, 1989a; Jackson & Griggs, 1990). One theoretical proposal that has been advanced to account for a wide range of psychological investigations of human reasoning, including the observed variations in performance of the selection task, is that of Evans (1984). Evans proposes that a two-stage process underlies human inference. The first ("heuristic") stage is unconscious and selects "relevant" information. Information deemed irrelevant at this stage is not processed further. The second ("analytic") stage operates on this selected information to generate inferences. The suggestion is that prior knowledge will influence the initial selection of relevant information and thereby affect reasoning performance. Errors occur when people have difficulty in selecting the appropriate features for consideration—which preempts their ability to appreciate the logical relationships involved. If a person fails to attend to some crucial element of a problem, then, however reasonable their subsequent logical approach, they are likely to be unsuccessful in solving the problem. Confirmation that some degree of logical competence is present in individuals who fail to correctly solve the problem is provided by the fact that when subjects are presented with evidence that logically falsifies the rule they will generally recognize this immediately.

It can be seen that this two-stage model is generally compatible with the discussion above of the role of expertise in problem solving. Experts may benefit from their superior ability to identify the relevant attributes of problem situations in advance of any subsequent analytic processing of the information they initially selectively attend to.

The evidence from the studies reviewed above supports the view that experts not only know more, but that their knowledge is functionally significant to problem-solving *strategy;* it changes the manner in which experts approach problems and helps them to analyze problems within their domain of expertise in a more proficient fashion. (One is reminded of the oft-cited finding that Eskimos apparently have a great many words for distinguishing between types of snow (Whorf, 1940) and the associated Whorf hypothesis that this will improve the discriminability with which snow is perceived.[1]) Thus far, then, one might well feel relatively confident about the value of expertise. However, the research considered up to this point has been primarily concerned with one role for expertise—namely, that of providing definitive answers to problems that may be

---

[1]There has been, of course, much controversy surrounding the Whorf hypothesis; but whether or not Eskimos, and others with enriched vocabularies for particular domains, benefit merely through possession of superior vocabularies, because the vocabularies functionally assist thought, or whether the vocabularies are merely reflective of greater effort to discriminate, need not concern us here. Presumably the extended vocabulary of experts is, at the very least, reflective of more sophisticated modes of analysis, or specialist jargons would not evolve—though the idea that experts develop and use jargon in order to conceal their thoughts from outsiders rather than to assist their thinking has its advocates (Johnson, 1980).

solved with the application of relevant knowledge. Yet, in many situations where experts are called upon to pronounce, such absolute answers to issues are very often unavailable; the necessary knowledge needed to specify the answer is not possessed by anyone—not even the most knowledgeable expert. In such cases experts may give their judgments concerning likely (and unlikely) causes and outcomes.

EXPERTISE AND JUDGMENTS UNDER UNCERTAINTY

As well as relying on expert knowledge, we tend to rely on expert *judgment* in those situations where not all the causal factors are fully known or understood. In the courts this function of expert advice is formally acknowledged; expert witnesses are the only witnesses who are permitted to provide opinion, that is, to give information other than facts (Cooke, 1990).

Many important conclusions and decisions are based on opinions or judgments, provided by experts, concerning the likelihood of uncertain events, such as the outcome of surgery, the guilt of a defendant, or the future level of interest rates. Doctors advise treatments, solicitors may recommend what to plead in court, and brokers will suggest when to buy and sell stocks and shares.

The apparent public acceptance of the practice of seeking and quoting expert judgment and opinion could be taken to imply something of the nature of lay theories concerning the nature of knowledge and the quality of human judgment. It appears to be accepted that human knowledge is viably partitioned into different domains and that within particular domains an individual may acquire a superior understanding—expertise. Such a view is supported by the studies cited above. Furthermore, given the acceptance of expert judgments of likelihood, it seems to be understood that, although the experts' knowledge may on occasion be imperfect for determining what will happen, the expert will be able to reliably indicate the appropriate likelihoods.

Hence it would appear that two logically separable competences are imputed to the expert: firstly that he or she will be conversant with whatever knowledge there is in the field, and secondly that, when this knowledge fails to be sufficient to specify a conclusion, the expert will be able to use his or her limited knowledge to synthesize a proper judgment of the likelihoods.

In courts of law, an expert opinion ". . . is deemed to be a fully reasoned conclusion drawn from the scientific facts" (Haward, 1981, p. 168). Whatever degree of reassurance may be provided by the fact that expert opinion purports to be "fully reasoned" will depend on what views one holds of the quality of expert reasoning and judgment. *Can* experts reliably use limited knowledge to make appropriate judgments? In a well-known series of classic papers Kahneman and Tversky (see Kahneman, Slovic, & Tversky, 1982) have presented evidence that people, including some who could be described as experts, can have considerable difficulty in reasoning correctly with uncertainty and that judgments of uncertainty may be biased and distorted as a function of the cognitive processes that characteristically underlie human judgment.

Kahneman and Tversky found that when evaluating probabilistic information or assessing likelihoods from limited knowledge, experimental subjects used heuristic methods that made them liable to neglect relevant information or be strongly influenced by weak or irrelevant information. For example, when asked to estimate the likelihood that a particular individual was a lawyer or an engineer, experimental subjects were influenced by a description of the individual but failed to consider base-rate information. Thus, subjects told that the individual was drawn from a group containing 30 lawyers and 70 engineers produced the same estimates as subjects told that the individual was drawn from a group containing 70 lawyers and 30 engineers. Kahneman and Tversky attributed this neglect of base-rate information to the operation of a representativeness heuristic. The subjects were estimating likelihood by making a judgment of the degree to which the individual was representative of, or similar to, the stereotypes of lawyers and engineers, and so ignored the relevant information concerning base rates.

Another heuristic used for probabilistic judgment is availability. This heuristic is invoked when people estimate likelihood or relative frequency by the ease with which instances can be brought to mind. Instances of frequent events are typically easier to recall than instances of less frequent events, so availability will often be a valid cue for estimates of likelihood. However, availability is affected by factors other than likelihood. For example, recent events and emotionally salient events are more easy to recollect. It is a common experience that the perceived riskiness of air travel rises in the immediate wake of an air disaster. Kahneman and Tversky demonstrated that people incorrectly judge that words beginning with r are more common than words that have r as their third letter. As aficionados of crossword puzzles will know, it is much easier to retrieve words by their first letter than their third letter. Judgments made on the basis of availability then are vulnerable to systematic bias.

The research reported by Kahneman and Tversky and others has stimulated a strong reaction in the psychological literature. Their case has been challenged. It has been claimed that their studies of judgmental fallibility should not be taken as having pejorative implications for the rationality of human reasoning any more than visual illusions undermine our faith in our perceptual competence (Cohen, 1981). It has been argued that many of the observed errors of judgment merely reflect mathematical or scientific ignorance (Cohen, 1981), or that they are caused by implicit suggestions subtly conveyed in the wording of the problems (MacDonald & Gilhooly, 1990) or that they may be of limited validity to the circumstances prevailing in real-world decision making (Berkeley &

Humphreys, 1982; Ebbeson & Konecni, 1980; Winkler & Murphy, 1973), and the judgments made by experts operating within the sphere of their expertise (Beach, Barnes, & Christensen-Szalanski, 1987).

The study of *expert* judgment has therefore become an area of particular significance to the wider debate concerning the general competence of human judgment. The performance of naive experimental subjects, making judgments on areas where they have no particular knowledge or training, on tasks that may not model any realistic situation, may not reflect the real world judgments of experts. The performance of experts operating in situ, it has been argued, ought to be the proper focus for any examination of the competence of human judgment and reasoning.

EVIDENCE FOR INCOMPETENT EXPERT JUDGMENT

Medical Diagnosis

The literature reporting investigations of expert judgment provides several instances of poor judgment or faulty reasoning—some of which have serious potential consequences. Eddy (1982) reports alarming evidence of fundamental errors in the probabilistic reasoning employed by physicians to make diagnoses of breast cancer on the basis of X rays. X rays can give an indication as to whether or not a lesion is malignant. X rays are used as a basis for making decisions as to whether or not surgery, involving the removal of tissue for further examination, is merited. However, the indication from the X-ray test is not perfectly reliable; some malignant lesions will be incorrectly classified as benign and some benign lesions will be classified as malignant. Consequently the task of diagnosis can be viewed as a process of statistical inference.

Eddy set a sample of physicians the task of estimating the likelihood that a patient had cancer given that, prior to the X ray, their examination of the patient indicated a 99% probability that the lesion was benign but that the X-ray test was positive and had indicated it was malignant. They were told that research into the accuracy of the test showed that 79.2% of malignant lesions were correctly diagnosed and 90.4% of benign lesions were correctly diagnosed by the test.

As 90.4% of the patients with benign lesions will be correctly diagnosed, 9.6% will not be and thereby show positive on the test, along with 79.2% of those that do develop cancer. But of course there are many more women who do not develop breast cancer than women who do develop the disease. Consequently the population of people who show positive on the test consists of a small proportion (9.6%) of the vast majority of people who do not develop the disease (99%), plus a large proportion (79.2%) of the tiny minority of the people who do develop the disease (1%).

Bayes' theorem can be used to combine the information about the reliability of the test with the physicians prior probability judgment to assess the correct likelihood that the patient has cancer. Bayes' theorem tells us that the likelihood of cancer, given a positive X ray, is:

p(cancer/positive) =

$$\frac{p(positive/cancer)p(cancer)}{p(positive/cancer)p\ (cancer)\ +\ p(positive/benign)p(benign)}$$

where p(cancer/positive) is the probability that the patient has cancer given she has a positive X-ray test result; p(positive/cancer) is the probability that, if the patient has cancer, the test will be positive (79.2%); p(cancer) is the prior probability that the patient has cancer (1%); p(benign) is the prior probability that the lesion is benign (99%); p(positive/benign) is the probability that, if the lesion is benign, the test will incorrectly indicate that the patient has cancer (as 90.4% of benign lesions are correctly diagnosed by the test then 9.6% are incorrectly diagnosed malignant). Substituting the values into the formula gives:

$$p(cancer/positive) = \frac{(.792)\ (0.01)}{(.792)\ (0.01)\ +\ (0.096)\ (0.99)}$$

$$p(cancer/positive) = 0.077$$

The probability of cancer, in the light of the positive test, is therefore nearly 8%. However, most of the physicians misinterpreted the information about the reliability of the test and estimated the likelihood of cancer to be about 75%. When asked about their reasoning the physicians report that they assumed that the probability of cancer given a positive test result (p[cancer/positive]) is equal to the probability of a positive X ray in a patient with cancer (p[positive/cancer]). They can therefore be said to have used a representativeness heuristic in that they judged the likelihood of cancer in patients with a positive test in terms of how typical (or representative) they were of patients with cancer. It is clear that they failed to properly consider the impact on the outcome of the very low incidence of the disease (base rate) together with the tendency of the test to (falsely) show positive test results.

In reviewing the medical literature on mammography, Eddy found a strong tendency to equate p(cancer/positive) and p(positive/cancer). Not surprisingly this basic confusion is interpreted as indicating a lack of understanding of the formal procedure for combining probabilistic information. Eddy documents cases where, if published procedures were to be followed, the true probabilities of risk of cancer would be massively misjudged.

Confirmation that, in practice, real decisions are taken on the basis of such misunderstandings is provided by Dawes (1983). He cites a case of a doctor performing mastectomy operations on women judged to have high risk of breast cancer. The surgery was justified on the grounds that "one in two or three with DY breasts will develop cancer sometime between ages 40 and 60." It turns out that the conclusion was based on the estimated probability that a woman with cancer will have DY breasts (p[DY/cancer]). However, the relevant probability (p[cancer/DY]) is approximately one in eight.

Eddy argues that the correct use of base-rate information could be developed to enhance the diagnosis of cancer. Where different populations with differing base rates for diseases are identifiable, the information can critically affect the interpretation of test results. Women who, during the course of examination, present no symptoms of breast cancer have a 1% chance of developing the disease. If, during the course of screening, they produce a positive test result, Eddy calculates that the likelihood of cancer is 2%. In contrast, 8% of women with an abnormal physical examination develop cancer. If they test positively, Eddy calculates that their probability of developing the disease is 40%—the chance for this population is a factor of twenty greater.

There is considerable evidence that the medical profession is confused about the relevance of base rates to medical diagnosis. Some evidence that efforts are made to consider base rates is given by the use of maxims in medical schools such as "When you hear hoofbeats, think of horses, not of zebras," and "Common things occur most commonly." Unfortunately, though, there are other maxims that denigrate the use of base rates, e.g., "The patient is a case of one," and "Statistics are for dead men." Eddy (1982) cites a medical textbook (DeGowin & DeGowin, 1969) which actually states:

> Statistical methods can only be applied to a population of thousands. The individual either has a rare disease or doesn't have it; the relative incidence of two diseases is *completely irrelevant* to the problem of making his diagnosis.

It seems plausible to conclude that gross errors of this kind might be eliminated if courses in the application of Bayes' theorem to probabilistic inference were recognized as a basic aspect of medical training. Although this would doubtless improve matters, it would be fanciful to imagine that it is a simple or complete panacea. The process of acquiring medical expertise, and the nature of that expertise, do not facilitate the application of statistical reasoning. In fact, some of the basic characteristics of medical training and knowledge are quite imposing impediments to the formulation of optimal clinical judgment.

In order to make a clinical diagnosis the doctor must make a statistical inference that involves assessing the probability that a patient has the disease, given some pattern of symptoms (p[disease/symptoms]). However, according to Eddy and Clanton (1982), medical knowledge is not organized like this. A good deal of medical education is disease-oriented. Most medical texts will discuss the probability that patients will present a certain pattern of symptoms, given that they have the disease (p[symptoms/disease]). This information is not sufficient for making a diagnosis and the focus on it may well encourage the false notion that p(disease/symptoms) is the same as p(symptoms/disease). The confusion between the two probabilities may be further engendered by the type of instruction that trainee physicians receive. On ward rounds, patients with certain diseases are examined and the co-occurrence of symptoms is noted. But, people with the symptoms but without the disease (healthy people not in the hospital and patients with similar symptoms and different diseases) will not be subject to the same scrutiny. As a consequence, the diagnostic significance, or *diagnosticity*, of a given set of symptoms may be overestimated.

Some of the problems in adopting Bayesian methods for diagnosis are quite formidable. The gathering of all the necessary component information would be a considerable effort. Base rates for particular diseases and probabilities for symptoms in the absence, as well as the presence, of each disease would be required.

But even when precise statistical information concerning base rates and diagnosticity of symptoms is unavailable, insights can still be gained from applying a Bayesian analysis to medical diagnosis. Evans (1989b) adopts a Bayesian perspective in discussing the recent disquiet in Britain concerning the disputed diagnoses of child sexual abuse by pediatricians in Cleveland. He points out that it is significant that critics of these doctors pointed to other possible accounts of the symptoms that the Cleveland doctors were so sure implied child sexual abuse. In this context the claim from the doctors making the diagnosis that they had a "special interest" in child sexual abuse is of particular interest. It may be that by focusing on a particular domain of knowledge an expert may become more prone to a confirming bias in reasoning. Thus, the specialists are interested in how consistent the evidence is with the hypothesis they are testing and may fail to consider its consistency with alternative hypotheses. In the very act of specializing, doctors may be more likely to overlook alternative causes of the symptoms that they take to have particular diagnostic significance to their specialty; for example, they may become removed from other experiences and sources of information which might tell them that the symptoms they attend to are more equivocal with respect to some diagnostic classifications within their specialty. This is another example of the risk of doctors' judgments incurring bias by being disease-oriented.

Arguably, the findings of Murphy and Wright (1984) discussed earlier have some relevance to this analysis. They suggested that concepts in the experts' domain become less distinctive with experience; experienced clinical psychologists assigned behavioral features to more than one diagnostic category. According to their critics, the Cleveland pediatricians failed to appreciate the similarity of the diagnostic category to other diagnostic categories; with respect to the features (symptoms) they focused on, the concept (diagnostic category) of abuse was less distinctive than they assumed. It would be interesting to know to what extent this was caused by their stated practice of specializing removing them from the more global experiences that might have encouraged them to reason otherwise.

There is also a broad analogy with the findings of Sweller et al. (1983) discussed above, in particular their notion that the development of effective problem-solving strategies is encouraged more by exploring the problem space in a relatively undirected fashion rather than by pursuing specific goals. The experiences of experts may well be highly filtered and attenuated by their operating circumstances; as we have seen, this can have adverse consequences. Paradoxical though it seems, experience—the very characteristic that we assume is quintessential to the competence of experts—may actually conspire against effective judgment and reasoning.

Christensen-Szalanski, Beck, Christensen-Szalanski, and Koepsell (1983) have supplied empirical evidence that experience can bias the judgments of doctors. They discovered an availability bias in physicians' estimates of the risk (mortality rate) of various diseases. They compared experts (physicians) with students and found that both groups overestimated the risks. In general, physicians were more accurate than the students, but the estimates of both groups were found to be biased by actual encounters with people with the disease. Christensen-Szalanski et al. suggest that experts and nonexperts may use similar thought processes but make differently biased judgments because of their different experiences of the risky events.

Evans (1989b) comments on the fact that the Cleveland pediatricians making the diagnoses of child abuse asserted a belief that the prevalence of abuse in the general population (the base rate) was much higher than that of medical colleagues who disputed the diagnoses. In the absence of objective base-rate data, doctors' estimates of base rates will be critical to diagnosis. A tendency to overdiagnose would lead to the conclusion that a disease is more common than it actually is, which in turn might then lead to an increased tendency to diagnose. Consequently a vicious circle may be created gradually eroding the accuracy of diagnosis.

Evidence that physicians overconfidently diagnose is provided by Christensen-Szalanski and Bushyhead (1981), who explored the validity of the probabilities given by physicians to diagnoses of pneumonia. They found that the probabilities were poorly calibrated; thus the proportion of patients who turned out to have pneumonia was far less than the probability statements implied. These authors had previously established that the physicians' estimates of the probability of a patient having pneumonia was significantly correlated with their decision to give a patient a chest X ray and to assign a pneumonia diagnosis.

One reason why doctors' judgments under uncertainty are liable to be poor may be that they tend to conceal uncertainty rather than attempt to deal with it rationally. Katz (1984) has pointed out that, while doctors are quite willing to discuss the theoretical uncertainties regarding the decisions concerning diagnosis and treatment, this is rarely acknowledged explicitly to the patient. Doctors may argue that patients would not appreciate discussion of uncertainty, finding it difficult to understand, and even stressful to the point of undermining the patients' health. Thus doctors may adopt the appearance of certainty in the belief that it acts as a placebo for the patient.

Katz challenges this practice, suggesting that by "donning a mask of infallibility" the doctors are able to manipulate the patient and maintain their professional control. Efforts to dispel doubt will result in limited attempts to explore the uncertainties leading to overconfidence in judgment and resulting in suboptimal decision making. Furthermore, doctors' professional status is threatened by this practice; they may create lowered perceptions of their competence from disappointed patients who have suffered bad outcomes.

The idea that motivation to explore uncertainty will materially affect resultant judgments receives support from the work of Mayseless and Kruglanski (1987). These authors have specifically considered the effects of what they describe as epistemic motivations on subjective probability assessments. They hypothesized that people who have a high need for structure will tend towards early closure on judgmental problems. A person operating with a high need for structure will, they suggest, inhibit the generation of competing alternatives to a given hypothesis. In theory it is possible to continue generating further and further hypotheses consistent with any body of evidence. But, if no alternative hypotheses come to mind that are also consistent with the evidence, then the given hypothesis may turn into a firm or subjectively valid fact.

The functional opposite of this tendency is what Mayseless and Kruglanski term fear of invalidity. This motivation is inspired by the desire to avoid judgmental mistakes, when these are perceived as being costly. While need for structure may promote a "cognitive freezing" of the epistemic process, fear of invalidity might lead to an unfreezing. Individuals operating with a high fear of invalidity are hypothesized to have an increased tendency to generate alternatives to a currently entertained hypothesis, as well as being more sensitive to information inconsistent with the hypothesis.

In a series of empirical tests of these ideas, Mayseless and Kruglanski measured subjects' initial confidence in a hypothesis, their changes in confidence in the light of information, and the number of alternative hypotheses they generated. They found that subjects' initial level of confidence in a hypothesis was higher when they had high, rather than low, need for structure and when they had low, rather than high, fear of invalidity.

They also found that the magnitude of shifts in confidence prompted by new information were greater in subjects induced to operate with a high need for structure or a low fear of invalidity. This they argued is because the tendency to interpret new information in competing ways according to different hypotheses may ambiguate its meaning and thereby lessen its impact. Subjects under the different motivational states would be differentially motivated to interpret the information in competing ways. Confirmation that these effects were mediated by a differential tendency to generate alternative hypotheses under different motivational states was also experimentally demonstrated. As predicted, the tendency to generate alternative hypotheses was greater for subjects with high (rather than low) fear of invalidity and for subjects with low (rather than high) need for structure. This study demonstrates that the level of confidence in a particular hypothesis is not always determined exclusively by purely cognitive considerations and may be significantly influenced by motivational factors. Consequently a full consideration of the effects of the operating environment of experts on performance is appropriate; Katz's suggestion that doctors' judgment suffers because they are motivated to dispel doubt rather than explore uncertainty plausibly applies to experts in other fields as well.

A further potential impediment to the learning of good judgment from experience is the hindsight bias. This is the experimentally demonstrated tendency for people to give higher subjective likelihoods to events once they know that they have occurred (in hindsight) than they would to the same events if they don't know the outcome (Fischhoff, 1975). Arkes, Saville, Wortmann, and Harkness (1981) have observed this effect in physicians giving probabilities to diagnoses. They asked physicians to read a case history and then assign likelihoods to each of four possible presented diagnoses. One group was told nothing about the correct diagnosis while the others were told that one of the presented diagnoses was the correct one. Knowledge of the supposedly correct diagnosis increased the subjective probability of that diagnosis; hence the probabilities for the diagnoses were influenced by hindsight.

The subjects used by Arkes et al. had a good deal of knowledge about the relationships between symptoms and disease, and yet were still prey to this effect. The hindsight bias shows that doctors are reasoning backwards, from knowledge of the diagnosis to an interpretation of the diagnostic significance of the symptoms. They were, presumably unconsciously, attempting to make their perception of the symptoms fit the given diagnosis rather than make a diagnosis that fitted their perception of the symptoms. Such retrospective interpretation of the symptoms may well occur in situations where a second opinion is sought and, clearly, is to the detriment of accurate diagnosis.

The doctors in the hindsight conditions of the experiment were in a similar situation to that which will frequently occur in their education and training— examining a patient with a known diagnosis and reviewing the relationship with the symptoms. If, because of the hindsight bias, doctors fail to experience surprise when they learn of outcomes, they will assume that their ability to gauge the likelihood of outcomes is more accurate than it actually is. This would cause overestimates of the diagnosticity of symptoms and result in overconfidence.

Overconfidence of judgments made under uncertainty is commonly found in probabilistic judgment experiments (see Lichtenstein, Fischhoff, & Phillips, 1982) and has been recorded in the judgments of experts. We have already noted this in the medical domain, but it has been found elsewhere. Wagenaar and Keren (1986) found overconfidence in lawyers' attempts to anticipate the outcome of court trials in which they represented one side. As they point out, it is inconceivable that the lawyers do not pay attention to the outcomes of trials in which they have participated. Nonetheless it is possible that the circumstances in which the lawyers, and other experts, make their judgments, and the circumstances in which they receive feedback, combine to impede the proper monitoring of feedback necessary for the development of well-calibrated judgments. A consideration of the reports of well-calibrated experts supports this notion; they all appear to be cases where some explicit unambiguous quantification of uncertainty is initially made and the outcome feedback is prompt and unambiguous.

The most commonly cited example of well-calibrated judgments are weather forecasters' estimates of the likelihood of precipitation (Murphy & Winkler, 1984), but there are a few other cases. Keren (1987) found highly experienced tournament bridge players (but not experienced nontournament players) made well-calibrated forecasts of the likelihood that a contract, reached during the bidding phase, would be made, and Phillips (1987) reports well-calibrated forecasts of horse races by bookmakers. In each of these three cases, the judgments made by the experts are precise numerical statements and the outcome feedback is unambiguous and received promptly and so can be easily compared with the initial forecast. Under these circumstances the experts are unlikely to be insensitive to the experience of being surprised; there is very little scope for neglecting, or denying, any mismatch between forecast and outcome.

Wagenaar and Keren (1986) concluded from their consideration of the factors responsible for poorly calibrated judgment that:

> There is little reason to believe that experts possess a mysterious sixth sense, an innate intuition, or an undefinable fingertipfeeling. Experts will be well calibrated only after they have learned to adjust the parameters in their prediction model on the basis of a formal analysis. (p. 103)

It seems quite likely that many experts operate in conditions where such an analysis is difficult or impossible. Sometimes the outcomes will be in the remote future or may be attributable to interventions (perhaps by the expert) designed to change the outcomes. Thus doctors may take actions that change the outcomes implied by a diagnosis, and thereby remove feedback that might confirm or refute the diagnosis. In any case, as doctors do not typically record precise numerical indices of their uncertainty, they may well forget what their original judgments were by the time outcome information is available.

Interpretation of Legal Evidence: A Case Study

Much of the research into expert judgment has scrutinized medical judgment, but there are other important areas of expertise that, under examination, reveal evidence that cognitive biases adversely affect the interpretation of evidence. At the time of writing there is, in England, a judicial inquiry taking place into the convictions of a group of people for possessing explosives (*The Independent*, 1990a). The only evidence against these people at the time of their trial was forensic evidence from thin-layer chromatography (TLC) tests on swab samples from the accused. The test results indicated the presence of minute quantities of the explosive nitroglycerine on the hands and, in one case, the gloves of the accused. At the time of the trial the results of the tests were represented by forensic experts as conclusive.

Subsequently it has become clear, though this was not mentioned at the original trial, that the TLC test will also respond positively to the presence of a different explosive called PETN which is also found in wholly innocent items such as tablets for angina. The judicial inquiry commissioned experiments to investigate the validity of the TLC test and discovered that one person handling explosives can contaminate others, either via direct contact or via such objects as towels and cups and glasses. It has since emerged that the policeman who took swabs from four of the accused had earlier been in contact with nitroglycerine explosives, and therefore might have contaminated them (*The Independent*, 1990a). No control tests were carried out by the forensic experts (e.g., on the policeman) to test for the possibility of contamination. Furthermore, the inquiry has established that there were no written procedures governing how the tests were to be conducted; it was left up to the forensic expert involved (*The Independent*, 1990b). Apparently it has even been found that tests on randomly selected members of the public (who, presumably, have not been handling nitroglycerine) can produce "rogue" positive test results (*The Independent*, 1990c).

Why was it that what now looks like insufficient care was taken with the test procedure by the experts? Why were no sufficiently rigorous attempts made to establish whether the positive test results might have been produced by circumstances other than the criminal ones that the court was led to believe were responsible? Some people might be tempted to attribute such states of affairs to professional carelessness or even conspiracy, but clearly there is scope to explain the behavior of the forensic experts in terms of the cognitive biases discussed in the psychological analysis of errors of reasoning and judgment above. Thus, according to this perspective, the forensic experts appear to have overestimated the diagnosticity of the TLC test. This in turn can be attributed to a failure to appreciate the importance of investigating the likelihood of a positive test result from someone who had *not* handled explosives. At the judicial inquest, counsel for the forensic experts argued that the forensic experts did not appreciate the relevance of the fact that the test responded positively to PETN (*The Guardian,* 1990). Counsel for the forensic experts argued that there was no deliberate conspiracy to misrepresent the evidence; the realistic explanation was that they were all caught up in "compartment thinking"; their minds were working a particular "tramline" that led them to ignore aspects of the evidence (*The Independent,* 1990c).

As with the pediatricians, they appear to be mainly interested in how consistent the evidence is with the hypothesis they are testing and fail to consider its consistency with alternative hypotheses. The focus on evidence consistent with the hypothesis and failure to seek out evidence that might mitigate against the hypothesis under consideration has parallels with the performance of experimental subjects on Wason's selection task. One might also speculate on the impact of epistemic motivations on the reasoning of people evaluating criminal evidence. To what extent do opinions concerning the guilt of suspects affect the rigor with which the uncertainties associated with evidence are explored?

In the judicial inquiry counsel for the accused have, appropriately, focused attention on the credibility of alternative explanations of the forensic evidence. Yet even in doing this they provide evidence of incompetent probabilistic reasoning. One barrister pursued the hypothesis that the positive test results may have occurred due to contamination of the forensic tests. He drew attention to the fact that the forensic notebooks showed, but for two results out of sequence, a gradually diminishing number of positive results in the order that the tests were performed on the seven accused, and claimed that the odds against this were about 20,000 to one against (*The Independent,* 1990d). In fact, there are factorial 7, only 5,040, different ways of arranging seven elements.[2]

One wonders how such probabilities are interpreted by the courts. Clearly, the probability of evidence assuming some hypothesis ($p[E/H]$) is not the same as the probability of the hypothesis in the light of the evidence ($p[H/E]$). Accord-

---

[2]From the account of the inquest it is not quite clear how imperfect the sequence was (it is not possible to have just one result out of sequence) but, adopting the most conservative assumption, that two adjacent test results were swapped about, adds another six possible outcomes. The chances of one of these seven occurring by chance is one in 720.

It is possible that if the exact opposite trend had been found in the testing sequence that this could also be interpreted as consistent with a contamination hypothesis. If so, assuming a similar tolerance for results out of sequence, there are another seven outcomes to be added to the set of outcomes that would be regarded as suspicious—the chance of any one of these occurring by chance is one in 360. Although this is a factor of more than fifty less than the probability cited at the inquest, it is, of course, still an impressively improbable result. The point of this discussion, though, is simply to point to the fact that probabilities cited by legal experts may be ineptly reasoned. Given that the principle criterion for the courts is probability ("beyond reasonable doubt" is the phrase a jury is given to define the critical probability for a conviction), this can be viewed as a rather disturbing state of affairs.

ingly, in the case discussed above, the probability of guilt is not simply the probability of observing, by chance, a positive test result; though, if the courts reason with probabilistic evidence in the same fashion as doctors appear to, they may well assume that the likelihood of a hypothesis in the light of evidence is the same thing as the likelihood of the evidence assuming the hypothesis. Dawes (1983) gives an example of a real case in the USA where the court appears to have become very confused over just this distinction.

Wagenaar (1988, Chapter 6) has proposed that, in courts of law, experts should be restricted to testimony concerning the probability of obtaining evidence on the assumption that the competing hypotheses of interest are true (p[E/H]). The job for the court is to determine the likelihood of hypotheses given the evidence (p[H/E]). This, Wagenaar argues, should not be commented on by experts and is for the court to determine. Although this principle may be ethical, in the light of the argument here it cannot be assumed that, unaided, the court will be competent to properly estimate p(H/E).

DOES THE POSSESSION OF EXPERTISE IMPROVE PROBABILISTIC REASONING?

Although, as we have seen, experts can make errors when reasoning probabilistically, there is some evidence that the possession of expertise may enhance probabilistic reasoning. Nisbett, Krantz, Jepson, and Kunda (1983, study 4) claimed that increased familiarity with a domain of knowledge leads to a greater tendency to reason probabilistically within that domain. In their experiment, subjects were told about a small sample of extreme behavior followed by a larger sample of less extreme behavior and asked for their preferred explanation as to the discrepancy between the two samples. Nisbett et al. hypothesized that expert subjects would generalize less and recognize that the discrepancy could be due to chance factors. They presented their subjects with the task of selecting their preferred explanation for why some footballers, who excelled at the preseason practice session, failed to perform up to that standard during the course of the season. Those subjects with experience of playing in team games were more likely than those without such experience to eschew a causal explanation (e.g., the players did not try so hard as they did at the practice) and select the statistical explanation (that the performances at the practice were not typical of their ability). A similar effect was observed for subjects with varying degrees of acting experience reasoning about the performance of actors.

A quite opposite conclusion can be drawn from the research conducted by Gilovich, Vallone, and Tversky (1985) who found that both basketball fans and professional players suffered from an erroneous belief concerning the chances of scoring. They tended to believe that a player's chance of hitting a shot are greater following a hit than following a miss. They termed this a belief in the "hot hand" or "streak shooting." However, a detailed analysis of the shooting records of two professional teams and a controlled experiment with a university team provided no evidence of a correlation between the outcomes of successive scoring attempts. Thus, people with huge experience of playing the game, or who at least attend enthusiastically to the causality of the game, were liable to invoke causal explanations for what were in fact chance outcomes.

How can the results of these two studies be reconciled? The conclusion from Gilovich et al.'s study seems quite inescapable: people with a great deal of experience had quite erroneous concepts of the causality of the game as a result of their failure to reason probabilistically. Nevertheless, the experienced subjects in Nisbett et al.'s study seem to demonstrate a greater tendency to reason probabilistically. It seems likely, though, that the criterion for demonstrating probabilistic competence is weaker in Nisbett et al.'s study than Gilovich et al.'s; indeed, the major aim of Nisbett et al.'s paper is the search for evidence of appropriate statistical reasoning with problems that are easier than those examined by researchers in the Kahneman and Tversky tradition. So, a subject selecting the statistical explanation in the former may nonetheless still be quite likely to suffer from the fallacy revealed in the latter. This argument is supported by the prevalence of the hot-hand fallacy (91% of fans and all of the eight professional players questioned believed in it) and the relatively modest numbers selecting the statistical explanation in Nisbett et al.'s study (fewer than 60%).

It also seems possible that the evidence for probabilistic competence in Nisbett et al.'s study is, at least in part, artifactual. Perhaps the reason why the subjects with experience in Nisbett et al.'s study found the probabilistic explanation relatively more compelling is not actually because they are reasoning probabilistically, but because they found the alternative causal explanations less credible. Experience in a given domain might well lead to a diminished respect for the causal explanations listed. It seems reasonable to conclude that greater experience of a domain of knowledge does not, of itself, guarantee a competent approach to dealing with uncertainty in that domain.

A similar argument concerning the a priori plausibility of causal hypotheses could be used to help explain the apparently compelling nature of the fallacious belief in the hot hand. It could reasonably be claimed that the prevalence of the hot hand fallacy is due to the relative imbalance in salience of the different (causal and probabilistic) hypotheses. When discussing the evidence for the hot hand fallacy with students, I have been struck by the number of people who strongly doubt that there can really be no connection between the scoring chances of successive shots and are easily able to generate plausible causal reasons why there might be an association. Gilovich et al. noted that there was a particularly strong belief that certain players were streak shooters (even though they weren't) and suggest this may be due to the availability heuristic rendering episodes of shooting consistent with that view more salient than the evidence inconsistent with that view. Again we can see a type of confirmation bias affecting the interpretation of evidence.

Another type of systematic bias found to afflict the judgments of both novices and experts is that induced by problem *framing*. Tversky and Kahneman (1981) report evidence that quite arbitrary ways in which the same risky dilemma is described can influence the way in which people respond to it. They label this as the influence of problem framing. Individuals presented with a negatively framed choice (i.e., making a decision to prevent losses) were more likely to choose risky alternatives, while those provided with positive frames (i.e., making a decision to protect gains) were more likely to avoid risk and opt for certain outcomes.

They presented physicians and students with the problem of deciding what to do in the hypothetical event that a new disease was threatening to kill 600 people. Program A would save 200 people, while program B would give a ⅓ chance that all 600 would be saved and a ⅔ chance that none would be saved. Here the description of the problem is positively framed (it discusses the lives that can be *saved*), and the majority of respondents chose program A (the outcome identified with certainty). However, if the same problem was presented with a negative frame (in terms of the lives that will be *lost*), then there was a reversal in the preferences of both the physicians and the students. When program A was described as leading to the death of 400 persons and program B as giving a ⅓ chance that nobody will die and a ⅔ chance that 600 will die, then the majority of physicians and students chose program B.

Neale and Northcraft (1986) looked for an influence of framing effects on the negotiating behavior of students and experts (professional corporate real estate negotiators) in a simulated negotiating task. Following Tversky and Kahneman's work, they hypothesized that if, in negotiations, people consider what they stand to gain from a particular offer, then they will be more likely to accept it than risk the deal collapsing by holding out for an uncertain better offer. However, people contemplating the same offer in the domain of loss (e.g., by comparing it with what might have been achieved) will be more likely to opt for the risky alternative (hold out for a better deal) and hence complete fewer transactions. They found that while experts outperformed the students, both conformed to the framing hypothesis; those framed in the domain of loss completed fewer transactions.

Another judgmental bias to which, evidence suggests, experts are not invulnerable is an anchoring bias. This was originally identified by Tversky and Kahneman (see Kahneman, Slovic, & Tversky, 1982, Chapter 1) as a by-product of the anchor-and-adjust heuristic. The literature on the anchor-and-adjust heuristic suggests that some initial reference point (even an arbitrarily chosen one) will significantly influence estimates because judges do not adjust sufficiently from it. Thus, Tversky and Kahneman found that subjects using a pointer wheel to indicate their estimates of such quantities as the percentage of African countries in the United Nations were influenced by the initial starting position of the pointer.

This sort of experimental demonstration is vulnerable to the charge that it is contingent on the use of student subjects making judgments on matters where they possess very little relevant knowledge. However, Wright and Anderson (1989) report a study which shows that increased familiarity with a domain of knowledge did not reduce anchoring effects on students' probability judgments. A high (or low) anchor was induced by asking subjects to state whether a probability was greater than or less than .75 (or .25) before they gave their estimates of the exact likelihood.

In order to investigate whether similar biases occur with experts in real-world information-rich settings, Northcraft and Neale (1987) asked professional estate agents and a sample of students to make valuations of real properties. They were taken to visit the property and the surrounding area and were provided with all the information that they might use to make valuations in practice. Northcraft and Neale also provided the estate agents and students with a listing price which reflected the seller's best guess as to the value of the property. They found that the valuations produced by the experts and student subjects were systematically influenced by variations in the listing price. Interestingly, although the students conceded that the listing price information did influence them, the professional experts flatly denied that the listing price had any influence on their judgments. Northcraft and Neale concluded that experts are susceptible to heuristically driven biases and are less likely to admit, or even realize, that the heuristics are responsible for their decisions.

The idea that experts may not know how they are making their judgments is consistent with Evans' (1984) two-stage theory reviewed above and receives empirical support from a number of different studies. For example, Berry and Broadbent (1984) examined the performance of their subjects on a computerized control task. Over a series of trials, subjects in the experiment had to adjust the value of the workforce of a factory in order to achieve some target level of production. They found that, after practice, subjects were capable of consistently achieving the target, yet they showed very little or no ability to demonstrate the knowledge they had when posed direct questions in a postexperimental questionnaire.

Kirwan, Chaput de Saintonge, Joyce, and Currey (1983) studied rheumatologists' evaluations of "disease activity" in arthritic patients. They found that rheumatologists' ratings of the importance they placed on different symptoms was quite different to the relative impact the symptoms actually had when they were judging patients. This lack of insight has been found in a number of studies of this type. Judges appear to strongly overestimate the importance they place on minor cues, and underestimate their reliance on major cues (Slovic, 1972). An intriguing result is reported by Slovic, Fleissner, and Bauman (1972), who found that the longer stockbrokers had been in business, the less insight they had into their weighting policy.

These studies clearly have disturbing implications for the elicitation of valid expert knowledge for use in expert systems, but they also may help explain why expert judgments under uncertainty may be biased. Wagenaar and Keren (1986) have suggested that one cause of overconfidence is a trust in inferential reasoning without consideration for its fallibility. Clearly, if experts have very little idea of *how* they are making their judgments, then it will be very difficult for them to assess their vulnerability to systematic bias under any particular prevailing set of circumstances.

There is some evidence that the act of giving an explanation for the occurrence of an event may in itself induce bias in judgment. Higher-event likelihoods have been reported from subjects who explained an event, compared to subjects who did not formulate explanations (Ross, Lepper, Strack, & Steinmetz, 1977). Anderson and Wright (1989) looked for the presence of the "explanation effect" in accountancy students' and experienced auditors' judgments of the likelihood that the balance of accounts were materially in error. They found that written explanations for the occurrence of the target event resulted in an explanation effect for the students, but not for the experienced auditors. This is evidence for a debiasing impact of expertise, but auditors may not be typical of all experts. As Anderson and Wright point out, explanation of conclusions is a fundamental aspect of audit practice. As we have seen, other experts may not be motivated to provide detailed justifications for their probabilistic opinions. The fact that the novices were vulnerable to the effect suggests that there may be occasions when the explanation effect does infiltrate the reasoning of some experts.

CONCLUSION

What can be concluded from this review of the research into the competence of experts? At the beginning of this chapter, it was suggested that there was a general acceptance of the related concepts of expert and expertise. The psychological evidence reviewed here challenges that acceptance. Plainly, experts' decisions are not invulnerable to error and bias. But, rather more obviously, experts' decision making clearly generally benefits from the possession of expertise; in spite of the observations made here, when ill, I would rather be treated by an experienced physician than a complete novice.

Nevertheless, it needs to be emphasized that the psychological research has unearthed real problems. Some have argued against this view, claiming that reports of poor performance do not have the rather bleak implications that have been ascribed to them (Cohen, 1981) and that reports of good performance have been unreasonably overlooked (Beach et al., 1987). For example, the point has been made that because subjects have no difficulty with some versions of the selection task, they do not lack the basic logical competence that some have claimed is lacking. Cohen (1981) has argued that, in this context, poor performance on the selection task can be attributed to what he terms a "cognitive illusion." The term cognitive illusion is selected deliberately in order to invoke the analogy with visual illusions and to prompt comparison with their interpretation; despite the undeniable existence of visual illusions, we do not take them as evidence of any fundamental incompetence of visual cognition. A counterargument is that the apparent competence demonstrated by performance on certain versions of the selection task may be as illusory as Cohen claims the incompetent performances are (Evans & Pollard, 1981). Nonetheless, illusion or not, errors resulting from faulty reasoning can have serious consequences.

To be fair, Cohen does not claim that these errors will not necessarily occur in real situations "if the circumstances that cause the illusion occur naturally." Consequently, the niceties of the argument concerning what interpretation should be placed on poor performance need not interest us; once errors of reasoning and judgment have been located in experts, then the case for caution in the use of expert judgment is established.

The discussion above of the contrast between the studies of Nisbett et al. (1983), showing evidence for statistical reasoning, and Gilovich et al. (1985), revealing the hot-hand fallacy, illustrates a general characteristic of the inferences that can be drawn from tests of the competence of experts (or novices, for that matter). Evidence that some set of individuals produce competent judgment, as defined by performance against some standard, does not establish the general case that their performance, perhaps in other situations, will necessarily be competent (perhaps by other normative standards). Consequently, studies reporting good performance will not necessarily provide reassurance as to the underlying level of competence, and hence the projected overall quality of performance. However, reliable evidence for incompetent judgment will always establish that there is some kind of limitation to underlying competence, and hence possible future levels of performance.

It may be tempting to suppose that, because the psychological research identifying errors in expert judgments necessarily also defines a correct standard or method, a check, or even ready remedy, for judgmental error could be easily devised. As much was suggested in the discussion of the relevance of base rates to medical diagnosis earlier in this chapter. Certainly, in some circumstances, decision support systems can be utilized in the reasonable hope of avoiding, or at least minimizing, the prospect of judgmental error. For example, the integration of different bits of information into a coherent judgment of uncertainty is something that a wide range of different experts appear to find difficult, even though (to the further detriment of the judgments) they may not realize it. Under those circumstances it might seem reasonable to suggest that a computer, suitably programmed to perform some form of Bayesian integration, does the bits that the expert gets wrong or finds difficult.

A limitation of this strategy is that it may not always be obvious, which is the bit that the expert gets wrong. Some biases may be completely masked by complex environmental and psychological factors. As we have seen, it is not always possible for an expert to state the reasoning behind their judgments (and even where they can this activity may engender further bias); for some experts, their expertise may defy easy formulation into a set of rules (Vaux, 1990).

Among those concerned with the practical use of the implementation of expert knowledge into expert systems there is recognition of the notion that expert judgment is plagued with biases (Jacob, Gaulteney, & Salvendy, 1986), though what should be done about it remains vague. If expert systems are to be based on an emulation of the expert then there is clearly a risk of emulating the expert's errors. Carefully planned procedures for eliciting expert knowledge may help reduce the bias in an expert system, but there is no current test available, nor is there ever likely to be, to check and eliminate all biases in the knowledge elicited from humans.

Perhaps one thing that would help is a greater recognition of the limitations of expert knowledge; efforts to locate likely sources of bias in a given realm of expertise might form the basis for the design of training programs. As far as I am aware, the basic training of doctors, forensic scientists, and others whose activities necessarily involve them with intuitive statistical inference, does not typically include reference to Bayes' theorem.

The tone of this chapter has been rather pessimistic about the value of expertise. Plainly, there is much to be said for the competence of experts; this is something that they themselves emphasize by such things as the constitution of professional bodies and, not least of course, their fees. What this chapter claims, however, is that there is also much to be said about their incompetence.

REFERENCES

Anderson, U., & Wright, W. F. (1989). Expertise and the explanation effect. *Organizational Behavior and Human Decision Processes, 42,* 250–269.

Arkes, H. R., Saville, P. D., Wortmann, R. L., & Harkness, A. R. (1981). Hindsight bias among physicians weighing the likelihood of diagnosis. *Journal of Applied Psychology, 66,* 252–254.

Beach, L. R., Barnes, V., & Christensen-Szalanski, J. J. J. (1987). Assessing human judgment: Has it been done, can it be done, should it be done? In Wright, G. & Ayton, P. (Eds.), *Judgmental forecasting.* Chichester: Wiley.

Berkeley, D., & Humphreys, P. (1982). Structuring decision problems and the "bias heuristic." *Acta Psychologica, 50,* 201–252.

Berry, D. C., & Broadbent, D. E. (1984). On the relationship between task performance and associated verbalisable knowledge. *Quarterly Journal of Experimental Psychology, 36A*, 209–231.

Chi, M., Feltovich, P., & Glaser, R. (1981). Categorization and representation of physics problems by experts and novices. *Cognitive Science, 5*, 121–152.

Chi, M., Glaser, R., & Rees, E. (1982). Expertise in problem solving. In R. Sternberg, (Ed.), *Advances in the psychology of human intelligence*. Hillsdale, N.J.: Erlbaum.

Christensen-Szalanski, J. J. J., Beck, D. E., Christensen-Szalanski, C. M., & Koepsell, T. D. (1983). Effects of expertise and experience on risk judgments. *Journal of Applied Psychology, 68*, 278–284.

Christensen-Szalanski, J. J. J., & Bushyhead, J. B. (1981). Physicians use of probabilistic information in a real clinical setting. *Journal of Experimental Psychology, Human Perception and Performance, 7*, 928–935.

Cohen, L. J. (1981). Can human irrationality be experimentally demonstrated? *The Behavioural and Brain Sciences, 4*, 317–370.

Cooke, D. (1990). Being an "expert" in court. *The Psychologist, 3*, 1990, 216–221.

Dawes, R. M. (1983). Is irrationality systematic? *The Behavioural and Brain Sciences, 3*, 491–492.

DeGowin, E. L., & DeGowin, R. L. (1969). *Bedside diagnostic examination*. 2nd ed. London: Macmillan.

de Groot, A. D. (1965). *Thought and choice in chess*. The Hague: Mouton.

de Groot, A. D. (1966). Perception and memory versus thought: Some old ideas and new findings. In Kleinmuntz, B. (Ed.). *Problem solving*. New York: Wiley.

Ebbesen, E. B., & Konecni, V. J. (1980). On the external validity of decision-making research: What do we know about decisions in the real world? In Wallsten, T. S. (Ed.), *Cognitive processes in choice and decision behavior*. Hillsdale, N.J.: Erlbaum.

Eddy, D. M. (1982). Probabilistic reasoning in clinical medicine: Problems and opportunities. In Kahneman, D., Slovic, P., & Tversky, A. (Eds.), *Judgment under uncertainty: Heuristics and biases*. Cambridge University Press.

Eddy, D. M., & Clanton, C. H. (1982). The art of clinical diagnosis: Solving the clinicopathological exercise. *The New England Journal of Medicine, 306*, 1263–1268.

Evans, J. St. B. T. (1984). Heuristic and analytic processes in reasoning. *British Journal of Psychology, 75*, 451–468.

Evans, J. St. B. T. (1989a). *Bias in human reasoning: Causes and consequences*. Brighton: Erlbaum.

Evans, J. St. B. T. (1989b). Some causes of bias in expert opinion. *The Psychologist, 2*, 112–113.

Evans, J. St. B. T., & Pollard, P. (1981). On defining rationality unreasonably. *The Behavioral and Brain Sciences, 4*, 335–336.

Fischhoff, B. (1975). Hindsight ≠ foresight: The effect of outcome knowledge on judgment under uncertainty. *Journal of Experimental Psychology: Human Perception and Performance, 1*, 288–289.

Gilovich, T., Vallone, R., & Tversky, A. (1985). The hot hand in basketball: On the misperception of random sequences. *Cognitive Psychology, 17*, 295–314.

Golding, E. (1981). *The effect of past experience on problem solving*. Paper presented to the British Psychological Society at Surrey University.

Griggs, R. A., Cox, J. R. (1982). The elusive thematic-materials effect in Wason's selection task. *British Journal of Psychology, 73*, 407–420.

Griggs, R. A., & Ransdell, S. E. (1986). Scientists and the selection task. *Social Studies of Science, 16*, 319–330.

The Guardian (1990). *QC condemns deliberate silence*. June 16th, p. 3.

Haward, L. R. C. (1981). *Forensic psychology*. London: Batsford Academic and Educational Limited.

Hunter, I. M. L. (1977). Mental calculation. In Johnson-Laird, P. N., & Wason, P. C. (Eds.), *Thinking: Readings in cognitive science*. Cambridge University Press.

The Independent (1990a). *Maguire inquiry puts convictions to a severe test*. May 29th, p. 5.

The Independent (1990b). *No record made of bomb case test*. May 30th, p. 3.

The Independent (1990c). *DPP criticised by Maguire lawyers*. June 16th, p. 3.

The Independent (1990d). *Scientists recalled to the Maguire inquiry*. June 5th, p. 3.

Jackson, S. L., & Griggs, R. A. (1990). The elusive pragmatic reasoning schemas effect. *Quarterly Journal of Experimental Psychology, 42A*, 353–373.

Jacob, V. S., Gaulteney, L. D., & Salvendy, G. (1986). Strategies and biases in human decision making and their implications for expert systems. *Behaviour and Information Technology, 5*, 119–140.

Johnson, D. (1980). Doctor talk. In Michaels, L., & Ricks, C. (Eds.), *The state of the language*. University of California Press.

Johnson-Laird, P. N., Legrenzi, P., & Legrenzi, M. S. (1972). Reasoning and a sense of reality. *British Journal of Psychology, 63*, 395–400.

Kahneman, D., Slovic, P., & Tversky, A. (1982). *Judgment under uncertainty: Heuristics and biases*. Cambridge University Press.

Katz, J. (1984). Why doctors don't disclose uncertainty. *Hastings Centre Report, 14*, 35–44.

Keren, G. B. (1987). Facing uncertainty in the game of bridge: A calibration study. *Organizational Behavior and Human Decision Processes, 39*, 98–114.

Kirwan, J. R., Chaput de Saintonge, D. M., Joyce, C. R. B., & Currey, H. L. F. (1983). Clinical judgment in rheumatoid arthritis: II. Judging "current disease activity" in clinical practise. *Annals of the Rheumatic Diseases, 42*, 648–651.

Larkin, J., McDermott, J., Simon, D., & Simon, H. (1980a). Expert and novice performance in solving physics problems. *Science, 208*, 1335–1342.

Larkin, J., McDermott, J., Simon, D., & Simon, H. (1980b). Models of competence in solving physics problems. *Cognitive Science, 4*, 317–345.

Lichtenstein, S., Fischhoff, B., & Phillips, L. D. (1982). Calibration of probabilities: The state of the art to 1980. In Kahneman, D., Slovic, P., & Tversky, A. (Eds.), *Judgment under uncertainty: Heuristics and biases*. Cambridge University Press.

Macdonald, R. R., & Gilhooly, K. J. (1990). More about Linda *or* conjunctions in context. *European Journal of Cognitive Psychology, 2*, 57–70.

Mayseless, O., & Kruglanski, A. W. (1987). What makes you so sure? Effects of epistemic motivations on judgmental confidence. *Organizational Behavior and Human Decision Processes, 39*, 162–183.

Murphy, A. H., & Winkler, R. L. (1984). Probability forecasting in meteorology. *Journal of the American Statistical Association, 79*, 489–500.

Murphy, G. L., & Wright, J. C. (1984). Changes in conceptual structure with expertise: Differences between real-world experts and novices. *Journal of Experimental Psychology: Learning Memory and Cognition, 10*, 144–155.

Neale, M. A., & Northcraft, G. B. (1986). Experts, amateurs and refrigerators: Comparing expert and amateur negotiators in a novel task. *Organizational Behavior and Human Decision Processes, 38*, 305–317.

Newell, A., & Simon, H. A. (1972). *Human problem solving*. Englewood Cliffs, N.J.: Prentice-Hall.

Nisbett, R. E., Krantz, D. H., Jepson, C., & Kunda, Z. (1983). The use of statistical heuristics in everyday inductive reasoning. *Psychological Review, 90*, 339–363.

Northcraft, G. B., & Neale, M. A. (1987). Experts, amateurs and real estate: An anchoring and adjust perspective on property pricing decisions. *Organizational Behavior and Human Decision Processes, 39*, 84–97.

Phillips, L. D. (1987). On the adequacy of judgmental probability forecasts. In Wright, G., & Ayton, P. (Eds.), *Judgmental forecasting*. Chichester: Wiley.

Ross, L., Lepper, M. R., Strack, F., & Steinmetz, J. (1977). Social explanation and social expectation: Effects of real and hypothetical explanations on subjective likelihood. *Journal of Personality and Social Psychology, 35*, 817–829.

Selnes, F., & Troye, S. V. (1989). Buying expertise, information search and problem solving. *Journal of Economic Psychology, 10*, 411–428.

Simon, D., & Simon, H. (1978). Individual differences in solving physics problems. In R. Siegler (Ed.), *Children's thinking: What develops?* Hillsdale, N.J.: Erlbaum.

Slovic, P. (1972). Psychological study of human judgment: implications for investment decision making. *Journal of Finance, 27*, 779–799.

Slovic, P., Fleissner, D., & Bauman, W. S. (1972). Analysing the use of information in investment decision making: A methodological proposal. *Journal of Business, 45*, 283–301.

Sweller, J., Mawer, R. F., & Ward, M. R. (1983). Development of expertise in mathematical problem solving. *Journal of Experimental Psychology: General, 112*, 639–661.

Tversky, A., & Kahneman, D. (1981). The framing of decisions and the psychology of choice. *Science, 211*, 453–458.

Vaux, J. (1990). Replicating the expert. *New Scientist*, March 3rd, 55–58.

Wagenaar, W. A. (1988). *Identifying Ivan: A case study in legal psychology*. New York: Harvester.

Wagenaar, W. A., & Keren, G. B. (1986). Does the expert know? The reliability of predictions and confidence ratings of experts. In Hollnagel, E., Mancini, G., & Woods, D. D., *Intelligent decision support in process environments*. Berlin: Springer-Verlag.

Wason, P. C. (1966). Reasoning. In Foss, B. M. (Ed.), *New horizons in psychology*. Harmondsworth, England: Penguin.

Whorf, B. L. (1940). Science and linguistics. *Technology Review, 42*, 227–231, 247–248.

Winkler, R. L., & Murphy, A. H. (1973). Experiments in the laboratory and the real world. *Organizational Behavior and Human Performance, 10*, 252–270.

Wright, W. F., & Anderson, U. (1989). Effects of situation familiarity and financial incentives on use of the anchoring and adjustment heuristic for probability assessment. *Organizational Behavior and Human Decision Processes, 44*, 68–82.

CHAPTER 5

Epistemic Strategies
Causal Thinking in Expert and Nonexpert Judgment

Lee Roy Beach

The purpose of this chapter is to explore the nature of epistemic strategies, one of the two classes of strategies in the contingency model of judgment and forecasting proposed by Beach, Barnes, and Christensen-Szalanski (1986; see also Beach, Christensen-Szalanski, & Barnes, 1987), and to examine the development and use of these strategies by both experts and nonexperts. I will begin by reviewing the circumstances that led to formulation of the model, followed by a description of the model. Then I will demonstrate that considerably more is known about epistemic strategies than may at first appear. This will be followed by an examination of the use of epistemic strategies by experts in an important judgment task; the point being that this use is not atypical of many other judgment tasks. Finally, I will use what has gone before to broaden and clarify the contingency model of judgment and underscore its relevance to understanding and supporting judgmental expertise.

BACKGROUND

A central feature of the judgment literature is its diversity of views concerning the quality of human judgment and decision making. While the battle lines

Lee Roy Beach • Department of Management and Policy, College of Business and Public Administration, University of Arizona, Tucson, Arizona 85721.
Expertise and Decision Support, edited by George Wright and Fergus Bolger. Plenum Press, New York, 1992.

are not drawn as clearly as they once were, there still are two rather distinct camps (Jungermann, 1983). One camp, the pessimists, regards the processes and products of various normative models from statistics and probability theory as the criteria against which human judgmental processes and products should be compared. It looks at the judgment literature and finds orderly, but disturbing, errors which it attributes to reliance upon cognitive shortcuts, called heuristics, that systematically bias judgment. The most commonly cited heuristics are representativeness, availability, and anchoring and adjustment (Tversky & Kahneman, 1974; Kahneman, Slovic, & Tversky, 1982). The list of biases that are assumed to result from the use of heuristics is long: the law of small numbers (Tversky & Kahneman, 1971), the illusion of validity (Kahneman & Tversky, 1973), the regression fallacy (Kahneman & Tversky, 1973), the imaginability bias (Tversky & Kahneman, 1974), the base-rate fallacy (Kahneman & Tversky, 1972; Bar-Hillel, 1980), the conjunction fallacy (Tversky & Kahneman, 1983), and so on.

The other camp, the optimists, does not take the indefensible position that human judgment is infallible. However, it contends that the evidence presented by the pessimists does not constitute a strong case against human judgment. The optimists argue that the normative models that are used as the criteria in evaluating judgment often are not appropriate to the task that the experimenters present to their subjects (e.g., Cohen, 1979; Corbin, 1980; Hogarth, 1981). They also argue that experimenters and subjects frequently do not have the same understanding of the experimental task, and as a result the subjects may be doing something entirely different from what the experimenter supposes they are doing—which also makes the use of normative criteria questionable. It is this latter argument that is the point of departure for the present work.

It is clear that subjects often do not understand what the experimenter is asking of them. For example, Christensen-Szalanski and Beach (1982) found that 20% of the subjects in a standard judgment research task refused to give a judgment at all—they simply did not know what to do. Because the number of nonresponding subjects usually is not reported in the literature, the prevalence of misunderstanding is difficult to estimate. However, confusion appears to be common. For example, Phillips (1983) had students in an advanced seminar in decision research interpret some of the problems that are commonly used in judgment research. Different members of the seminar gave different interpretations of the problems, and the group as a whole was able to deduce the "correct" interpretations only by working backward from the "correct" answers provided by the original experimenters.

These and related findings (e.g., Kahneman & Tversky, 1973), prompted Berkeley and Humphreys (1982) to suggest that subjects construct "small worlds" when faced with experimental judgment problems, and that the form of the small world that a particular subject constructs depends at least as much upon what he or she is trying to do and upon the meaning attached to the problem as it does upon the problem's formal characteristics. The difficulty is that experimenters have not ensured that the subjects' small worlds correspond to the small worlds that they, the experimenters, think are appropriate.

TWO KINDS OF REASONING

Building upon Berkeley and Humphreys' (1982) suggestion, Barnes (1984) performed an experiment that demonstrated the marked difference between subjects' and experimenters' perceptions about the nature and demands of various judgment tasks—as well as the impact of those differences on the resulting judgments. The subjects were 15 undergraduates who had never taken statistics and who thus were typical of the subjects in the judgment literature. They were presented with 15 judgment problems that had been used in previously reported studies to demonstrate judgmental errors. Five problems had been used to demonstrate that subjects tend to ignore sample sizes (the law of small numbers; Tversky & Kahneman, 1971), five had been used to demonstrate that subjects tend to ignore or underuse base rates (the base-rate bias; Kahneman & Tversky, 1972), and five had been used to demonstrate that subjects tend to judge the probability of the conjunction of events as higher than the probabilities of the constituent events (the conjunction fallacy; Tversky & Kahneman, 1983).

To begin, the subjects read the 15 problems and sorted them into classes of similar problems and labeled each class and described what was similar among the problems in the class. It was found that the labels and definitions of similarity did not at all reflect sample size, base rate, or conjunction—the three normative concepts that the original experimenters had used to generate the problems. Instead, the subjects divided the problems according to content—"math problems" or "problems about people." In short the problems that the experimenters would have grouped together got distributed among several of the subjects' groups, indicating that the subjects conceived of (framed) the problems in a very different way from that of the experimenters.

Then the subjects were asked to make a judgment for each problem while talking aloud about what they were thinking. In some cases what was said revealed that the subjects grasped the feature that the experimenters would have regarded as essential, and their answers were fairly similar to what the experimenters would regard as accurate. In other cases, however, their approach was substantially different from what the experimenters would have regarded as appropriate, and their answers were correspondingly different.

However, granting their approach, their answers usually were justifiable. In general, "probabilistic" reasoning tended to predominate for sample-size problems, "causal" reasoning tended to predominate for conjunction problems, and the two kinds of reasoning were used about equally for base-rate problems.

However, close examination of the problems revealed that content, rather than the normative concept, was the underlying determinant of the predominant kind of logic. These results conform to the conclusions drawn by Nisbett, Krantz, Jepson, and Kunda (1983): problems that encourage recognition of chance, repeatability, and *sets* of persons, objects, or events tend to elicit "probabilistic" reasoning, and problems that involve individual persons, objects, or events tend to elicit "causal" reasoning. For example, two of Barnes' five base-rate problems were about diseases in groups of people and virtually all subjects used "probabilistic" reasoning for them. The other three base-rate problems involved individual persons and most of the subjects used "causal" reasoning.

The lessons to be learned from Barnes' (1984) study are that in the laboratory tasks that comprise the major portion of the judgment literature: (1) subjects and experimenters often differ about the nature of judgment problems, but experimenters (who, after all, write the journal articles) condemn those differences as errors even though charity and prudence suggest they be interpreted merely as differences; and (2) subjects are able to use different kinds of reasoning for what they perceive to be different kinds of judgment problems. It was these results, together with a wish to add some order to what has become a very confused and contradictory literature and to address the question of differences in motivation and expertise among judges, that prompted the formulation of the contingency model of judgment (Beach, Barnes, & Christensen-Szalanski, 1986).

THE CONTINGENCY MODEL OF JUDGMENT

The model is fashioned after the Beach and Mitchell (1978) contingency model for decision strategy selection. The general idea is that *judges* use different judgment strategies for different judgment *tasks* encountered in different judgment *environments,* and that the final judgment is contingent upon the characteristics of all three.

Judgment Strategies

Each judge is assumed to have a unique repertory of judgment strategies. However, because of the difficulty of speaking generally, across judges, about these unique repertories, the model posits two classes of strategies. One class corresponds to what was referred to above as "probabilistic" reasoning and one corresponds to what was referred to as "causal" reasoning—called *aleatory* and *epistemic* reasoning, respectively. (This division was suggested by Tversky & Kahneman [1983], although they did not use precisely these labels.)

Aleatory reasoning is the logic of gambling (an aleator is a dice player), and is the basis of modern probability theory. Basic to this reasoning is the principle of extentionality which asserts, in essence, that all elements in a particular set are mutually intersubstitutable (Suppes, 1957). Statements about the characteristics of the elements are based solely upon class membership and not upon unique properties; the focus is on the set and not on the individual elements (just as the unemployment rate refers to the problem for the aggregate rather than the plight of the individual). From this viewpoint the fact that each throw of a die is a unique event is irrelevant to statements about the probabilities of the possible outcomes of that throw; a five on one throw is the same as a five on any other throw, a three is the same as any other three, etc. The uniqueness of the events is not pertinent.

Epistemic reasoning means that judgments, be they stated as probabilities or in any other form, derive from the judge's knowledge about the unique characteristics of the specific elements of interest and about the causal network in which they are embedded, as well as their various set memberships. This class of strategies requires that element-specific knowledge not be ignored because it is central to the judgment, and set membership is merely one aspect of it.

Of course, both classes of reasoning strategies can generate judgments that can be stated as probabilities, although the judgments are derived in different ways and the stated probabilities are not necessarily the same. For example, when assessing the probability of measurable precipitation, a weather forecaster using aleatory reasoning would depend entirely upon probability data, regarding present weather conditions as a member of a set of previously observed, similar conditions that have resulted in precipitation on a specific proportion of occasions. In contrast, a forecaster using epistemic reasoning might look at satellite photographs and mentally project the progress of various weather fronts and their subsequent influences on the local weather; the mental projection would rely upon the forecaster's cognitive model of how fronts progress through the particular locale for which the forecast is being made, and upon his or her knowledge about what causes precipitation.

In short, the contingency model begins with the assumption that judges have unique repertories of judgment strategies that can be divided into two broad categories, aleatory and epistemic. However, while aleatory strategies have been the focus of forty years of research, considerably less has been done in regard to epistemic strategies. This is because probability theory provided precise points of reference for the evaluations of judgments. As we have seen, a strong argument can be made that this may not have been a wholly profitable paradigm. Nonetheless, it motivated most of the existing literature.

In contrast, there may be no precise reference points for the evaluation of epistemic reasoning. Recognition of this possibility has slowed investigation of epistemic reasoning—primarily resulting in amiable acknowledgment of its existence, but not a great deal more. While I cannot promise to wholly rectify this situation, I hope that what follows will make it clear that psychology knows more about epistemic reasoning than might be supposed on the basis of the judgment literature alone, and that this knowledge may be profitably applied in understanding epistemic judgment strategies, particularly the epistemic strategies used by experts.

Judgment Task

Barnes' (1984) research, as well as that by Nesbitt and his colleagues (1983) and that reported more recently, for example by Gigerenzer, Hall, and Blank (1988), all indicate that the various characteristics of the judgment task influence the judge's selection of a strategy for making judgments. Tasks that involve repeated events, aggregates of persons or things, and that are stated in numerical terms or that are normally couched in statistical terms (e.g., sports records) encourage use of aleatory strategies. Tasks that involve unique events, individual persons, and that are not stated in numerical terms encourage use of epistemic strategies.

Judgment Environment

The model conceives of strategy selection as directed by the characteristics of the judgment task, limited of course by the richness of the judge's repertory. However, simply selecting a strategy, even a perfectly appropriate strategy, does not assure that the resulting judgment will be appropriate or adequate. Most strategies can be applied in either a rigorous, comprehensive manner or in a loose, approximate manner, or the rigor of their application can be somewhere between these two extremes. For example, you can calculate exactly the amount of interest you will have paid on a loan over the course of its life, or you can make an informed estimate, or you can make a wild guess. All three judgments may be driven by the same underlying knowledge about how interest on loans works, but that knowledge is sharpened by the use of formulas and a calculator in the first case, by use of some sort of rule of thumb in the second case, and by who-knows-what in the third case. The point is that a strategy can have several manifestations, each of which is more or less rigorous and precise than another.

The judgment model views the characteristics of the judgment environment as determining the rigor with which the judge will implement the strategy that is selected to deal with the particular judgment task at hand. A review of the relevant literature (Beach, Barnes, & Christensen-Szalanski, 1986) suggests that these characteristics are: (1) the judge's perception of the extrinsic *benefits* of making an accurate judgment; (2) the judge's perception of whether the judgment will be *revisable* in the light of further information or in the light of feedback about the success of the enterprise in which the judgment is used; (3) the judge's perception of whether the judgment task is within his or her area of *competence*;

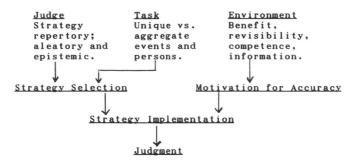

Figure 1. A schematic of the contingency model for the selection of judgment strategies.

and (4) the judge's perception of the adequacy (quality and amount) of the *information* available. In general, the higher the perceived benefits of being accurate, the less the opportunity for revision, the more the task is in his or her area of competence (error undermines reputation), and the more adequate the available information, the more the judge strives for judgmental accuracy by more rigorous use of the selected judgment strategy.

Figure 1 contains a schematic of the contingency model for the selection of judgment strategies. The model's major conceptual weakness, in general as well as in reference to expert judgment, is that the nature of epistemic strategies needs further explication. To address this weakness, we must take a short side trip into cognitive psychology.

COGNITION AND CAUSALITY

Consider the wonderful ability of people to infer causality and to use their inferences to explain the past and predict the future. Observation of this ability raises questions about its generality and utility, and about what makes experts different from nonexperts in terms of appreciation of causality in specific domains. Even if it were desirable, space limitations prevent a detailed review of the psychological literature on causality, so I will limit myself to a brief description of two early landmarks, included to indicate the breadth of what has been done, and a somewhat expanded description of a third landmark.

The first landmark is the classic work of Michotte (1963) using the "Michotte machine" in which a disc upon which two lines are drawn is rotated behind a screen that contains a slot through which the observer sees two small blocks, A and B. Depending upon how the lines are drawn on the disc, the blocks can be made to appear to move back and forth in the slot in a variety of patterns and speeds. Typical of Michotte's findings was that when block A was made to move quickly across the slot and touch block B, followed by both of them moving to the end of the slot, observers reported that A had *pushed* B. Or, when A rushed across and touched B and then A slowed down while B rushed to the end of the slot, observers reported that A had *hit* B. In these and other cases, A's physical energy seemed to the observer to have been transmitted to B, the commonsense notion of physical causality. In all cases the perception of causality was immediate and wholly compelling.

The second landmark study is by Heider and Simmel (1944), who made an animated silent film in which the only "characters" were a small triangle, a small circle, and a large square, all three of which moved in and around a large rectangle on the two-dimensional movie screen. Observers of the film all found themselves inferring that the triangle was in love with the circle who was the unwilling recipient of the attentions of the square. The triangle tried to protect the circle from the square who, in anger, proceeded to break up the house (the rectangle) in which the lovers had taken refuge. The point is, the movements of these simple geometric figures led nearly all observers to perceive motivated (caused) behavior where in fact none existed except by inference, and nearly all construct a storylike scenario that neatly summarized their perceptions.

The research begun by Michotte (1963) and Heider and Simmel (1944) is carried on in more recent studies of people's ability to evaluate the causal relationships between various experimentally presented cues, as well as of their ability to make causal attributions for observed events (Dickinson, Shanks, & Evenden, 1984; Downing, Sternberg, & Ross, 1985; Einhorn & Hogarth, 1986; Schustak & Sternberg, 1981; Shanks, 1986). However, review of this line of inquiry would take us far afield.

The third landmark is more pertinent to judgment by experts and nonexperts. It cannot be illustrated by a single study because it consists of thirty years or so of behavioristic research on "learning." The behaviorist tradition eschewed description of behavior in anything like cognitive terms, focusing instead upon the rather mechanistic concepts of classical and operant conditioning as the foundations of behavior. However, with the advent of the cognitive revolution it became safe to rethink the conditioning literature and to recast it in cognitive terms.

The most thorough treatment of conditioning in cognitive terms is by Holyoake, Koh, and Nisbett (1989). It consists of a rule-based performance system that is linked to a mechanism for inductive learning. A simpler treatment of conditioning in cognitive terms by Beach (1973) reflects the same general view as the Holyoake, Koh, and Nisbett (1989) treatment and is expositionally more convenient for the present purpose. The central assumption in both treatments is that creatures, animals, and people formulate if-then propositions that guide their behavior. The principles of conditioning (motivation, reinforcement schedules, shaping) specify the conditions that promote induction of these propositions. The principles of stimulus and response generalization and of discrimination specify the conditions that promote application of these propositions. The principles of extinction specify the conditions that promote modification or rejection of these propositions.

PREDICTIVE PROPOSITIONS

In Beach's (1973) terms, classical conditioning is interpreted as a "what-to-expect" if-then proposition, where antecedent conditions S_1 give rise to an expectation about subsequent conditions S_2, written $S_1 \rightarrow S_2$. Operant conditioning is interpreted as a "what-to-do" if-then proposition, where antecedent conditions S_1 give rise to an expectation about subsequent conditions S_2, conditional upon the subject's intervention R_1, written $S_1 \rightarrow R_1 \rightarrow S_2$.

The theme that is common to both kinds of propositions is that they permit the actor to predict the future using causal if-then logic. What-to-expect propositions are the most obvious: if so-and-so occurs, then you can expect such-and-such to happen too, usually because so-and-so causes such-and-such. These are not necessarily hard-and-fast rules; they tend to be loosely coupled causal linkages—more causal than correlational, but not wholly deterministic.

What-to-do propositions are what-to-expect propositions in which the actor intervenes in an attempt to influence the future, to cause a desired state of affairs (S_2) to come about. They permit one to predict the future on the premise that by acting appropriately (R_1) in the present situation (S_1) one can predictably transform the situation (i.e., produce S_2). Of course, it is possible to imagine other actions and other outcomes, which gives rise to choices among alternative courses of action. The point is that the essence of both propositions is their usefulness for predicting the future.

We all form if-then predictive propositions on the basis of the things we experience, read, and are told. Propositions inferred from experience tend to be rather simplistic in that the events involved must be fairly concrete and proposition formation often is dependent upon fairly immediate feedback. However, people have ways other than inference from experience for forming propositions.

One way is by being taught the proposition by someone who already possesses it, and the other is by the use of intellect to construct a proposition. In the first case, propositions are acquired either through observing someone using them, or through instruction by someone about what is to be expected if so-and-so occurs or if you do such-and-such (Bandura, 1969). More often than not, propositions are acquired by a mixture of both observation and instruction. This, of course, is the purpose of providing explicit training and supervised experience to nonexperts, to shorten the time and effort they must invest in learning the causal relationships in their intended domain of expertise.

The other way people have of acquiring propositions is through the use of their intellect. Training and experience provide a foundation for the appreciation of the second-order, nonobvious, causal relationships that is the hallmark of the expert's understanding of a domain. In part, this consists of seeing commonalities in causal propositions across apparently different situations within the domain—of identifying propositions that transcend specific circumstances and that lend consistency and predictability to the domain as a whole. And, in part, it consists of hypothesizing causal factors (gravity, evolution, personality) that provide unifying explanations for observed events.

For many years the study of intellectual proposition making, both expert and nonexpert, relied upon an analogy with scientific proposition making (e.g., Piaget, 1929; Brunswik, 1956). The analogy was valuable, because it suggested that intellectual propositions are in fact rather complex theories that are tested against reality and modified when they are found wanting. However, times change and so do analogies. The newer analogy is that of a reader of a story (Bruner, 1986). The reader takes the information as it unfolds and constructs a cognitive representation that interrelates the important events, lets him or her maintain a global overview or zoom in on details as needed, and permits the reader to anticipate (predict) the story's ending. Although the ending provided by the author need not be the same as the reader's (sometimes, as in a mystery novel, it is best if it is not), it must be consistent with the reader's cognitive representation or it will be rejected as implausible, ill-constructed, illogical, or merely irksome.

Current research related to the new analogy is illustrated by the work of Pennington and Hastie (1986, 1988) on their "Story Model." Jurors are presented with prosecution and defense evidence about a crime. The experimenters observe the ways in which the evidence is cognitively represented by the jurors, and how that representation is related to their verdicts. It is found that representation is a storylike narrative, that the precise form of the narrative is influenced by the order in which the evidence is received, that different people constructed different narratives, that relationships among events internal to the narratives are inferred when no direct information is available, and that the verdicts follow reasonably from the narratives. Moreover, the ease with which a coherent narrative can be constructed determines the jurors' confidence in the resulting verdict.

The general conclusion is that intellectual propositions that interrelate complex sets of events are formulated as meaningful representations that have internal consistency and that can be used to predict (or, in this case, to postdict guilt or innocence). However, these intellectual propositions do not appear to be as detailed as scientific theories, nor as logically tight (although we do not know how lacking in details or logically tight scientific theories are when they are in the heads of scientists rather than in books and journals), and they do not appear to be as rigorously subjected to testing (although we do not know how rigorously scientific theories are tested in the heads of scientists either).

EPISTEMIC STRATEGY IN USE

Now let us turn to an interesting example of experts, physicians, using epistemic, causal reasoning in medical diagnosis, a task that often is regarded by decision researchers as requiring Bayesian aleatory reasoning. Eddy and Clanton (1982) examined 50 case reports published in the *New England Journal of Medicine* in 1974 and 1979. The cases were detailed reports of clinicopathological conferences (CPCs), which are a regular feature of the *Journal* and which . . . "are the offspring of the case method of teaching instituted at the Harvard Law School in the 1870s and introduced to the Massachusetts General Hospital in 1910 by Dr. Richard Cabot. Drs. Castleman and Dudley [1960] have explained the purpose of the CPC as 'an exercise in deductive reasoning. . . . It is less important to pinpoint the correct diagnosis than to present a logical and instructive analysis of the pertinent conditions involved' " (p. 1263). The purpose of analyzing the 50 cases was to infer the strategies that the participating physicians used when diagnosing the illnesses presented in CPCs.

It was found that the physicians' diagnostic process followed six steps: aggregation of initial information about the case, selection of a "pivot" finding from the initial information, use of the pivot to generate a cause list (possible diseases), pruning of the cause list, selection of the diagnosis, and validation of the diagnosis.

Step 1 involves learning about the patient's presenting symptoms and a history of his or her illness. Often a great deal of information is available, so the physician reduces the size of the problem by combining information into an aggregate: "Given a patient who presents with extreme polyuria, nocturia, polydipsia, and a urinary specific gravity below 1.003 in the absence of exogenous vasopressin, a discussant aggregated these four elementary findings into the aggregate finding of diabetes insipidus" (p. 1265). Aggregated findings are not the same as a diagnosis because the former pulls together only a limited set of highly related symptoms, while the diagnosis pulls together diverse sets of aggregated findings. "Hence, the recognition of a pattern of findings is sufficient for aggregation, whereas diagnosis often requires . . . more extensive reasoning . . ." (p. 1265).

Step 2 involves selection of pivotal findings, one or possibly two salient symptoms that can be focused upon while temporarily ignoring the others. Often these are symptoms that are known to be generally important, and that are stressed during medical education. "The powerful role of pivots in the diagnostic process is reflected in the fact that, although most medical knowledge may be stored according to disease, certain rather common findings receive separate attention (e.g., a coin lesion in the lung, protein-urias, and abdominal pain). When possible, these are the signs or symptoms chosen as pivots" (p. 1265).

Step 3 involves generation from memory of a cause list, which is a list of diseases that could have caused the pivotal symptom. Note that the logical flow now is reversed—initially it was from symptom to disease, but now it is from disease to symptom (the latter being the way in which knowledge is acquired in medical school).

Step 4 involves pruning the cause list by considering the diseases on the list one at a time and comparing them with the nonpivotal symptoms. Because only the pivotal symptoms were used to construct the list, in most cases the list is severely pruned when the other symptoms are reconsidered. To put this in terms of my favorite theory, image theory (Beach, 1990; Beach & Mitchell, 1987), the pruning process is an example of screening (Beach & Strom, 1989; van Zee, Paluchowski, & Beach, 1989). Each incompatibility between the disease in question and the nonpivotal symptoms reduces the plausibility of the disease being the cause of the illness; at some point a rejection threshold (Beach, 1990; Beach & Mitchell, 1987) is reached and the disease is pruned from the list. Returning to Eddy and Clanton (1982), "This is a comparison rather than a calculation, and it uses knowledge of the characteristics of diseases instead of requiring estimation of the probabilities of a disease, given the findings" (p. 1266). In short, pruning is an epistemic process rather than an aleatory process such as Bayesian inference. Pruning proceeds until only one disease remains on the list or, if more than one remains, the survivors constitute a tentative differential diagnosis.

Step 5 is the diagnosis. If only one disease survived pruning, it is the diagnosis. If more than one survived, Eddy and Clanton found that the physicians considered the survivors two at a time, comparing the ability of each to explain the case—the disease with the characteristic features that most closely matched the patient's symptoms was retained and the other one was eliminated. This pair-by-pair method quickly whittled down the list, usually to a single survivor, which was the diagnosis.

Step 6 involves reviewing what has been done, including reconsidering whether the final diagnosis is wholly adequate. Occasionally, the surviving disease is unable to comfortably fit all of the observed symptoms, whereupon the physicians tend to repeat the entire process using one of the unexplained symptoms as a new pivot.

CPCs are artificial diagnostic problems in that they are simulations, there is no patient present, and the information is limited to that which is presented. On the other hand, they probably are more complex than most actual diagnoses because in the latter patients usually present one or two classical symptoms and the diagnosis and treatment are immediately evident.

The drawback of the CPC artificiality for our present purpose is that the process ends with identification of the disease. In real life the diagnosis is merely a transition point. As noted above, in the majority of cases identification of the disease that is causing the patient's symptoms simply calls up a preformulated course of treatment that is automatically applied in much the same manner as a response is elicited by a stimulus in a conditioning study (what Klein [1987] has called "recognitional decision making").

On the other hand, in the minority of cases the sequelae of diagnosis are more interesting—knowledge about the specific disease process, knowledge comprised of causal rules that the physician possesses about how this particular syndrome operates, is used to predict what would happen if this, that, or another intervention were implemented. In all instances the diagnosis is used to explain and predict. It is just that in the first instance explanation and prediction are rather passive, although they may be effective, while in the second instance they are active and creative. The first undoubtedly would have been of interest to behavioristic researchers, but judgment and decision researchers are much more interested in the second.

However all that may be, the point of describing the Eddy and Clanton (1982) work in such detail is to illustrate how experts, physicians, use their causal knowledge to deal with what other experts, decision researchers, regard as an aleatory task. It is my contention that expert knowledge far more frequently involves causal thinking than it does aleatory thinking, and that efforts to understand and improve expert judgment must begin with this fact.

Moreover, it perhaps is inappropriate to assume that aleatory strategies necessarily are better than epistemic strategies. Certainly it is inappropriate to evaluate judgments derived from epistemic strategies in terms of their congruence with those prescribed by aleatory strategies unless, or until, the latter can be convincingly and independently demonstrated to be the correct criterion—and I very much doubt if that often can be done.

BROADENING THE JUDGMENT STRATEGY MODEL

Based upon the foregoing, it seems reasonable to identify epistemic judgment strategies as narrative cognitive representations—networks of causal propositions that permit explanation of the past and prediction of the future on the basis of assumptions about the present state of things and about constraints on what could have happened or can happen as events unfold. The constraints limit the admissible transformations on the present to create explanations about the past or conjectures about the future. The constraints may be independent of possible interventions, in which case the transformation describes the natural development of events. Or, the constraints may be conditional upon interventions, in which case the transformation describes the interaction of both natural development and the influence of actors. Unless the judge is trained in statistics (and usually in spite of such training), the logic is causal—prior events are perceived as causing subsequent events.

To elaborate: the general idea, based upon Pennington and Hastie (1986, 1988), is that when the judge is presented with background information he or she constructs a narrative, a structured representation that gives coherence to the presented information and that permits inferences about the reasons for past events and predictions about future events. The inferences are about parts of the narrative that are not available in the information but that are needed to make it coherent. The predictions are about how the narrative might develop, either naturally or as a result of intervention. The predictions may be either forecasts about eventualities with appended statements of confidence (probabilities) about the degree to which they are causally determined, or they may be only confidence statements for eventualities that someone else (the experimenter, for example) suggests.

Thus, I could contemplate moving from my present home to some other town and forecast that I will find a house to buy within two months, appending a confidence statement of the form, "the probability is about .80." Or, I can be asked by someone else what I think the probability is that I will find a house to buy within two months of arriving in the new town, to which I respond, "About .80." Either way, my probability assessment is a function of my inability to construct a faultless bridge from the present to the future (the purchase of a house in the new town). There is enough ambiguity in my "house hunting" narrative, the verbal-pictorial story I tell myself, that I am not wholly confident that the goal will be achieved in two months. Of course, were the time extended to a year, my confidence would go up.

The problem with all of this, or at least *a* problem, is that it presumes the construction of the narrative. Where does that narrative come from? Here we turn to Eddy and Clanton (1982). First of all, like Eddy and Clanton's physicians, people in general, and experts in particular, possess narratives associated with similar past contexts that they can draw upon. When a context (S_1) is encountered, its features are used to probe memory (Beach, 1964; Hintzman, 1986). If the probe locates a memory that is virtually the same as the present context, the context is said to be recognized and the narrative that is associated with it is deemed applicable, however roughly, to the present context. If the probe locates memories that merely resemble the present context, the context is said to be identified, in which case the similar memories constitute an ad hoc definition (frame) of the context (Beach, 1990) and the narratives associated with each of them provide the material for construction of a narrative for the present context.

In either case, memory provides the foundation upon which present information can be used to build a narrative. An expert, as a result of training and greater experience, has more in memory upon which to draw than does a nonexpert.

Having a foundation, we still have the problem of how the narrative actually gets constructed—information from memory will color it, but more is needed to give it a solid structure. It can be demonstrated that people very quickly recognize the themes and plots of the stories they read (Bruner, 1986). This implies that they possess a store of prototypic plots that are evoked by the presenting features of a story and then are modified as the story unfolds, with resulting coherence and predictability. I suggest that in much the same way prototypic narratives are used in conjunction with narratives from memory and with the information about the present context in order to tailor a unique narrative for the present context and to predict how the context may develop. Quite simply, these prototypic narratives *are* the epistemic strategies in judges' repertories of judgment strategies. And, again, an expert possesses more, and more finely developed, domain-specific prototypic narratives than does a nonexpert.

The notion of prototypic narratives as causal models is not as remote as it may seem. Very similar ideas are a mainstay of social psychology, where they are called implicit theories. For example, people apparently use implicit theories of personality, usually involving enduring traits, to explain and predict other people's behavior. For members of a single culture these theories may be more similar than different, but there still are notable individual differences that reflect differences in training and experience. One person may typically explain events in terms of good and evil, God and the Devil; others may explain them in terms of competition and achievement, love and rejection, courage and cowardice, pride and prejudice. Of course, an individual has multiple implicit theories, multiple prototypic narratives, each primarily reserved for a specific sort of context, S_1.

Implicit personality theories are but one, albeit important, example of the kinds of narrative structures I suggest are the basis of epistemic judgment strategies. Research on attitudes (Abelson, 1981) and stereotyping (McCauley, Sitt, & Segal, 1980), mental models for economics (Hogarth, Michaud, & Mery, 1980) and politics (Axelrod, 1976) as well as for physical processes such as electricity (de Kleer & Brown, 1983) and mechanics (Hegarty, Just, & Morrison, 1988), in addition to studies of metaphor and analogy (Gentner & Stevens, 1983), all suggest the breadth and variety of prototypic narratives. Perhaps the mechanism that underlies the construction of narratives for projective tests such as the TAT, which are reputed to provide insight into primary themes, also underlies narrative construction when unambiguous information about S_1 is available. In fact, some variation on the projective technique might prove valuable as a research tool for investigating epistemic judgment strategies.

The fact that narratives are formed so quickly and effortlessly suggests the existence of an easily accessible mode of narrative construction, probably by recourse to prototypes that can absorb the particulars of the presenting context (S_1). Perhaps one's store of prototypes is organized as a hierarchy of episodes, with related episodes occupying adjacent parts of the structure and applying to related kinds of events (Trabasso & van den Broek, 1985). These episodes can be used to revise narratives for familiar contexts or used to custom-design a narrative when the context has not been encountered in the past.

SUPPORTING EXPERT JUDGMENT

In all of the preceding we have assumed that the causal narratives constructed by experts basically are the same as those constructed by nonexperts, but that they are better informed, more elaborate, and, perhaps, more accurate. Although there is evidence (e.g., Chase & Simon, 1973) that experts are sensitive to structural similarities among contexts that nonexperts overlook, this does not refute the assumption that the narratives are fundamentally similar. However, even casual observation reveals that experts often have difficulty constructing accurate narratives. They also often have difficulty drawing appropriate conclusions (judgments) from their narratives, irrespective of the narratives' accuracy. The question is whether the view of causal thinking that has been advanced here provides useful guidance for designing systems to support and improve narrative construction and the use of those narratives in making judgments.

Begin by assuming that epistemic, causal reasoning is cognitively represented as narratives, however fragmentary and however inaccurate they may be. Further assume that expertise comes about by: (1) elaboration of and correction of these narratives as a result of training, experience, and deliberative thought; and (2) increased ability to discriminate crucial, often subtle, contextual cues that permit retrieval of appropriate narratives from memory. It follows that a judgment support system must focus upon extending these two aspects of expertise.

Elaboration of Narratives

The first focus of a support system must be to provide a useful summary of the judgment context—a summary that is congruent with the judge's method of cognitively representing that context so that it can be easily integrated into the judge's representation. This involves skillful use of graphic and textual presentations, the guidelines for which can be obtained from the literature on educational communications.

Presentation of an accurate summary assumes prior research to ascertain what belongs in it. Usually this research will begin with a review of existing literature, often starting with training texts and working backward to more detailed sources. Sometimes it will require original empirical work. Often it will reveal holes in what is known about the domain of interest, holes that must be represented as such to the judge.

The causal statements in the summary will be a combination of the two basic propositional forms, what-to-expect and what-to-do. What-to-expect propositions are descriptive if-then statements about the various themes in the narrative. What-to-do propositions are conjectural in that they are conditional upon some action on the part of the judge or some other actor in the narrative. As such, there can be as many what-to-do propositions as there are possible actions—each with its conjectured results.

In addition to causal statements, the narrative must contain information statements that describe the constraints under which the what-to-expect and what-to-do propositions operate. Information statements are descriptions of the context itself, the task, and the environment. The causal statements are descriptions of process within that context.

Once the summary of the context is presented to the judge, there are two ways in which he or she can use it. One way is to embellish or to correct his or her own narrative and then proceed to use the revised version to subjectively construct scenarios that can be used for explanation or prediction—i.e., for judgment generation. The second way is for the judge to use the summary narrative as it is presented to objectively construct scenarios with which to generate judgments. That is, in the first case the judge constructs scenarios in his or her head, and in the second case he or she uses the support system to construct the scenarios. Let us examine each of these in turn.

Jungermann and Thüring (1987) have presented a model of cognitive-scenario construction and use that provides a picture of how narratives arc used subjectively to generate judgments. Their model has four steps, of which the first consists of framing the situation (identifying it) and retrieving relevant knowledge about it from memory. In the second step, if-then propositions and information about constraints are used to construct a causal network (Thüring & Jungermann, 1986), using both known causal relationships from memory and inferred causal relationships. The latter derive from the four cues to causality identified by Einhorn and Hogarth (1986): covariation of events, their temporal order, their spatial and temporal contiguity, and their similarity—to which Beach (1990) added a fifth, knowledge about some actor's intention to cause events to occur.

In the third step, the network is treated as a simulation. Plausible values are assigned to its various component propositions to represent the status of a context (past, present, or future). Each unique set of plausible values constitutes a different scenario, not all of which are admissible because of limits set by the causal propositions and the contextual constraints. The fourth step consists of observing the logical results of assigning different plausible values to the propositions. These results are answers to the question, "What if x were the case?" The x in question being a particular scenario, a particular set of plausible starting conditions for the component propositions that make up the causal network. The answer to the question constitutes the judgment that follows from those starting conditions.

This subjective use of narratives to generate judgments need not remain encapsulated in the head of the judge. It should be possible to externalize the process, possibly using computers, so that the judge can use the support system's summary as a simulation. He or she would assign plausible values to the components of the summary and the computer would grind through the causal logic to generate judgments. The judge's role primarily would be to determine the plausibility of the starting values as descriptors of the context in question.

Discrimination of Contextual Cues

The second focus of a support system for expert judgment must be to help the judge discriminate the crucial features of the context so that relevant knowledge from memory can be brought to bear. If the support system is intended to virtually replace the judge with a computer simulation, this focus becomes one of helping the judge determine appropriate starting values for the propositions. Simple checklists derived from the summary itself may suffice.

If, on the other hand, the intention is to support elaboration and correction of the judge's own narrative, helping him or her determine starting values is necessary but not sufficient. The system also must teach the judge to recognize structural similarities among superficially different contexts so that memory probes retrieve a broader range of relevant memories. It is this ability that appears to be the hallmark of expertise (Chase & Simon, 1973) and its inclusion is the greatest challenge in designing a support system. Perhaps the research on mental set, creativity, and the breaking of mental blocks will prove valuable here.

Finally, it is clear that support of expert judgment must go beyond merely aiding in the construction of better narratives, using scenarios to generate judgments, or training judges to discriminate contextual cues. These efforts influence only one part of the overall picture of the judgment process that is described by the contingency model of judgment (Beach, Barnes, & Christensen-Szalanski, 1986). Attention also must be paid to factors that influence the judge's motivation to be correct, the rigor and energy he or she will invest in using the support system. This means that the benefits of the system must be apparent, the degree of finality of the judgment must be made clear, the degree to which the judge will be held responsible for the judgment must be evident, and the quality of the information the system is supplying must be indicated. In short, unless the judge sees a need to bother with the support system, the work put into its design will be of no avail. However, if conditions motivate the judge to learn to use the system, and if the system is comfortable to use because it is congruent with the judge's cognitive representation of the context and its demands, it may be possible to decrease the time it takes to make experts out of nonexperts and to increase the quality of the resulting judgments.

REFERENCES

Abelson, R. P. (1981). Psychological status of the script concept. *American Psychologist, 36,* 715–729.

Axelrod, R. (1976). *The structure of decision.* Princeton, N.J.: Princeton University Press.

Bandura, A. (1969). *Principles of behavior modification.* New York: Holt.

Bar-Hillel, M. (1980). The base rate fallacy in probability judgment. *Acta Psychologica, 44,* 211–233.

Barnes, V. E. (1984). The quality of human judgment: An alternative perspective. Unpublished doctoral dissertation, University of Washington, Seattle, Wash.

Beach, L. R. (1964). Recognition, assimilation, and identification of objects. *Psychological Monographs, 78,* 22–37.

Beach, L. R. (1973). *Psychology: Core concepts and special topics.* New York: Holt, Rinehart & Winston.

Beach, L. R. (1990). *Image theory: Decision making in personal and organizational contexts.* London: Wiley.

Beach, L. R., Barnes, V. E., & Christensen-Szalanski, J. J. J. (1986). Beyond heuristics and biases: A contingency model of judgmental forecasting. *Journal of Forecasting, 5,* 143–157.

Beach, L. R., Christensen-Szalanski, J. J. J., & Barnes, V. E. (1987). Assessing human judgment: Has it been done, can it be done, should it be done? In G. Wright & P. Ayton (Eds.), *Judgmental forecasting.* London: Wiley.

Beach, L. R., & Mitchell, T. R. (1978). A contingency model for the selection of decision strategies. *Academy of Management Review, 3,* 439–449.

Beach, L. R., & Mitchell, T. R. (1987). Image theory: Principles, goals, and plans in decision making. *Acta Psychologica, 66,* 201–220.

Beach, L. R., & Strom, E. (1989). A toadstool among the mushrooms: Screening decisions and Image Theory's compatibility test. *Acta Psychologica, 72,* 1–12.

Berkeley, D., & Humphreys, P. (1982). Structuring decision problems and the "bias heuristic." *Acta Psychologica, 50,* 201–252.

Bruner, J. (1986). *Actual minds, possible worlds.* Cambridge, MA: Harvard University Press.

Brunswik, E. (1956). *Perception and the representative design of experiments.* Berkeley, CA: University of California Press.

Castleman, B., & Dudley, H. R. (1960). *Clinicopathological conferences of the Massachusetts General Hospital: Selected medical cases.* Boston, Mass.: Little, Brown.

Chase, W. C., & Simon, H. (1973). Perception in chess. *Cognitive Psychology, 4,* 55–81.

Christensen-Szalanski, J. J. J., & Beach, L. R. (1982). Experience and the base-rate fallacy. *Organizational Behavior and Human Performance, 29,* 270–278.

Cohen, L. J. (1979). On the psychology of prediction: Whose is the fallacy? *Cognition, 7,* 385–407.

Corbin, R. M. (1980). A theory of choice should not be based on choice alone. In T. Wallsten (Ed.), *Cognitive processes in choice and decision behavior.* Hillsdale, N.J.: Erlbaum.

de Kleer, J., & Brown, J. S. (1983). Assumptions and ambiguities in mechanistic mental models. In D. Gentner & A. L. Stevens (Eds.), *Mental models.* Hillsdale, N.J.: Erlbaum.

Dickinson, A., Shanks, D. R., & Evenden, J. (1984). Judgment of act-outcome contingency: The role of selective attribution. *Quarterly Journal of Experimental Psychology, 36,* 29–50.

Downing, C. J., Sternberg, R. J., & Ross, B. H. (1985). Multicausal inference: Evaluation of evidence in causally complex situations. *Journal of Experimental Psychology: General, 114,* 239–263.

Eddy, D. M., & Clanton, C. H. (1982). The art of diagnosis: Solving the clinicopathological exercise. *The New England Journal of Medicine, 306,* 1263–1268.

Einhorn, H. J., & Hogarth, R. M. (1986). Judging probable cause. *Psychological Bulletin, 99,* 3–19.

Gentner, D., & Stevens, A. L. (Eds.). (1983). *Mental models.* Hillsdale, N.J.: Erlbaum.

Gigerenzer, G., Hall, W. & Blank, H. (1988). Presentation and content. The use of base rates as a continuous variable. *Journal of Experimental Psychology: Human, 14,* 513–525.

Holyoake, K. J., Koh, K., & Nisbett, R. E. (1989). A theory of conditioning: Inductive learning within rule-based default hierarchies. *Psychological Review, 96,* 315–340.

Hegarty, M. Just, M. A., & Morrison, I. R. (1988). Mental models of mechanical systems: Individual differences in qualitative and quantitative reasoning. *Cognitive Psychology, 20,* 191–236.

Heider, F., & Simmel, M. (1944). An experimental study of apparent behavior. *American Journal of Psychology, 57,* 243–259.

Hintzman, D. L. (1986). "Schema abstraction" in a multiple-trace memory model. *Psychological Review, 93,* 411–428.

Hogarth, R. (1981). Beyond discrete biases: Functional and dysfunctional aspects of judgmental heuristics. *Psychological Bulletin, 90,* 197–217.

Hogarth, R. M., Michaud, C., & Mery, J. L. (1980). Decision behavior in urban development: a methodological approach and substantive considerations. *Acta Psychologica, 45,* 95–117.

Jungermann, H. (1983). The two camps on rationality. In R. W. Scholz (Ed.), *Decision making under uncertainty.* Amsterdam: North Holland.

Jungermann, H., & Thüring, M. (1987). The use of causal knowledge in inferential reasoning. In J. L. Mumpower, O. Renn, L. D. Phillips, & V. R. R. Uppuluri (Eds.), *Expert judgment and expert systems.* Berlin: Springer-Verlag.

Kahneman, D., Slovic, P., & Tversky, A. (1982). *Judgment under uncertainty: Heuristics and biases.* New York: Cambridge University Press.

Kahneman, D., & Tversky, A. (1972). Subjective probability: A judgment of representativeness. *Cognitive Psychology, 3,* 430–454.

Kahneman, D., & Tversky, A. (1973). On the psychology of prediction. *Psychological Review, 80,* 237–251.

Klein, G. A. (1987, July). *Naturalistic models of C(3) decision making.* JDL 1987 C2 Research Symposium. Washington, D.C.

McCauley, C., Stitt, C. L., & Segal, M. (1980). Stereotyping: From prejudice to prediction. *Psychological Bulletin, 87,* 195–208.

Michotte, A. (1963). *The perception of causality.* London: Methuen.

Nisbett, R., Krantz, D., Jepson, C., & Kunda, Z. (1983). The use of statistical heuristics in everyday inductive reasoning. *Psychological Review, 90,* 339–363.

Pennington, N., & Hastie, R. (1986). Evidence evaluation in complex decision making. *Journal of Personality and Social Psychology, 51,* 242–258.

Pennington, N., & Hastie, R. (1988). Explanation-based decision making: Effects of memory structure on judgment. *Journal of Experimental Psychology: Learning, Memory and Cognition, 14,* 521–533.

Phillips, L. (1983). A theoretical perspective on heuristics and biases in probabilistic thinking. In P. Humphreys, O. Svenson, & A. Vari (Eds.), *Analysing and aiding decision processes.* Amsterdam: North Holland.

Piaget, J. (1929). *The child's conception of the world.* New York: Harcourt Brace.

Schustak, M. W., & Sternberg, R. J. (1981). Evaluation of evidence in causal inference. *Journal of Experimental Psychology: General, 110,* 101–120.

Shanks, D. R. (1986). Selective attribution and the judgment of causality. *Learning and Motivation, 17,* 311–334.

Suppes, P. (1957). *Introduction to logic.* Princeton, N.J.: Van Nostrand.

Thüring, M., & Jungermann, H. (1986). Constructing and running mental models for inferences about the future. In B. Brehmer, H. Jungermann, P. Lourens, & G. S. Sevon (Eds.), *New direction in research in decision making.* Amsterdam: North Holland.

Trabasso, T., & van den Broek, P. (1985). Causal thinking and the representation of narrative events. *Journal of Memory and Language, 24,* 612–630.

Tversky, A., & Kahneman, D. (1971). The belief in the law of small numbers. *Psychological Bulletin, 76,* 105–110.

Tversky, A., & Kahneman, D. (1974). Judgment under uncertainty: Heuristics and biases. *Science, 185,* 1124–1131.

Tversky, A., & Kahneman, D. (1983). Extensional versus intuitive reasoning: The conjunction fallacy in probability judgment. *Psychological Review, 90,* 293–315.

Van Zee, E. H., Paluchowski, T. F., & Beach, L. R. (1989). Information use in screening and in choice. Unpublished manuscript, University of Washington, Department of Psychology, Seattle, Wash.

CHAPTER 6

Sociological Perspectives on the Nature of Expertise

Andrew Sturdy, Innes Newman, and Peter Nicholls

INTRODUCTION

The purpose of this chapter is to review some of the principal sociological perspectives on the nature of expertise and to highlight the partiality of these perspectives. Thus, the discussion is not concerned with the sociology of knowledge in the tradition of Kuhn (1962) or Habermas (1971) or Foucault (1970). Nor is the intention to explore all relevant theories with the aim of reaching some conclusive outcome on the nature of expertise. Rather, the objective is to suggest a way forward for developing a theoretical framework as a tool for understanding the nature of expertise as it is practiced. To this end, empirical data are presented.

The following discussion is divided into three parts. Firstly, the structural theoretical perspectives are explored. This includes a presentation of the commonsense or functionalist view of the role of experts and demonstrates the way in which sociologists might question this understanding of expertise. Here, attention is drawn to prevalent alternative perspectives which focus on societal power relationships.

In the second part, these structural perspectives are critically examined by employing a subjectivist approach to analyze empirical data from a study of the role of management consultants (MCs) as purveyors of expertise in the commercial context. In this exploration of the relationships between MCs and their

Andrew Sturdy, Innes Newman, and Peter Nicholls • Bristol Business School, Coldharbour Lane, Frenchay, Bristol BS16 1QY, England.
Expertise and Decision Support, edited by George Wright and Fergus Bolger. Plenum Press, New York, 1992.

clients, the focus is the subject which receives relatively little attention within structural perspectives and becomes lost in either the structure or process of society.

Finally, by revealing expertise in action, the chapter concludes by questioning the claims and practice of "experts," contends the concepts of expertise as technical rational or "rule-based" phenomena, and suggests a direction for theoretical development on the nature of expertise.

THEORETICAL PERSPECTIVES

One commonsense notion of expertise is grounded in expectations of a relatively long formal educational process combined with years of practical experience where theoretical knowledge and learning-on-the-job are synthesized as they are applied. Here, expertise is not prey to personal predilections because it is viewed as objective, measurable, and even scientific in nature. There is, then, a sense in which expertise is felt to be detached from persons who, or occupations which, profess to own it. Indeed, in functionalist theories, expertise is considered to serve a positive function in society whereby experts are the vehicle through which this function is delivered (for example, Parsons, 1954). Maintaining the efficient functioning of society requires observance of a status quo insofar as expertise must be recognized, certified, and practiced. This is reflected in social stratification where occupational experts, often referred to as professionals, reside in upper strata and are commensurately accredited with higher prestige, status, and financial rewards (for example, Bottomore, 1965).

For example, the medical profession possesses a particular expertise. For practitioners, accumulating this expertise requires years of theoretical study based on scientific rules and procedures. Complementary periods of guided application of this theoretical knowledge precede the testing and certification of medical expertise. With respect to certification, the individual is bestowed with the right to practice medicine. Medical expertise functions to maintain the health and welfare of citizens, thus, medical practitioners are the vehicle through which this function is delivered within society. To writers in the functionalist tradition, it is no coincidence that medical experts are highly respected and well paid because, it is argued, this is indicative of the value that society places on the those who profess medical expertise and of the years of sacrifice required to attain the mandatory credentials. Indeed, much orthodox functionalist analysis has focused on the nature or attributes of experts rather than on expertise.

The isolation of attributes peculiar to occupational groups recognized as experts or professionals has been a concern of orthodox sociological analysis (Klegon, 1978). For example, from a review of various taxonomies, Millerson (1964) listed: (1) skills based on theoretical or abstract knowledge; and (2) an obligatory adherence to an ethical code which governs working practice, as two of the six most frequently mentioned of traits associated with professionalism. Little contention seemed to exist regarding the "core" or "essential" occupation characteristics of professional experts (Greenwood, 1957; Gross, 1958; Kornhauser, 1962; Barber, 1963; Carr-Sanders & Wilson, 1964; Voller & Mills, 1966). Where any ambiguities were observed, they were either functionally differentiated (Parsons, 1954), cast to the "fringes" of professional work organization (Parsons, 1968), or conceptualized in terms of a possible "scale" of professional expertise (Moore, 1970).

Take British accountants as an example. The role of their expertise may be considered as the regulation of firms' financial activities and the presentation of a "true and fair view" of the firms' financial state to the outside world. Legislation dictates that accountants performing this role must be qualified as auditors and the professional body—the Institute of Chartered Accountants (ICA)—demands adherence to the code of ethics. The ICA, however, is only one of several accountancy bodies; each one may bestow credentials but these qualifications confer different expertise for different purposes: such as the Institute of Management Accountants which confers accounting expertise specifically tailored to the requirements of business management. Accountancy is, therefore, a functionally differentiated profession. Moreover, there are differences attached to accountancy qualifications in terms of technical difficulty, earnings potential, and status, and there is a different order of qualification known as the Accountancy Technician which is technically less demanding, thus indicating a lower technical ability and associated with a lower level of work responsibilities, salary, and status. There is, then, a scale of professional accountancy expertise.

Nevertheless, while the unitary or objectivist model of expertise retains its patrons (Hall, 1975), other analysts have regarded it as tantamount to an uncritical acceptance of experts' own claims and idealized public conceptions: in effect, a "sociologists' decoy" (Roth, 1974). Critiques of functionalist-oriented analysis of expertise have derived principally from structuralist Marxist perspectives and a heterogeneous composite of sociologists who have drawn attention to the processes of formation and publicization of expertise and the strategies employed by experts to legitimate and maintain societal work and power boundaries.

Employing concepts from both Marx and Weber, Hughes (1958, 1963, 1971) developed a line of reasoning which highlighted the professional system of licensing competence and its "fictional" components: in essence, the basis of the professional mandate. Hughes perceived as fictions the exclusive claim to esoteric knowledge and specialized skill and the historical appropriation of the "title" profession as a mechanism for achieving occupational middle-class dignity (also Reader, 1967)—what Elliot (1972) has since referred to "status professionalism."

In this context Anthony and Crichton (1969) provide an interesting example of the personnel profession during the twentieth century: when, it seems, the struggle for "professionalism" was won by finally discarding the "welfare image" which represented its humble origins. According to Niven (1967), this was the result of a purposeful strategy beginning in the interwar years when welfare workers assumed a definition of their role as an aspect of management and the name of their association was changed to incorporate "Industrial": thus emphasizing their niche in society. Skills, such as interviewing and record keeping, were extended to cover wider areas of labor administration and control and were to set the profession on course for recognition in the years of postwar full employment when the control of labor became a more urgent or focused problem. The task of persuading employers to enlist the services of specialist welfare workers with a managerial brief was facilitated by renaming the association once again: in 1947 it became the Institute of Personnel Management (IPM). There is a clear connection between "Institutional" representation and professional aspiration: for personnel specialists, the latter continued to the point where, in the 1970s, professional ideology and values had completely overshadowed a concern for employee welfare. Instead, the focus of activity shifted to "efficiency" as personnel "experts" consolidated their interests in alignment with employers (cf. Watson, 1979, p. 198).

Personnel professionals, however, continue to experience difficulties in their claim to exclusive expertise vis-à-vis their managerial counterparts. Because, on the one hand, line managers are disinclined to accept that responsibilities relating to human relations and social skills are the sole prerogative of the personnel function. And, on the other hand, professional control of personnel activities appears somewhat partial. For example, membership in the IPM is not a prerequisite for personnel managers; some analysts have been surprised by their rarity within companies and the lack of any formal qualifications possessed by those who are employed (Daniel & Millward, 1983). This relationship between professional activity and professional control of activity has been highlighted by Johnson as a further critique of functionalist analysis which he views as:

> theoretically confusing concepts of professional activity with institutionalized forms of control of activity. (1972, p. 37)

Although forms of control may differ, the capacity to exercise control stems from a common base. This is the uncertainty that clients experience because of their lack of expertise which is fostered by professionals to ensure that expert knowledge remains inacessible to the client. Johnson argues that professional mystification of knowledge and the ability to maintain and/or expand its boundaries is the source of professional autonomy and power potentialities.

This focus on professional strategies deriving from political power spawned the development of the influential "critical" perspective. Drawing on Marxian structural class analysis, the myths of impartiality and objectivity are exposed as legitimations of the professional monopoly of expert knowledge and autonomy which share its roots with the dominant ideology of capitalist society (Heraud, 1973; McKinley, 1973; Gyarmati, 1975). The twin focus of concern lies in the

> inherently political nature of internal professional activity itself [and] the significance of professionalism and professional employment for the wider issue of the location and exercise of power in society as a whole. (Esland, 1976, p. 17)

Thus, expertise or, more accurately, the claim to expertise, emerges as a tool utilized by certain occupational groups to legitimate the right and efficacy of monopoly perpetuated by self-regulation. Moreover, the reproduction of employment and, therefore, social relationships is inherently harnessed to the inequitable distribution of political power, authority, and wealth characteristic of class-divided capitalist society.

To illustrate this approach, Marxist analysts have frequently pointed a finger at the accountancy profession which has successfully defended its claim to self-regulation on the ground that the decisions surrounding who and how members enter the profession must be made by the profession itself. No external organization is qualified to judge because only the profession understands the conceptual complexity and sophistication of accounting regulations. Yet, so the argument goes, the same profession actually creates the complexity, then monopolizes its understanding by instituting a prolonged and stringent regime of theoretical study, practice, and examinations for potential professional members.

In addition, because the accountancy profession is part of the very fabric of capitalist social relationships (via, for example, cost accounts or profit and loss accounts), it has a vested interest in reproducing those relationships. It comes as no surprise, then, that the profession is assisted by the power of the state, say through legislation or participation in government committees, and by the power of immense industrial and commercial enterprises where accountants are board directors and members of employers' associations.

Further, empirical support for this "critical" approach to expertise as a political lever has emerged from studies of professionals at work. Jamous and Pelliole (1970) distinguished between technical (codifiable) and indeterminate (esoteric) aspects of professional knowledge and further demonstrated how the knowledge base can be shaped so as to serve the needs of practitioners (also see Elliot, 1973).

There are, however, two major ontological difficulties with the critical perspective. Firstly, Turner and Lodge (1970) have contended that the "macro-stratification assumptions" underlying the class approach to analyses of the professions dissolve what is distinctive about occupations and the productive work they embrace. More recently, as emphasized by Fielding and Portwood (1980), there has been increased interest in the heterogeneity between and within specialized areas of expert work activity. For example, Armstrong's (1986) account has documented the competition between organizational experts and Johnson's (1976, 1977a, 1977b) analyses of industrial accountants have both prompted awareness of possible horizontal cleavages within professional sectors. This, Johnson argues, is generated by the ability of elites to maintain the indeterminancy of expertise while nominal colleagues are excluded from the clique. Experts, then, have lost their assumed monolithic and omnipotent characterization.

Secondly, the critical perspective tends to present a static structural analysis. This is problematic because there is no easy accommodation of process and change. However, some writers within this tradition have taken account of changes in capitalist societies. Carchedi (1976), for example, has highlighted the rise of the joint stock company and the development of the managerial strata: roles which have replaced but still execute the functions of the former owners of capital. Carchedi argues that the work of management focuses essentially on the appropriation, realization, and allocation of the surplus value of labor work; oversimplified, this is "profit." Managers as agents of capital are, therefore, concerned principally with the control and coordination of labor and other resources to ensure that profit is forthcoming. In a further rejection of managerialist ideology, Armstrong (1989) contends that management expertise is mistakely viewed as a set of qualities and abilities necessary for the performance of "some theoretical specification of the managerial task." Rather:

> In a fundamental sense it is the social relationships within capitalist management hierarchies which *define the management task itself.* (p. 311 [emphasis added])

Thus, managerial expertise "depends heavily on the priorities and prejudices of whoever appoints the agent," usually top management or "principals," as Armstrong puts it. The essential feature of this "agency" relationship is seen as a form of "trust"—principals must trust agent managers to perform effectively and efficiently on behalf of capital. However, since securing and maintaining trust is expensive, the dynamic undertone of this relationship is the search by principals for ways in which trust might be cheapened or dispensed with. Expertise is rewarded and occupational groups, either within or external to the company, prosper according to their ability to offer economies by substituting trust with control in the agency relationship.

For instance, it may be less expensive for a senior manager to pay an accountant to monitor the activities of production managers than to pay these latter the commensurate amount for creating a trust relationship with them. Alternatively, Armstrong also draws attention to nineteenth-century engineering projects which were characterized by contract labor arrangements, thus dispensing altogether with the need to trust full-time engineering employees. Yet, the need reappeared "in the person of the consulting engineer" and in personal relationships with the large contractors.

Paradoxically, in Armstrong's analysis, the mystification of expert knowledge as a source of power disappears only to reappear in a functionalist disguise. In other words, the important point now is not that expertise is mystified and monopolized by experts, but how expertise is used and the effect its use has on the relationships within capital—say, the relationships within management and between management and professionals. However, Armstrong implies that the nature and use of expertise is determined by the rational, and presumably conscious, goals of principals to cheapen trust. So, although this argument is presented in terms of dynamics and dialectics, principals emerge as monolithic and rational. Seemingly, the problematic of process and change remains except insofar as trust relations are characterized by interdependence. However, this relation is by no means peculiar to agents and principals, it is also pertinent to agents and labor.

By contrast, a more general recognition of change has been addressed by a composite of sociologists and probably most closely appraised theoretically in what Klegon (1978) has called the "processual" approach. Here, the expert occupations lose their collective quality to become

> loose amalgamations of segments pursuing different objectives in different manners and more or less delicately held together under a common name at a particular period in history. (Strauss, 1975, p. 10)

Thus, the focus shifts to the dynamics of professionalization and the "different manners" (traits in taxonomic analysis) or strategies for, say, achieving upward social mobility (Haug & Sussman, 1973) or maintaining occupational control over work activity (Child & Fulk, 1982).

The "processual" approach also recognizes the dual nature of strategies exercised by expert occupations in that not only do they constitute internal enclosure mechanisms, that is, controlling occupational entry and practice by regulating the accumulation, delivery, and evaluation of expertise: but also these strategies act as external legitimations of the exclusive right to exercise expertise in a particular occupationally defined manner, in effect, control of relevant labor market segments (Friedson, 1977). There is, then, an exposure of the interface between the occupational facets of expertise, identity, and ideology and wider socioeconomic and political conditions. Consequently, as Klegon (1978) suggests, the organization, operation, and control of expert occupations needs to be related to processes, other institutional mechanisms, and arrangements of power in wider society.

Each of the three major sociological approaches—functional, critical, processual—claims to make a contribution to understanding the nature of expertise in society. However, by juxtaposing them, all may be viewed as partial and disregarding of subjectivity. To illustrate this point, the discussion now turns to a case-study examination of management consultants as an occupation claiming management expertise.

CASE STUDY OF MANAGEMENT CONSULTANTS

The emergence of management consulting can be located at the turn of the twentieth century when the drive towards efficiency of factory-based production spawned the development of managerial scientism (Parker, 1988). Since labor was constituted as a commodity comparable to machines, the application of engineering principles to labor work appeared, to factory owners and managers, not only consistent but a highly desirable strategy aimed at increasing production efficiency while maintaining or reducing cost. Thus, the raison d'être of consulting engineers was to improve the productivity of industrial workers, thereby gaining competitive advantage for their clients. This they did by implementing rational (and rationalizing) techniques such as time and motion studies and task fragmentation. Hence the "pioneers" of management consultancy were industrial engineers who plied their trade as efficiency experts (Parker, 1988), by offering technical rational solutions to management problems.

This was the generalized image of consultants until post-World War II, when several American companies began expanding the horizons of management consultancy by embracing wider issues, such as operations management, financial and resource planning, control systems, organization structure, and marketing strategies (Sturdy, Nicholls, & Wetherly, 1989). Today, practitioners worldwide are estimated to number over 100,000 with a turnover in excess of $10 billion (*Economist*, 13.2.88). All of the large U.K. accountancy firms have lucrative management consultancy divisions which sometimes exceed accountancy revenue. Here also advice on business strategy with an emphasis on competitive advantage has grown, although it has been a focus since the 1960s. More generally, management consultancy has displayed the stereotypical image of an accepted profession. For example, the Institute of Management Consultants (IMC) was founded in 1962 and is deemed to be the recognized professional body for management consultants (MCs) in the U.K. The IMC offers services to members, has established qualifications for a graded membership structure, and may institute disciplinary proceedings against those who transgress the Code of Professional Conduct (IMC, 1989). The Code is underpinned by three principles: high standards of service to the client; independence, objectivity, and integrity; and responsibility to the profession (IMC, 1989).

From the outset, then, consultants have laid claim to a commonsense, valuable, and experience-oriented expertise and have sought recognition of it by purporting to apply objective, measurable, and scientific formulae which function to improve industrial, and managerial, efficiency. Latterly, this has surfaced in the form of an IMC principle and in various "scientific" techniques applied to business and Information Technology (IT) strategy formulation based upon a rationalist pretext that "without clear strategic thinking, the organization will lose competitive advantage" (for example, Wightman, 1987). Hence, it could be submitted that a functionalist perspective certainly appears a useful reflective framework for the analysis of management consulting expertise and a legitimation of it.

By contrast, company managements are the clients of MCs. The latter work on behalf of management and may thus be viewed as third-party agents of capital. Moreover, managements and MCs share similar training and career paths, moving between consultancies and business organizations. Since managements and MCs clearly share a managerial ideology, which is the defining characteristic of capitalism, there will be a mutual interest in reproducing capital relations of production with its attendant implications for political power positioning, prestige, and financial reward.

Unsurprisingly, hostility towards MCs by employees' representatives is still evident. "The failure to take account of employee and trade union views seems all the more surprising since the LRD survey shows that in nearly one third of cases, the introduction of management consultants led to industrial relations problems, with one in six studies leading to actual job losses. . . . The survey shows that trade unionists have many criticisms of consultants" (LRD, 1988:4/5).

Moreover, if certain evolutionary features are considered, for example, the development of consultancy within established accountancy practices, the internationalization, concentration, and professionalization of MC firms and the expansion of MCs interests in firms with a particular emphasis on providing advice to top management, then the compelling logic of the critical perspective becomes difficult to counter. Correspondingly, professional expertise is regarded as a source of power used to legitimize privilege and financial reward or employed by principals to cheapen/substitute for trust in competition with other agents.

And yet, neither is the processual approach irrelevant. Certainly, MCs cannot be said to constitute a homogenous group. There are sole practitioners, small, medium, and large firms. From the total IMC membership of 3300, it is clear that the vast majority of U.K. practitioners do not feel the necessity to join their professional body. Moreover, MC firms portray different images, specialize in different functional areas of consulting, address their expertise to different organizational levels and forms, and exercise a plethora of different strategies to penetrate a client company. Additionally, the fortunes of MCs have not always been buoyant or rising, as seems to be the case today—encouraged in no small measure by the propensities of the present political regime in the U.K. Either MCs en masse have experienced a downturn in demand for their services such as during the recessionary years of the early 1970s (Cheadle, 1989, p. 9): or individual specialist firms have come in and gone out of favor. For example, the strategy advisors who felt the first wave of success in the 1960s have largely been ignored until a few years ago (*Economist*, 13.2.88).

Thus, what appears to emerge from a closer appraisal of MCs is a tension between the perception of MCs as bastions of capitalist power and simultaneously "subject to characteristic tendencies of capitalist development" (Sturdy, Nicholls, & Wetherly, 1989, p. 14). Further perplexities arise in the partiality of their formal professionalization, their segmentalist nature, and the multifaceted interface between their occupational expertise, identity, and ideology and wider socioeconomic and political conditions. The processual perspective, then, leads to a position which dispels some of the structuralist assumptions adhering to both functionalist and critical approaches.

All three approaches, it seems, may advance understanding of the nature of expertise. However, an inherent feature of all purely structuralist perspectives is the implicit assumption that practice is "determined" by a macroview of expertise. Consequently, individual practitioners, at the behest of clients, merely allow expertise to flow, whereupon it is, in a sense, immediately recognized and accepted. There is no cognition of uncertainty, of negotiation, of compact or rejection in the transaction processes of expertise. While structuralist sociological perspectives do not deny the existence of the subject at the level of action, there is a tendency to present the subject, in this case the MC, as passive or wholly determined by functional/structural obligations. If a sociologist is disinclined to perceive the subject as passive/determined or expertise as taken-for-granted, an alternative sociological approach must be adopted. This concern leads inevitably to deeper analysis at the level of subjectivity and practice. Thus, the discussion now turns to empirical evaluation, the implications of which are discussed in the concluding part.

There is, first of all, documented evidence that expertise expressed in rational models of organizational behavior and equally rational solutions to business problems is not uncritically accepted by prospective MC clients and thus suggests that MCs' expertise is not taken for granted:

> . . . in the 1970s management consultants were accused of redefining their brief to match their preconceptions and fabricated solutions according to a pre-determined model. (*Economist*, 13.2.88)

Increasing client familiarity with MCs' models has led to demands for more originality. This has not escaped the attention of some MC firms who attempt to market their expertise exactly upon this issue:

> It follows that if we have no cloned solutions we cannot have cloned consultants either. A notable feature of ABC Consultancy is the variety of skills and experience which our professionals have. This allows us to fit the professionals to the problem rather than trying to fit the problem to the standard approaches. (ABC Consultants' publicity material)

The move to competitive tendering by clients would suggest some rejection of the marketing hype. The impetus for competitive tendering arose in the public sector and has been endorsed by recent legislation (Local Government Act 1988;

see Fredman & Morris, 1989). Similarly, most private-sector firms enter into some form of negotiation which indicates a challenge to the financial rewards claimed by MCs as legitimate exchange for their expertise, viz. the comments of one IT manager:

> In 1984 we commissioned an external consultant. We chose ABC who were becoming quite well known for their methodology . . . they were also into strategic planning and were much cheaper than bigger names like DEF and GHI, people like that want to charge you the earth.

There is also a degree of cynicism targeted at the occupation:

> an MC is someone who will borrow your watch to tell you the time and then sell it to someone else;
>
> an MC can tell you 500 different ways to make love but can't get a date;

These jokes may arise as a defensive diversion or a form of protection against the perceived challenge MCs pose to clients' identity as competent. Nevertheless, it is perhaps this cynicism together with the questioning of MCs' formal expertise and the fees they claim which have added impetus to MCs' strategies of resource allocation, research, project preparation, and work extension: insofar as MC firms establish specialist units on the basis of business trends indicated in market research surveys and, before any formal meeting, investigate a potential client with close attention paid to any possibilities of "problems."

For example, one account from an MC noted how MC firms only invest resources, that is, building or augmenting expertise and supplying support services, in sectors where there is a sufficient rate of change. The rationale is that where change is rapid, business is likely to be problematic, therefore, company managements are likely to be anxious, vulnerable, and, thus more receptive to the prospect of commissioning external consultants to solve business problems. His firm undertook market research which identified insurance companies as a sector undergoing considerable change and indicated a growth of the marketing function and computer networking within these companies. The potential for this information to generate business derived from the way it was used to give the impression that the firm understood the insurance sector.

There were two techniques for exploiting this information. Firstly, having identified a growth in the marketing function within insurance companies, direct contact (effectively cold calls) to the IT departments of these companies yielded answers to enquiries as to whether their IT resource was felt to be fulfilling marketing requirements. If not, the MC replied by saying that his firm could be of some assistance. Secondly, "courting" was a process which identified, say, the computer network managers of the top twenty insurance companies. The initial contact started with general questions as to what the company was doing in the networking area. Subsequent contacts became more focused and suggestive. For example, "Have you thought of this?" then, "Perhaps we can help you?"

Research can also take the form of project preparation, as one MC suggested:

> We try and identify what the business issues are before we ever meet the company and draw out the IT implications of that. So we don't go in and say "we've got a lovely IT strategy for you," we say . . . "is the fact that you're finding it hard to attract suitable labor an issue" and "yes it is" . . .

Now the question arises as to the necessity for these elaborate strategies intended to create the impression of MCs expertise if this expertise is determined at the level of practice. Alternatively, perhaps these strategies indicate the awareness of MCs that their expertise is not taken for granted, is not automatically accepted by firms on the basis of an occupational reputation for such expertise on a structural level. Indeed, MCs do not merely react to an apparent demand, but are obliged to proactively sell their expertise. The reasons for this are speculative. MC firms are, of course, in competition with each other but, as a group, perhaps it has not been successful in monopolizing its expertise: for example, universities and polytechnics offer similar expertise. Or, as Sturdy, Nicholls, and Wetherly (1989) have noted, MCs may be viewed as challenging or competing with the identity of managements (their clients) as "experts."

Reasons notwithstanding, the inherently political nature of these selling activities becomes more visible when the potential arises for extending work within a company. Here, the point is that the technical expertise which MCs offer becomes inextricably bound to their political skills. For example, deft political maneuvering is necessary not only to translate the potential into work but also to overcome the dilemmas faced by MCs when, on the one hand, fee income could rise considerably yet, on the other hand, this conflicts with the objective, boldly stated in promotional literature, to encourage client self-reliance. For some MC firms, though, the dilemma appears not to exist: one MC blandly reported that the purpose of "getting in at a high level" in a company was that it enabled investigation of other issues which could "generate more business." The longer-term strategy was aimed at developing respect so that the "presence" of MCs became "a natural component of the development and implementation of systems."

This position was expressed in different ways:

> What we're looking for in the first place is, what we call in the trade, "hooks," or symptoms where we say "well, we recognise the symptoms" but internally they haven't been recognised yet and we say, almost like a doctor, "if these are the outward symptoms, then the underlying must be something like this or that" and *it is part of our skill* to translate the symptoms into work.

Yet publicity material often cites aims of achieving "solutions of lasting value," "optimum permanent results," and "self-reliance."

> We build up the organization's own skills for effective management and control.

> We know that productive and lasting change cannot be imposed from outside but must be produced inside.

> We involve client's staff in our findings on a day-to-day basis so that potential misunderstandings are eliminated, duplication is avoided and future self-reliance is enhanced.

Against the stated aim, the emergent dilemma does not go unnoticed by MCs:

> Sometimes this leads to further assignments but we are careful to ensure that the prospect of future work does not bias our immediate recommendations.

Indeed, this conflict of interest is a matter of wider debate between MCs (Hindley, 1989): and, in practice, the involvement of MCs often creates client dependence, largely due to the skill of MCs in seizing work opportunities and elaborating and mystifying hitherto undetected "problems":

> Once they (MCs) are in there, they get the Board level relationships going and they will carry out a range of operations on behalf of the BOD.

> That'll be going on about April and we've already talked about possible future assignments . . . that's a nice long term arrangement, I've been there 7 years and they're still calling me back which is nice.

> We know ABC because L uses them for senior level recruitment. One day in conversation with the recruitment person with our manager, they said, "Oh, we could actually add something to your IT strategy that you've just told us about."

MCs are also seizing work opportunities by capitalizing on, if not creating, certain trends. For example, based on a rationalist premise that without clear strategic thinking the organization will lose competitive advantage, business strategy formulation has experienced a resurgence in popularity during the 1980s. This time, however, MCs are promoting the necessity of integrating business and IT strategies and this is also proving a lucrative source of additional assignments.

> Half the problem with IT strategy is that you start off and find that there are one year (business) plans and you say "you've asked us to provide, say, a 5–10 view on where you should go in terms of IT" . . . we end up working on a business strategy first before even considering IT implications.

In keeping with MCs' publicized image, "strategy" formulation expertise is offered on the basis of a technical and systematic approach. Why? The appeal of a technical rational approach to strategy has a number of facets. For example, as Morgan and Knights (1989, p. 38) have noted, "strategy" is of symbolic importance in the relationship between an organization and the outside world. The conception of "strategy" as planned and systematic reflects externally as a perception of the organization as controlled and ordered. This perception also exists internally.

> So the purpose or benefit of strategy is that . . . it actually concentrates efforts . . . at least any order is better than no order at all.

> The DP manager . . . now sleeps better since we helped him justify the installation of essential backup facilities.

The quest for control and order emerges as reassurance when, in a competitive marketplace, MCs can provide information about competitors' strategic positions.

> So we talked to one of the (MC) chaps and found it was "good practice" they called it . . . I said to L I don't actually think they'll come up with anything new and exciting, so if you did go ahead and spend the money, it would be for comfort . . . then said one day S thinks we should do it for comfort.

This reassurance is based on notions of systematization and measurement which, coupled with the underlying assumptions of related objectivity and impartiality, give rise to a belief that control, or better control, of untidy organizational life is effected. Problems are normalized. Thus, MCs conduct a dialogue of standardization emphasizing technicity—structured methodologies, corporate models, logical dialogue design, logical data structure, cost-benefit analysis—and, through the glossy brochure medium, promote this image to the world at large.

> We have developed an approach to strategic IT planning which has been successfully applied to client organizations of all sizes in every sector around the world.

> This experience has enabled us to develop our own systematic approach and methodologies and to use appropriate tools for IT project management.

> We provide objective evaluations of external systems.

Yet in practice, MCs are aware of the limitations of these rational approaches. Consequently the presentation of expertise changes.

> One of the things I would say about strategic methodologies is that, I mean we have methodologies that we follow but we follow them only to an extent and they provide guidance. . . . We do not have a checklist approach and I don't think we ever will.

Furthermore, corresponding to observations made by Jones (1989) on accounting techniques, technical rational approaches or solutions are explicitly partial: usable only for certain tasks or at certain hierarchical levels and otherwise must be tempered with different approaches and techniques. This is evident in the way that MCs both formally publicize and verbalize their approaches.

> ABC people are seasoned professionals . . . we encourage them to shun orthodoxy and think creatively and above all practically.

> Well, I think they're (techniques) used at two different levels. The strategy is to do with the high level where the complexities are greatest and cost benefit tends to be employed on a project-by-project basis.

> We've built a number of generic models . . . but in every case a generic model is a totally inadequate vehicle. The specific model that relates to any company reflects all the factors we've talked about—different factions with different levels of (hierarchical) importance, different cultures, values, ways of doing things.

The last reference to "culture, values, and ways of doing things" is a generalized expression of organizational features that MCs cannot explain in terms of their generic, that is, rationalist models. Clearly, if the substantive activity of MCs revolves around these issues labeled as "culture" or "values," a technical rational approach which depends on standardization and measurement can hardly be appropriate and must, therefore, be supplemented with other types of approaches involving different types of expertise. Objectivity, even in the form of "specific models" then emerges as little more than a ruse in dealing with the subjectivist reality of organizational life.

This dilemma for MCs is resolved by selling their services on the basis of "objective" techniques yet routinely employing substantively different techniques in order to deal with the subjectivist complexity of client environments. The technique of "active listening," for example:

> The key thing is to *listen*.

> . . . as a result of this *insistent looking for proper answers*.

> We use the technique of *creative tension* . . . By using various well proven *group techniques*.

> We use a variety of *interview and workshop techniques*.

In effect, the utilization of, at least some of, these techniques reflect an attempt to objectify subjective phenomena. However, the practice of MCs is thrown into another dilemma by this subjectivist complexity because company managements are not monolithic or unitary but comprise differing, sometimes conflicting, perspectives of various coalitions of interest. Here, perhaps, is the most transparent example of the tension between the rationalist approaches and solutions which MCs present to the outside world and the political and more "indeterminate" skills which are actually their stock in trade. Since these conflicting managerial views are clearly acknowledged by MCs, their approach tends to be oriented towards inculcating a unitary view of the organization and eliciting appropriate behavior. This is an inherently political process and MCs are obliged to exercise political and more "indeterminate" or covert skills, for it is in their interests to gain a majority commitment and support from their clients. Without this, they will fail, thus jeopardizing certainly their income, if not their reputation.

> I mean what it (implementing IT strategy) is about is vested interests, that's the bottom line.

> . . . let's get round those politics and get you to the end result.

> The other definition I have of IT strategy is that it's bloody war because within an insurance company there are so many different factions . . . So we're trying to merge together units which traditionally have gone their own way.

> Our role as agents provocateurs is, we're trying to get everyone to share their information for the greater good of the organization.

> So you've got to get strategies where everybody thinks that they're winning . . .or prepare the ground for someone to lose out. Otherwise you're going to fail.

> I think you've got to have both on your side. Both the DP and user because, unless you've got both of them vying for you, one or the other will stand in your way and you won't get any business.

What also emerges from this scenario is that MCs' attempts to inculcate a unitary view of the organization overflow into attempts to inculcate clients with their particularistic approach to management. Moreover, this process is carefully massaged, through "active listening" for example, in order to persuade clients that they themselves have visualized the solutions to their problems.

> The second thing was to get senior management making the decisions they needed to make . . . giving them the information and focusing their minds on the decisions . . . tell them what the decision that really needs to be made is and give them the up and down sides of that.

> You need to present the information to the strategists in a way that they can't fail to draw out the message themselves.

> We've been going through an education process (with the BOD) during the period of our regular meetings with them . . . The education process is ongoing and will continue.

There are, then, ideological and political functions served by MCs' expertise in client arenas since they attempt to transform managements' diverse and conflicting interests and methods into a single form of their own definition. In other words, part of their political skill in overcoming internal divisions is the achievement of at least a temporary consensus on their terms. These skills cannot be predetermined in the sense that they must be used and adapted as situations unfold: and they may be "indeterminate" since, in sensing how to respond, MCs are led by their experience rather than following guidelines set out in a predefined model. For instance, on the basis of past experience, they may anticipate management resistance or discomfort in their presence:

> they hate it at first then suddenly love it when they see it will help the business;

> they didn't always enjoy it at the time because it's an uncomfortable thing trying to answer questions they've been trying to dodge for years;

But they cannot know in advance who will be their antagonists and what form this antagonism will take: open hostility or a total refusal to impart information are just two possibilities. Nor, then, can they have any concrete preconceptions as to why antagonism might arise. It might be that managements feel threatened, demeaned, devalued, or suspicious of their colleagues' motives for commissioning external expertise. In any case, before the point is reached where managements are persuaded that they themselves have elaborated the solutions to problems, MCs need to apply a considerable repertoire of skills: some of which never appear on their rationalist curriculum vitae, some of which remain covert for the duration of the client relationship, and some of which cannot be determined prior to their application. There is, then, a sense in which expertise may be regarded as situationally specific and interactionist, that is, transpiring as a result of negotiation through interaction. Yet, without this expertise, the persona of MCs would be seriously compromised. What then, is the essence of expertise for MCs?

> It's funny how when you talk about IT strategy, actually you're talking about culture and people and group dynamics . . . (the consulting process) comes down, not so much to IT or business strategy but to interviewing techniques and human behaviour.

CONCLUSION

There are a number of points that need to be drawn from the foregoing analysis and related to the major sociological perspectives. For all these perspectives there is a sense in which expertise is a given phenomenon, somehow "out there" and detached from the individuals or groups claiming possession of it. They emphasize the recognized, technical, rational, or concrete nature of expertise which, in turn, assumes the subject to be passive or even wholly determined. The question asked here is whether this is the most appropriate approach for understanding the nature of expertise.

To begin with, certain trends, such as clients' demands for more originality than contained in MCs' rational models, competitive tendering, and the search for cheaper alternatives, indicate that MCs' expertise and their claim to high financial rewards are not simplistically taken for granted. Indeed, if this were so, would MCs be obliged to proactively sell their services and operationalize a raft of elaborate strategies for doing so? Moreover, the recognized function of MCs, which corresponds to their own definition, is increasing management efficiency and organizational competitiveness by the application of rational techniques. This, however, does not address the ideological and political functions which were highlighted as inherent elements of their practice and necessitated the application of a repertoire of skills which appear nowhere in their formal presentations to the outside world. Orthodox functionalist analysis of professional expertise has yet to embrace this scenario.

Neither does the "processual" approach account for skills which lie outside the formal definition of expertise. Another skill of MCs, for example, is their opportunistic grasping of further work. While some MCs are more open about this than others, it remains the case that the involvement of MCs often leads to client dependence. Leaving aside the issue of integrity, it is difficult to see how this could be interpreted as "regarding the client's interests as paramount" (viz. Principle 1 of the IMC Code of Professional Conduct). In any case, given the partiality of MCs' attachment to their profession, MCs expertise as a strategic element in the dynamics of professionalization underlined by the processual perspective does not appear to be mirrored in practice.

Furthermore, this partiality of professional attachment, together with their proactive selling and client trends, questions the concept of MCs as a professional group successfully monopolizing their expertise. Clearly, MCs do not appear to compromise a homogeneous professional entity. What is clear is that the expertise offered by MCs is not their sole prerogative; other groups offer the similar expertise designed to serve the same formal function. MCs, then, even if they created the knowledge, cannot be said to have preserved its mystification or, thus, its monopoly as a source of power. This presents a difficulty for the structural assumptions of "critical" analysts.

Nevertheless, within the critical tradition, Armstrong (1989) offers a different approach: that of the trust-based agency relationship within capital. Considering MCs as a third-party agent, at the behest of principals, with a brief of cheapening or dispensing with trust may be of some relevance. Certainly MCs have generally pitched their services more towards the top echelon of company hierarchies in recent years and they do encounter discomfort or resistance from certain sections of management. Furthermore, dispensing with trust implies a cancellation of the trust relationship. In this context, it is not unknown for even senior managers to be relieved of their duties shortly after the arrival of MCs in the company.

Cheapening trust, however, is a different matter. The search for cheaper alternatives between different MC firms may itself be regarded as way of cheapening trust. And MCs may be tendered and called in to institute control mechanisms which have both an agreed cost and lasting effect on the autonomy of certain managers but the likelihood of any sustained cheapening of the trust relationship between principals and senior managers without the sustained activity of MCs is a more moot point. While this must remain an open question here, as far as MCs are concerned, there is another difficulty with Armstrong's analysis.

Armstrong argues that the "qualities and abilities of managers depend heavily on the priorities and prejudices of whoever appoints the agent" (1989, p. 311), the agent in this case being the MC: thus by implication, so is the management task or management expertise. Now, despite some challenge to MCs' rational models and solutions, it is clear that these are the techniques that attract potential clients because they are felt to encourage the "right" sort of corporate image to the outside world, and because they are perceived as offering reassurance by promoting control and order over the untidiness of organizational life. Indeed, this control and order may be perceived as necessary by principals to overcome explicitly political problems, so the apparent legitimacy of MCs' independence and rationalistic solutions may be directed towards political ends.

However, the means, that is, the objective or rational techniques, must be seen as such because it is precisely this interpretation that enables their utilization. Otherwise, MCs would be perceived as merely harbingers of political scenarios to be avoided at all costs. Therefore, it is fair to assume that MCs' definition of their expertise as objective and rational is accepted, to a lesser or greater degree, by clients or principals. There is, in effect, an overt agreement between MCs and clients concerning what might be called this "formal agenda."

However, regardless of whether the ends are explicitly political or not, when it comes to practice, not only do MCs themselves experience tensions between their rationalist approach and its relevance but also partially discount the importance of rationalist techniques. Some even go as far as admitting in private that these techniques are not actually what their work is about. More pertinent is self-interest or "culture, values, and ways of doing things" which is tantamount to saying "we cannot explain our work in terms of technical rational solutions." There is, then, some discrepancy between clients' perception of expertise and MCs' practice of it. Yet, Armstrong's argument implies that the involvement of MCs is solely contingent upon, or simply responding to, the interests of principals which primarily relate to the continued accumulation of capital. Thus, MCs (or any third-party agents) cannot be seen as operating against these interests.

However, as has been indicated in the preceding part, in practice MCs necessarily operate in the context of a wide spectrum of different, and conflicting, interests of principals and other organizational groups. Here, to be effective, say in terms of achieving the aims of a brief and earning income, MCs utilize expertise which is essentially political, cannot be openly discussed, and is, therefore, covert. This, then, might be considered as the "hidden agenda" which is not addressed in Armstrong's analysis of the "agency" relationship as a fundamental feature of management.

A possible reason for this is that Armstrong assumes that principals are themselves rational and monolithic. The case study does not appear to support his view. Rather, even at top management level, much of the work of MCs involves creating the unitary view which is absent and dispelling management discomfort/resistance or ignorance. Once again, this requires the exercise of nonrational or political techniques, such as "active listening" and "creative tension," which may not be understood by clients, at least initially: or which may remain covert for the duration of their relationship. Moreover, because MCs are dealing with human beings who tend to be unpredictable, their expertise includes elements which cannot be programmed to surface in some predetermined order; some skills are used and adapted as situations unfold, and yet other skills are spontaneous, emerging as a result of negotiated interactions.

None of the three sociological perspectives addresses these elements of expertise. Yet, in practice, these elements constitute important, if not the most important, aspects of MCs' expertise. Expertise, as noted by one MC, is related to "human behavior"—or interactions. The argument here is that expertise may appear to be technical/rational, but the wholesale acceptance of this position is misleading because of its explicit partiality. Thus, sociological perspectives which accept expertise as taken for granted, functional, scientific, and objective are susceptible to the same criticism and may not be the most appropriate tool for understanding the nature of expertise as it is practiced. The case study of MCs presented above suggests that the more subtle elements of expertise—political, tacit, and possibly "indeterminate" skills—should be apprehended or rendered determinate.

There is, then, a perceived need for sociology to develop a framework for understanding the way in which these skills contribute to and constitute expertise. One possibility may be to suspend, or recognize as limited, structural and processual assumptions and take a more Weberian approach as a point of departure. This would imply a focus on subjectivity and the meaning that experts and their clients attach to expertise as it is practiced. For example, following Hughes (1963), it may be necessary to draw on symbolic interactionist insights. Thus, focusing on the manner of perceiving expertise as a result of negotiation between participants in an interactive process. This framework may also be applied to all levels and categories of expertise—from janitors to lawyers. Further, an ethnomethodological view would emphasize creative processes whereby persons continually shape their own meanings of expertise in a situational context (for example, Douglas, 1970). This would include all the elements of a situation— the place, people, interactions, events—which distinguish situations from each other and render them irreproducible. And in the context of any situation perhaps the concept of expertise should be broadened from its intellectual connotation to include skills that may be related to the constitution of perception, feeling, or emotion which underlie interpretation.

Finally, what emerges from this discussion carries implications for practitioners perceiving expertise as resting solely on technical/rational foundations. For example, those belonging to the computing fraternity continue to emphasize that their disciplines are built on sound engineering principles. Their response to a history of inefficiencies and problems has been more extensive application of the same principles to impose order and improve control, for instance, new techniques for measuring developer productivity or quantifying project risks.

Still, up to 50% of development projects overrun and quality "failures" cost the U.K. industry over £500 million per year (see Palmer, 1989).

It is tempting to speculate whether such "failures," at least partially stem from a disinclination of "software engineers" to question assumptions about the nature of expertise in their attempts to codify it. As the preceding analysis suggests, the concept of expertise may not fit neatly into technical/rational or rule-based solutions. Not only does expertise change and become redefined as it is practiced but expertise also has tacit and political dimensions. Fundamental problems, then, concern the codification of the tacit elements of expertise and, at least, a recognition that those responsible for structuring expertise are, in part, reproducing a political scenario.

REFERENCES

Anthony, P., & Crichton A. (1969). *Industrial relations and the personnel specialists.* London: Batsfield.

Armstrong, P. (1986). Management control strategies and inter-professional competition: The cases of accounting and personnel management. In D. Knights, & H. Willmot (Eds.), *Managing the labour process.* Aldershot: Gower.

Armstrong, P. (1989). Management, labour process and agency. *Work, Employment and Society, 3, 3,* 307–322.

Barber, B. (1963). Some problems in the sociology of the professions. *Daedalus, 92,* 669–688.

Bottomore, T. (1965). *Classes in modern society.* London: George Allen and Unwin.

Carchedi, G. (1975). On the economic identification of the new middle class. *Economy and Society, 4,* 1–86.

Carr-Sanders, A., & Wilson, P. (1964). *The professions.* London: Frank Cass and Co. Ltd.

Cheadle, N. (1988). The history and growth of management consultancy in the U.K. In J. Grosvenor (Ed.), *The Ivanhoe guide to management consultants.* Oxford: Ivanhoe Press/Institute of Management Consultants, 7–10.

Child, J., & Fulk, J. (1982). Maintenance of occupational control: The case of the professions. *Work and Occupations, 9, 2,* 155–192.

Daniel, W., & Millward, N. (1983). *Workplace industrial relations in Britain: The DE/PSI/SSRC Survey.* London: Heinemann Educational.

Douglas, J. (Ed.) (1970). *Understanding everyday life.* Chicago: Aldine.

Economist. (1988). A survey of management consultancy. 13 February.

Elliot, P. (1972). *The sociology of the professions.* London: Macmillan.

Elliot, P. (1973). Professional ideology and social situation. Reproduced in G. Esland, G. Salamon, & M, Speakman (Eds.), *People and work.* Edinburgh: Holmes McDougal (open University Press), 275–286.

Esland, G. (1976). Professions and professionalism. In B. Kansara, & J. Korer (Eds.), *Politics of work and occupation,* Milton Keynes: Open University Press.

Fielding, A., & Portwood, D. (1980). Professions and the state: Towards a typology of bureaucratic professions. *Sociological Review,* 1980, 28, *1,* 23–53.

Foucault, M. (1970). *The order of things.* London: Tavistock.

Fredman, S., & Morris, G. (1989). The state as employer: Setting a new example. *Personnel Management,* August 25–29.

Friedson, E. (1977). The future of professionalization. In M. Stacey et al. (Eds.), *Health and the division of labour*. London: Croom Helm.

Greenwood, E. (1957). Attributes of a profession. *Social Work, 2*, 44–55.

Gross, E. (1953). Some functional consequence of primary control in formal work organizations. *Sociological Review, 18*, 368–373.

Gymarti, G. (1975). Ideologies, roles and aspirations. The doctrine of the professions: Basis of a power structure. *International Social Sciences Journal, 27, 4*, 629–654.

Habermas, J. (1971). *Towards a rational society*. London: Heineman.

Hall, R. (1968). Professionalization and bureaucratization. *American Sociological Review, 33*, 92–104.

Haug, M., & Sussman, M. (1973). Professionalization and Unionism: A Jurisdictional Dispute. In E. Friedson (Ed.), *The professions and their prospects*. Beverly Hills, CA: Sage, 89–104.

Heraud, B. (1973). Professionalism, radicalism and social change. In P. Halmos (Ed.), *Professionalization and social change*. University of Keele Sociological Review Monograph, Number 20, 85–101.

Hindley, D. (1989). What price integrity? In *Management Consultancy*, November.

Hughes, E. (1958). *Men and their work*. Glencoe, Ill. The Free Press.

Hughes, E. (1963). Professions. Reprinted in G. Esland, G. Salamon, & M. Speakman (Eds.), *People and work*, Edinburgh: Holmes McDougal (Open University Press), 248–257.

Hughes, E. (1971). *The sociological eye* (2 vols.). Chicago: Aldine-Atherton.

Institute of Management Consultants. (1989). *The Ivanhoe guide to management consultants*, J. Grosvenor (Ed.). Oxford: The Ivanhoe Press/Institute of Management Consultants.

Jamous, H., & Pelloile, H. (1970). Changes in the French university hospital system. J. Jackson (Ed.), *Professions and professionalism*. Cambridge: University Press, 109–152.

Jones, C. (1989). What is social about accounting? Occasional paper in Sociology No. 7, Bristol Polytechnic.

Johnson, T. (1972). *Professions and power*. London: Macmillan. Klegon D. (1978) The sociology of the professions: An emerging perspective. *Sociology of Work and Occupations, 5, 3*, 259–283.

Johnson, T. (1976). Work and power. In B. Kansara, & J. Korer (Eds.), *Politics of work and occupation*. Milton Keynes: Open University Press, 36–61.

Johnson, T. (1977). The professions in the class structure. In R. Scase (Ed.), *Industrial society: Class, cleavage and control*. New York: St Martin's Press, 93–110.

Johnson, T. (1977b). What is to be known? *Economy and Society, 6, 2*, 194–223.

Kornhauser, W. (1962). *Scientists in industry*. Berkeley, CA: University Press.

Kuhn, T. (1962). *The structure of scientific revolutions*. Chicago: University Press.

Labour Research Department (LRD). (1988). *Management consultants: Who are they and how to deal with them*. London: LRD.

McKinley, J. (1973). On the professional regulation of change. In P. Halmos (Ed.), op cit, 61–84.

Millerson, G. (1964). *The qualifying professions*, London: Routledge and Kegan Paul.

Moore, W. (1970). *The professions: Roles and rules*. New York: Russell Sage.

Morgan, G., & Knights, D. (1989). Corporate strategy and organizational theory: A sociological critique. Paper prepared for the 9th EGOS Colloquium, West Berlin: July.

Niven, M. (1967). *Personnel management 1913–1963*. London: Institute of Personnel Management.

Palmer, D. (1989). Information systems. *Software Management*, October, p. 12.

Parker, H. (1988). The changing image of the management consultant. In J. Grosvenor, op. cit.

Parsons, T. (1954). The professions in the social structure. In *Essays in sociological theory*. Glencoe, Ill.: Free Press.

Parsons, T. (1968). *Professions*. New York: International Encyclopedia of the Social Sciences.

Reader, W. (1967). *Professional men: The rise of the professional classes in nineteenth century England*. Cambridge: University Press.

Roth, J. (1974). Professionalism: The sociologists decoy. In *Sociology of Work and Occupations, 1,* 6–23.

Strauss, A. (1975). *Professions, work and careers.* New Brunswick: Transaction Books.

Sturdy, A., Nicholls, P., & Wetherly, P. (1989). Management consultants and the politics of information technology strategy. Paper presented at the 9th EGOS Colloquium, West Berlin: July.

Turner, C., & Hodge, M. (1970). Occupations and professions. In J. Jackson (Ed.), *Professions and professionalization.* Cambridge: University Press.

Voller, H., & Mills, D. (Eds.) (1952). *Professionalization.* Egnlewood Cliffs, NJ: Prentice-Hall.

Watson, T. (1979). *The personnel managers.* London: Routledge and Kegan Paul.

Wightman, D. (1987). Competitive advantage through information technology. *Journal of General Management, 12, 4,* 36–45.

PART II

ISSUES IN THE INTERACTION OF EXPERTISE AND DECISION SUPPORT SYSTEMS

CHAPTER 7

Perspectives on Expertise in the Aggregation of Judgments

Gene Rowe

INTRODUCTION

Various approaches exist by which the response of a number of experts (or "judges") may be combined in order to attempt to achieve assessment superior to that which might be attained by merely accepting an individual recommendation. Such approaches have been classified, according to Ferrell (1985), into those of "mathematical," "behavioral," and "mixed" type. Briefly, "mathematical" approaches entail the statistical aggregation of a number of judges into a single estimate, while "behavioral" approaches allow the full interaction of group members until some form of consensus is achieved, and "mixed" type involves components of both these approaches.

Depending upon the type of aggregation attempted, the locus of expertise improvement will vary between that of the "individual" and of the "group." That is, implicit in the use of each of these kinds of technique are certain assumptions about the abilities or usefulness of the selected experts; whether it is economic or practical to try to enhance these individuals as judges/decision makers, and so on. In the case of mathematical approaches, experts are used to provide inputs into some statistical model, and then are dismissed: enhanced "group" judgmental validity is the sole concern and the individual is left with whatever biases or misconceptions help prior to the process. On the other hand, behavioral strategies rely upon the varied knowledge of the expert group mem-

Gene Rowe • Bristol Business School, Coldharbour Lane, Frenchay, Bristol BS16 1QY, England.
Expertise and Decision Support, edited by George Wright and Fergus Bolger. Plenum Press, New York, 1992.

bers to help in the resolution of faulty opinion, leading to interactions which should influence the judgments of the individual experts. As such, behavioral groups may be interpreted as providing a medium in which the debiasing of the individuals may take place, with improved individual abilities leading (it is hoped) to improved group validity. Mixed approaches provide an interesting attempt at harnessing the beneficial aspects of each approach while avoiding any of their detrimental aspects. We will consider the pros and cons of these various approaches later.

The importance of understanding the subtleties of the above aggregation approaches lies in the correct selection of technique to produce optimal gain from the specific panel of experts chosen. In this chapter we will try to elucidate the fundamental characteristics of each of the three mentioned approaches (considering distinct techniques within them), going on to demonstrate how key factors in the judgmental setting should influence procedure effectiveness. In doing this, we shall concentrate upon issues related to individual expertise, such as how it is used by particular aggregation techniques, how or whether it is improved through the aggregation process, and so on. Consequently, we are less interested in the purely mathematical (and less *human*) considerations related to the mathematical manipulations of the attained responses from judges. We will therefore quote no formulae: if the reader is more interested in the mechanics of combining judgments we refer them to Ferrell (1985) and Clemen (1989).

One further form of expertise which may be identified (apart from the individual and collective expertise of group members) must be that of the experimenter/monitor/consultant/overseer responsible for deciding upon which aggregation approach to use in the first place. In a way, contributing to this expertise is perhaps the raison d'être of this chapter, through explicating aggregation as a tool for enhancing expertise in its own right: by pointing to those *cues* that need to be considered when deciding upon which technique to use; by giving some indication as to their relative importance or *weighting;* and by pointing to considerations effecting how they might be *combined*. Thus, the very people who bear responsibility for conducting aggregation procedures are as answerable to the above criteria for expertise (as defined by Einhorn, 1974, and others) as those they use in their constructed groups. The widespread acceptance of aggregational approaches would seem to testify to the effectiveness of combining judgments, though "better performance" does not necessarily equate to "best performance": pointing the way to such optimality is a key theme of this work.

THE NEED FOR HUMAN JUDGES

Before considering how expert judgment should be aggregated and when any particular technique should be used over another, it is first important to consider whether human judgments need to be sought in the first place. In many circumstances, objective data may be available in a form useful for the construction of a mathematical model—such as when time-series data exist, as in the case of past performance of shares on the stock market, or data on a company's past profits, or whatever. By using techniques—such as regression analysis—one can fit identified predictor variables into extrapolational models (or perhaps econometric models), after which one may derive predictions on the criterion variable. Such models have frequently been shown to function well in comparison to the judgments/predictions derived from other techniques which use solely subjective components, i.e., with judges making judgments on the basis of the same objective input data. For example, Ashton and Ashton (1985) compared a variety of mathematical aggregation techniques of expert subjective judgment, but also developed a linear multiple regression model (on the basis of the original objective variables given to the experts) and found that this gave better predictions (less mean error) on the criterion (advertising pages to be sold), than any of the aggregations based on subjective inputs.

The above finding of the advantage of using objective over subjective inputs is typical (Ferrell, 1985), and has led various authors (e.g., Armstrong, 1986) to suggest that such statistical models be employed—over approaches using expert judgment—whenever this is feasible. However, in many cases this type of modeling is impractical or even impossible. This may arise in circumstances where the dependent variable is unobservable; when sufficient historical data on the relevant independent variables are unavailable; and when the data generating process on which a model may be based is expected to change over time (rendering the model inappropriate). Practical difficulties might also arise through the cost (in development time and capital) of producing the model, such that alternative easier approaches (like the group meeting) may be more acceptable in spite of the potential decline in the accuracy of judgment, i.e., a financial trade-off. Lack of the appropriate skills within an organization for building such models, along with organizational resistance (e.g., Dawes, 1982) may further hinder the implementation of this judgment-enhancing approach. In such situations, subjective estimation becomes a necessary input into the judgment equation—but how such inputs should be used or combined to produce the most accurate response is not always clear, and it is these issues we now move on to address.

MATHEMATICAL AGGREGATION OF EXPERT JUDGMENT

Composites formed by combining judgments have frequently been shown to outperform individuals in judgmental and forecasting tasks requiring subjective inputs (Lock, 1987), both quantitatively and qualitatively (Hill, 1982). The main reason proposed for such improvement relates to the idea of averaging out "random error," such as in eliminating random components of human judg- ment—like unreliability—which generally ensure that judges will give different ratings or responses, on the same question-item, when questioned on a number of different occasions. Because human judgment is so often limited due to unre- liability—and also due to bias, various authors (e.g., Hogarth & Makridakis, 1981) have argued that expert judgment is best aggregated statistically.

The simplest statistical aggregation approaches involve the equal weighting of the "group" members—essentially averaging all responses into a mean re- sponse. The use of simple averaging relies upon the assumption that the esti- mates being combined represent true values with an added zero-mean random error (i.e., no bias as such) where random error may be averaged out leading to a response centering upon the true value. However, when the individual judgments are not independent in a statistical sense (when correlation exists between the judges), and judges are suspected of having some degree of bias, then the errors of one judge are liable to be shared by the other judges (or at least by some of them), and simple averaging should produce a response centering upon the mean of the erroneous judgments rather than the true value (see Reagan-Cirincione & Rohrbaugh, this volume). A great deal of evidence exists pointing towards the pervasiveness of certain types of bias, not only in naive subjects in laboratory experiments, but also in truly "expert" judges taking part in real-world "ecologi- cally valid" studies. For example, judges have been shown to be generally overconfident in their estimates of values they believe they know something about, but underconfident on items about which they are less certain (Lichten- stein, Fischhoff, & Phillips, 1982); to show inappropriate adjustment of their estimates away from an initial anchor point (Tversky & Kahneman, 1974; North- craft & Neale, 1987), and so on. These issues are addressed in other chapters of this book.

Evidence would therefore suggest that the ideal condition for using a simple averaging strategy is perhaps not a common one. Instead it would seem that, in many situations, we will be confronted by a selection of estimates consisting of the true value plus random error, but with a mean that is nonzero (termed "B"). In this case, simple averaging will result in a judgment with smaller variance than the individual estimates, but which won't eliminate the mean error "B." However, even if there is a consistent bias, aggregation should still result in improved judgment, with a reduction in the impact of random individual errors, as long as the random components are not perfectly correlated. Still, since this leaves scope for improvement, a better strategy in these circumstances might be to select the best of the individual judges and to let his/her estimate stand as the group estimate. Though it is possible for the simple average to be better than the estimate of the best judge (if the true value falls between the best and worst judge estimates), this generally won't be the case (e.g., Sniezek & Henry, 1989; Hill, 1982).

Thus, we have a trade-off here: if we accept a simple average (while suspecting that the estimates will possess a certain regular bias) we accept that the group estimate will be suboptimal; but if we attempt to identify the best judge, then we remove the chance of deriving an estimate which is more accurate than the most accurate individual in the group, and risk an inappropriate selection, which will likely give a worse result than the simple group average.

Larreche and Moinpour (1983) have considered this dilemma as one of choosing between "integration" and "identification" methods (that is, between aggregation—mathematical or behavioral—and the selection of the best expert, respectively). They have suggested that integration methods are merely substitutes for our inability to identify the best expert a priori, which implies that if we did possess accurate identification techniques then we would not need to use aggregational procedures at all. This point bears some similarity to that of Jenkins (1974) who argued against the position of combining *forecast models* by claiming that the only reason one would need to do this would be if the models had not been properly defined in the first place. While this latter argument is true enough, it must be remembered that practical difficulties exist in the lack of comprehensiveness of any one modeling approach, and thus in the difficulty of unique model specification (Granger & Newbold, 1975; Bunn, 1989).

Similarly, the argument against integration/aggregation falls because of the lack of comprehensiveness of knowledge of any one expert (if omniscient experts existed and were obvious, then there would be no need of any judgment-aiding technique or research in the first place). Our use of integration approaches thus stems from our inability to select the "best" judge, and from the absence of such omniscients. As we have suggested, integration/aggregation also provides the possibility of gaining a judgment more accurate than the best individual; a possibility which is closed to the identification approach.

Of course, it is possible to combine both identification and integration methods, and, intuitively, this would seem to offer a valuable way forward. Indeed, this is precisely what takes place (or should take place) in everyday judgment and decision-making contexts, such as in the typical board meeting: the participants in such group judgments have, in effect, gone through some sort of selection procedure as a prerequisite to their attendance at such meetings— though whether the criterion for their selection may be adequate is another story. It seems somewhat ironic that most research into judgment and decision making, utilizing students as subjects, tends to conduct studies on integration methods without this identification component, thereby examining the effectiveness of such methods only in part and yet making grand declarations about effectiveness on the whole! This simply reflects the difficulty of transfering complex real-world phenomena into simplified yet controllable laboratory situations.

A more systematic approach to the encorporation of an identification component into statistical aggregation involves the use of differential and unequal weights on the estimates of the "group" members. However, unlike the identification approach which would allocate a weighting of "one" to the "best" group member and "zero" to the rest, here the opportunity for judgment better than the best individual does exist, since each individual has some input into the final equation and hence a final estimate more accurate than that of the best member may be attained. We will not consider all the mathematical complexities of the different weighting schemes here: rather, we will address the psychological issues of the weighting problem, namely, how we might discern those individuals who should be given greater weights than their fellows, i.e., the question of the identification of relative expertise. This issue naturally also bears relevance to the "behavioral" and "mixed" categories of aggregation techniques, notably in determining group composition, though it seems to us of most immediate pertinence to the issue of unequal weighting for "mathematical" purposes, hence we include it in this section. More specific issues on this topic will be considered where appropriate in those later sections.

There are several different ways by which expertise may be simply assessed, each way possessing notable pros and cons. Perhaps the easiest method involves the straightforward self-rating by the judge of his/her expertise or knowledgeability on the problem topic (or his/her confidence in the given estimates). Though easy, a number of important problems arise in such evaluations, most particularly the likely biased view we all possess as regards our self-perceived ability (a well-demonstrated bias leading to over- or underconfidence, as noted earlier). Alternatively, weighting may be achieved through some group-weighting process whereby each individual assesses his/her group companions for their relative expertise, with some form of combination of all assessments taking place thereafter, to determine the proportionate value of each individual's estimate (e.g., DeGroot, 1974; McKinnon, 1966). Naturally, for the latter method to be practical, one would require groups of judges who were well known to one another (a rarity in the highly artificial groups used in the vast majority of laboratory studies), while one would also have to hope that each individual was competent in the task of assessing their fellows (that is, competent in attributing expertise according to appropriate criteria).

Since human judgment has frequently been shown to be biased in a number of ways, the above procedures seem somewhat dubious in that they risk compounding any preliminary errors in the judgment task, with some form of second-order errors in the metajudgments. After all, an expert who was selected for his/her expertise on the problem area need not necessarily be an equal expert with respect to an ability at judging the expertise of their fellows—an assumption which is implicit in the idea of weighting judgment by this means. When one also considers the difficulties that may arise as a result of each individual's unique rating scales (a problem in all approaches employing the subjective ratings of a number of individuals), plus the uniqueness of each individual's experiences and perceptions of one another's judgmental performances and accuracies—then the problematic nature of all such weighting schemes is apparent.

A more objective weighting approach therefore seems desirable, though other problems arise when one attempts to weight individuals on the basis of performance measures. For example, there may not be enough data of an appropriate nature to adequately rate all the members of the group, perhaps because of different and noncomparable experiences of the individuals, or because the new problem to be assessed is subtly different from past problems, or because no concise objective measurements of past performance exist. Indeed, even if these criteria are satisfied, one still cannot dismiss the possibility that learning might have taken place since the latest performance on which assessment had occurred (e.g., Lock, 1987). In any case, the optimal situations where adequate objective measures might be obtained are also likely to be situations in which objective data/inputs are available for use in econometric/extrapolational models—in which case those potentially more valuable approaches might supplant any need to use subjective components in the judgment process in the first place (e.g., Armstrong, 1986). As we can see, the a priori identification of experts seems to be a major bottleneck in the practical application of the differential-weighting mathematical aggregation approach.

A considerable number of studies have examined the relative worth of various weighting schemes, and have generally found there to be little advantage (if any) in using differential over equal weighting. For example, Rowse, Gustafson, and Ludke (1974) used firemen as subjects in a task involving estimations of likelihood ratios, eliciting individual estimates plus other measures (such as self-ratings of confidence). The individual estimates were then combined mathematically in a number of ways, through the equal weighting of all the estimates, and through each of four differential weighting schemes, one of which relied entirely upon the individuals' self-confidence assessments, and with the other three deriving weights through various combinations of the self-confidence measures plus measures by each subject on their opinions on the ability of their peers. No objective measures of past performance in such a judgmental task were available. The results failed to demonstrate a statistical superiority of any one of these measures over the others.

Flores and White (1989) used business students to make forecasts (on the basis of time-series data), with three weeks of practice and feedback followed by the experimental trial. The subjects were formed into statistical groups of size two or three (as well as actual interacting groups which we will consider later), and had four statistical methods applied to their estimates. One set of measures were obtained through the equal weighting of group members; one through a weighted average developed on the basis of past accuracy in the trail rounds; one through a weighting based on self-assessed expertise; and one through a weighting based on the perceived confidence of the individuals in their own forecasts. For the forecasts on the Dow Jones Industrial Index, the judgments derived through use of past accuracy weighting showed the lowest mean absolute percentage error, followed by the self-rated expertise weighted forecasts, and with

ambiguities and conflict. It has also been suggested that the involvement of individuals within a group may have a beneficial impact on the motivations and commitments of the group members to do well and to produce the most accurate response possible (e.g., Lock, 1987).

The group process is perhaps best conceptualized as the process of selecting and applying a strategy for judgment or problem solving that is suited to the task and the resources of the particular group (Ferrell, personal communication). One such strategy, in line with our prior discussion on mathematical aggregation, is for the group to seek the best approach for weighting its members to make the best use of their knowledge (Hackman & Morris, 1975). (This is a conceptualization which is probably only applicable in certain cases and is not necessarily meant to say very much about the actual process and dynamics of the group meeting as such—though it will allow us to follow a certain line of argument from the preceding section.) From this perspective, we see that the group response may essentially equate to either an equal or differential weighting scheme; for the group interactions to be useful, the appropriate scheme should be selected and applied.

For example, according to Sniezek and Henry (1989), when there is low disagreement within the group, one might expect there to take place an equal weighting of group members with resulting accuracy no better than a simple averaging strategy; but when disagreement is high, one would expect a differential weighting of members, which may result in judgments better or worse than simple averaging, but which should be better if the group approach possesses any validity (i.e., the group members are able to select the best members to give the highest weightings). The group's ability to weight its members appropriately, and its potential to derive judgments better than its best member (and hence to exhibit "process gain") will depend upon a number of factors, such as the extent of bias within the group, and so on. (For example, with biased judgments process gain due to chance is less likely with an equal-rating approach than in cases of generally unbiased judgments—and when all individual judgments are biased the group may only outperform its best member by adopting a nonweighting scheme and producing a judgment *outside* the range of individual judgments—see Sniezek & Henry, 1989.)

Regardless of what the actual group process entails, of fundamental importance is the ability of group members to select from among themselves those individuals who are most likely to be accurate and valid, and to be convinced by, or place greatest onus or weight in, their judgments. Hence, a "weighting" conceptualization as used above would seem useful.

Thus, we might expect the greatest potential for using behavioral aggregation to arise in situations where there is a heterogeneity of group members (with varying opinions and low agreement, e.g., Lorge, Fox, Davitz, & Brenner, 1958; Steiner, 1972) since in low-disagreement situations we must presume that interacting groups possess little scope for improving upon simple averaging of the individuals. (Indeed, Rohrbaugh, 1979, reports that the similarity of initial individual judgment policies is inversely related to final group judgment quality.) In effect, when one decides to improve judgment through using a group process instead of using a statistical aggregation approach, one is deferring the whole aggregation method (including the choice of weighting scheme) from the organization/monitor/experimenter unto the discretion of the experts selected to take part in the group. Whether such a policy is wise may be determined by comparing group performance to the performance of equal and differential weighted statistical aggregates of the individuals.

Empirical evidence generally seems to support the efficacy of group judgment over average individual judgment over a wide range of tasks and circumstances (Nisbett & Ross, 1980; Hill, 1982; Lorge et al., 1958). Studies comparing groups with the best members of statistical aggregates have further revealed that groups may occasionally perform at the level of their best individuals or even show process gain in producing judgments better than the best member. Einhorn, Hogarth, and Klempner (1977) used students to judge the population of their home city, individually and in groups of three, and found the group outcomes to fit a "best member" model better than any of the other models considered (including an equal weighting model). Sniezek and Henry (1989) similarly used students in isolation, then groups of three (with a total of eighteen groups), to make judgments on the annual frequency of deaths from various causes. They then attempted to fit the group judgments to one of four models, of which the "best member" model proved the best fit to over one-half of the total of 270 judgments (again equal-weighting models were considered along with a "confidence-weighted" model), and, further, nine of eighteen actual group judgments proved superior to the best judgments of their members, in terms of mean absolute percentage error. Uecker (1982) has also shown performance to best-member standard using groups of accountants.

However, though performance up to and beyond best-member level has been demonstrated, group judgment is generally shown to fall short of this standard (e.g., Lorge et al., 1958; Hill, 1982; Hastie, 1986) and hence exibits "process loss" (Steiner, 1972). Various explanations have been posited to account for this (e.g., Martino, 1983; Janis, 1972; Ferrell, 1985). These include: (1) the social pressures often inherent within groups which may force conformity of opinion to the majority view, decreasing the influence of more knowledgeable minorities (e.g., Hoffman, 1965); (2) the overinfluence of the most talkative and strident individuals who need not necessarily be the best informed (triumph of vocal minorities); (3) the changing motives of groups where "reaching agreement" may become a goal in itself, leading to premature closure and satisfying (rather than optimizing), i.e., the acceptance of the first solution which greatly offends no one, and yet which no one agrees with wholeheartedly either; (4) the

(4) the motive change of individuals and their need to "win" (or at least not to lose face); and (5) the reinforcement of common biases, particularly when all group members share the same background. These factors and others serve to cloud the ability of groups to select the most appropriate opinion-combining strategy, or to select the most appropriate weighting for their members, and hence may lead to suboptimality of group judgments.

The presence of process loss in many group situations—due to the above factors—should not be surprising, and closely parallels the "differential mathematical weighting" problem: the same sort of problems which inhibit experimenters in identifying the best group members also inhibit the group members themselves. However, again, we must be wary in the conclusions we draw from experimental laboratory studies: various authors (e.g., Fraser & Foster, 1984) have commented upon a "nonsense group" tradition in research, in which laboratory groups often lack the defining characteristics of "real" groups, usually being bereft of past histories, expectations of future interactions, group norms, shared goals, perceptions of group membership, and so on. If laboratory groups are not comparable to "real" groups, then results and conclusions from laboratory studies cannot be fully generalized to the real world.

For example, in a "real" group we might expect the individuals to be better acquainted with one another than in the usual study group, and hence these should be more capable of correctly assigning appropriate weights to one another, deriving more accurate responses closer to the potential of the group. While, intuitively, this seems reasonable, it is also reasonable to suppose that several of the above process loss factors—such as the motive changes in groups, where individuals' needs to win supplant the original group motive of reaching the most accurate consensus—are liable to effect "real" groups as well, as shown in the case of "groupthink" (Janis, 1972). Thus, any difference in effectiveness between "real" and "artificial" groups may merely be of degree or quantity (of performance improvement), though qualitative differences in judgmental style and strategy cannot be ruled out and should be considered more thoroughly.

One way of combating the above negative influences may be through the instruction of groups in good communication strategy, e.g., Hall and Watson (1971). Eils and John (1980) demonstrated this by giving groups short guidelines on such strategies—including points such as "view initial agreement as suspect" and "avoid changing your opinion only to avoid conflict and to reach agreement"—and found that groups so instructed did significantly better than when not instructed, in a task involving the judging of the creditworthiness of loan applicants.

Although adding some structure to the group process may improve the flow of information between the individuals once the group has been formed, all this may be superfluous if the composition of the group is not appropriate so as to benefit from the manipulation. As suggested earlier, one should aim to use "behavioral aggregation" in situations in which the group members possess some variance of opinion: without disagreement it will be difficult for group members to distinguish between their judgments to find a basis for variable weighting, hence greater initial disagreement may lead to greater accuracy improvement of group judgment (e.g., Sniezek & Henry, 1989). Also, and perhaps obviously, it is necessary for the group members to possess some reasonable degree of knowledge on the topic of consideration, to ensure the opinion change takes place for the right reasons and not just as a result of normative pressures.

"MIXED" AGGREGATION TECHNIQUES

Thus far, we have largely differentiated "mathematical" and "behavioral" techniques according to the locus of responsibility for judgmental improvement. In the former approach, the overseer or monitor of the "group" mainly bears this responsibility, and the extent of any performance improvement must rely upon his/her choice of weighting scheme (once mathematical aggregation has been accepted as the modus operandi), and therefore the "expertise" improvement which should be sought is that of the overseer's ability to apply an appropriate aggregation technique. To the contrary, the behavioral approach relies upon some form of expertise enhancement in the actual group members per se in order to achieve a correspondent performance improvement in the ultimate response accuracy.

In the case of "mathematical" manipulations, it is almost implicit that the experts who are brought together to judge the problem scenario are seen/believed/expected (by the "overseer") to be either incorrigible (in that they cannot be dissuaded from their expected biases)—or at least practically so (i.e., performance on the judgment problem may be more easily enhanced through another means). With the adoption of a behavioral approach, the "overseer" essentially accepts that the interacting judges may debias themselves to the extent where measurable improvement in performance can be obtained. As we can see, the judgmental expertise of the "overseer(s)" plays the key initial role in both approaches (deciding the limitations of the group experts and hence which type or category of aggregation to employ); but the extent to which this is further required then depends upon that initial selection.

In the case of "mixed" approaches, the locus of responsibility for judgmental improvement is more spread across the above identified levels. That is, certain mathematical processes are substituted for behavioral ones (or vice versa) combining the two aforementioned approaches, and hence combining the potential recipients of "expertise" improvement (the overseers may be educated in the more appropriate selection of aggregation technique and means for mathematically aggregating the judgments of the experts, and the judges themselves may benefit as a result of the actual group process). In essence, one can interpret "mixed" approaches as ones which allow human judges the opportunity to debias themselves through the process of interacting with their fellows, while replacing those aspects of judgment or decision making at which those judges are expected to be incorrigibly fallible, such as in the combining/weighting of various statistical assessments (in line with Kleinmuntz's 1989 assertion that humans cannot be expected to do such tasks well, and should then be replaced by an appropriate computational/mathematical device).

Furthermore, "mixed" approaches attempt to deal with other aspects of "process loss" by supplying a more structured environment—essentially guiding the judges down the correct path, fencing out potential sources of distraction and inappropriate and confusing routes. The nature of such structuring—and how it is expected to work—shall now be shown through an examination of two of the more formalized "mixed" techniques, namely "Delphi" and the "Nominal Group Technique" (NGT).

Delphi

The Delphi technique was developed during the 1950s by workers at the RAND corporation as a procedure to "obtain the most reliable consensus of opinion of a group of experts . . . by a series of intensive questionnaires with controlled opinion feedback" (Dalkey & Helmer, 1963, p. 458). Initially, it was used in the realm of long-term forecasts of change, particularly in science and technology, though in later years it has come to be employed in a wide variety of other judgmental settings (e.g., see Linstone & Turoff, 1975; Martino, 1983; Parente & Anderson-Parente, 1987).

Specifically, Delphi aims to make use of the positive attributes of interacting groups (i.e., knowledge from a variety of judges), while removing the negative influences (such as the overinfluence of dogmatic minorities or dominant individuals). To this end, Delphi has four necessary characteristics: anonymity, iteration, controlled feedback, and statistical aggregation of group response. Anonymity is achieved through the use of questionnaires which allow group members to make their responses privately, thereby reducing the influence of forceful individuals, and also allowing members to change their minds, if they so wish, without risking loss of face (indeed, iteration of the process—presenting the questionnaire over a number of rounds—encourages such rethinking).

Controlled feedback takes place between rounds, in which each group member is presented with some indication of the opinion of their fellows, usually in the form of a statistical summary, and occasionally with written arguments from members who hold extreme opinions. Thus are all members allowed an input into the process, and not just the most vocal. At the end of the procedure, a statistical group response is obtained—usually expressed as the median or mean of statistical judgments, with indications as to the spread of opinion reflecting the degree of consensus on the issue. As noted above, this takes the complex task of combining judgments away from the judges and allows mathematical aggregation instead (using an equal weighting approach, though there is no reason why the Delphi "monitor" should not attempt some variable weighting of judges if he/she believes this may be beneficial).

The Delphi process is not rigidly defined, hence variations exist. In the "classical" approach (according to Linstone, 1978; Martino, 1983), the first round is unstructured, allowing the experts free scope to elucidate those issues they see as being important in the selected area of interest, after which the monitor/s consolidates the individual factors into a single set, producing the actual questionnaires which are returned to the judges on subsequent rounds. After each round, the judges' estimates are statistically summarized (usually into medians plus upper and lower quartiles) and returned to the group members for further consideration. In the third round and thereafter, the "panelists" have the opportunity to alter prior estimates on the basis of the group feedback, and, further, panelists whose responses fall outside the quartiles may be asked to give written argument as to why they think they are right in opposition to the majority view (such arguments also being fed back).

This procedure continues until a certain stability in responding is achieved whereby additional rounds are expected to result in only minimal changes in responses. The group median on the final round is then taken to represent the group judgment (with differences in the quartile figures indicating the degree of disagreement). Most commonly, however, round one is structured and the number of iterations rarely goes beyond two, while feedback tends largely to be limited to a single statistic representing the present group average (and rarely includes actual written arguments). It is important to state these latter variations since they apply most strongly to laboratory research, whence we get the majority of evidence as to the usefulness of the technique.

Though not unequivocal, experimental studies have generally shown that convergence of opinions (or at least of responses) does take place over rounds, and that such convergence tends to be towards more valid responses (e.g., Dalkey & Brown, 1971; Jolson & Rossow, 1971; Riggs, 1983). That is, the result on the final polling tends to be more accurate than the average (median/mean) of the first-round responses—which is an equal-weighted mathematical aggregation of responses. However, we must be wary of drawing grand conclusions on the basis of this: first, because such improvements as have been demonstrated have usually been small (and often statistically nonsignificant), and second, because of the limited nature of the majority of Delphi studies.

The first point is important because it relates back to a point we have previously noted: that practical factors should be considered when one selects an aggregation technique, and so, if Delphi improvements are minor, then it may be justified to use the simple first-round polling of experts (accepting a small decrement in performance relative to that which may be attained after further rounds of polling and feedback), for the sake of the savings one might make in terms of time/money, etc. The second point is relevant because, as we have attempted to demonstrate, the usefulness of any technique depends upon a number of subtle factors, such that superiority in one situation (with experts of a particular nature making a specific type of judgment) does not guarantee superiority in all other situations.

In the case of Delphi, experimental studies have generally used simplified versions of Delphi (structured first rounds, two iterations, small groups), using students as subjects, making short-term forecasts (of days or weeks into the future) or estimates on "almanac" type questions (questions whose answers are usually large numbers, the values of which are already known to the experimenters, and about which the subjects are presumed capable of making educated guesses—such as the tonnage of a certain material shipped from New York in a certain year). A number of interesting points can be made on the basis of these general characteristics.

The use of inexpert subjects is often justified by researchers on the basis of the inconclusiveness of studies in demonstrating a consistant advantage in using expert over inexpert subjects within Delphi panels. That is, while certain studies have revealed that greater increases in accuracy over Delphi rounds may be obtained through the selection of expert panelists (e.g., Dalkey, Brown, & Cochran, 1970; Jolson & Rossow, 1971; Best, 1974; Riggs, 1983; Larreche & Moinpour, 1983), other studies have failed to find such benefits (e.g., Winkler, 1971; Bender, Strack, Ebright, & von Haunalter, 1969; Salancik, Wenger, & Helfer, 1971; Brockhoff, 1975). With such ambiguity of findings, perhaps it is not surprising that researchers have tended to quote the latter set of studies to save themselves the difficulties of having to find truly expert panelists. Indeed, even studies which do attempt to consider individual expertise as a factor tend to make differentiations on the basis of the self-rating of (student) subjects.

The first point that arises here is that any real differences in expertise between such groups of high and low raters are liable to be small, all panelists coming from the same basic group. A second point concerns the appropriateness of self-rating as an accurate reflector of actual expertise: as we have noted earlier, such a measure will identify those who think they are expert, but this self-perception does not necessarily have to be correct, and is more than likely to be biased (in which case it is little wonder that studies have demonstrated "expertise" to be irrelevant in determining the value of Delphi). Once more we return to the bottleneck of identifying true expertise.

With subjects in Delphi studies generally possessing only superficial knowledge about experimental problem scenarios, and belonging to homogenous groups (hence sharing much of the little knowledge they have), it is difficult to see how they might benefit from interaction with their fellows, there being so little knowledge available for exchange. Furthermore, difficulties also seem to arise as a result of the nature of the feedback usually provided in the typical laboratory study, consisting merely of solitary statistics representing the group average response (and no written arguments or opinions).

This has to be a crucial issue, since the feedback is the intended means of conveying information from one panelist to the next: by limiting the scope of feedback one limits the scope for improvements. Thus, even if a Delphi panel is composed appropriately, with panelists who do have information to share, unless these are allowed to exchange that information in an effective way, then their valuable insights become useless. Deutsch and Gerrard (1955) made an important distinction between the "normative" and "informative" forces or incentives for opinion change of individuals within groups, the former factor acting through the desire of individuals to be accepted (or at least not rejected) by the others in the group, the latter factor leading to change on the basis of the informative arguments presented by the other group members.

It is the informative influence which is necessary for appropriate opinion change, with normative influences serving to distract individuals, potentially leading to process loss. When one considers feedback consisting of merely a statistic, it is difficult to see how the prime influence for change can be anything other than the normative factor, shifts in opinion coming from bandwagon effects (e.g., Hill & Fowles, 1975) rather than from the reasoned consideration of arguments (what arguments?).

So, does Delphi remove process loss? The technique as used in the majority of laboratory studies, we might argue, should be capable of ameliorating some of the difficulties which often arise in normal interacting groups, yet not resolve these problems completely. The main problem, however, must be that the highly restrictive approach to interactions among the panelists, and the information they are allowed to exchange, must reduce any possibility of process gain, thereby wiping out any benefits achieved through the removal of possible sources of bias.

However, if one were to conduct a Delphi using *genuine* experts who possessed different knowledge and presented feedback of a deeper nature—such as written arguments or justifications from each panelist—then one might expect far better results than those which have generally been attained in the laboratory—for the underlying rationale of the technique seems sound. What is surely needed to confirm the potential of Delphi is a number of careful studies taking a broader view of the approach, paying more attention to variables such as the nature of feedback and the composition of the Delphi panel, alongside a clearer analysis of the problems in which Delphi has been used, with the aim of matching the method more appropriately to the task.

The Nominal Group Technique

The basic idea behind the NGT is that, while interaction among group members may prove dysfunctional during the generation phase of problem solving (for the reasons leading to process loss), verbal interaction during the assessment or evaluation phase of problem solving may provide some positive influences concerning the clarification and justification of items generated, leading to improved judgment and decision making (Van de Ven & Delbecq, 1971; Delbecq, Van de Ven, & Gustafson, 1975). The process begins with each group member writing down ideas concerning the selected problem scenario, then selecting one of these for presentation to the remainder of the group. This is followed by a discussion of each point in turn (allowing some true interaction, unlike Delphi), after which each individual rates or rank-orders those ideas (in isolation); thence a mathematical aggregate of the result is obtained.

Relatively few studies have been conducted on the NGT, though the results from these have been encouraging. For example, Gustafson, Shukla, Delbecq, and Walster (1973) evaluated four methods of eliciting subjective likelihood ratio estimates, and found an NGT approach to perform best, outperforming individual estimates (statistical aggregation), estimates derived through normal interacting groups, and estimates from a Delphi-like condition. Other studies have also reported NGT to perform as well as, or better than, Delphi (e.g., Seaver, 1979; Fischer, 1981). However, we should also point out here that the above studies utilized Delphis of the simplistic variety noted earlier, with highly limited feedback and nonexpert subjects (e.g., Gustafson et al., 1973, used undergraduates judging likelihoods that a certain height or weight would describe a male or female—but assessing people's heights and ascribing relative probability estimates to height categories is hardly the sort of task one would expect people to indulge in and be "expert" at!). While the "naïveté" of the subjects is somewhat controlled for, in that this factor must also have effected the NGT (and other) conditions equally, the shallow feedback must have specifically limited the potential gain available from the Delphi technique, perhaps casting an unfair reflection upon its usefulness.

On the basis of studies so far conducted, it is difficult to know how to advise our "overseer" as to the usefulness or scope of mixed aggregation techniques. It may well be that the full potential of Delphi has yet to be demonstrated—and the same might be said for the NGT (Fischer, 1981, and Ferrell, 1985, have noted how the overall superiority of the NGT over other techniques has been shown to be only small). It is, perhaps, easy to see how each technique might be valuable, particularly in circumstances where one's experts are heterogeneous in terms of their knowledge and expertise, and might benefit from the interaction with their fellows.

"Interaction" is key and must be allowed, though restricted or channeled when it is suspected that nonrelevant factors (such as status or dogmatism) may adversely influence the judgment process, such that a mixed aggregation approach may excel a normal interacting group approach. It is difficult to predict how effective or useful NGT, Delphi, or some other mixed form of aggregation, will ultimately prove. The only way this may be determined is to consider a large range of judgment scenarios, varying key dimensions such as the *type* of judgment being made, the nature of the expertise of the group members, and so on. Further research would also seem warranted in the area of differential weighting of experts at the mathematical aggregation stage—and we have already mentioned some of the issues and dilemmas associated with this topic.

WHAT WORKS BEST AND WHEN?

The key variables that should influence one's choice of aggregation technique are: "task/judgment type," and "nature of experts" (including the number of experts). By and large, we have considered the influences of these variables *within* each category of techniques, rather than *between* them, and have largely refrained from comparing across the categories. In order to round off this analysis, we will now do this—though we will draw back on making specific conclusions because of the large gaps which we have identified as still existing in our knowledge.

Various authors (e.g., Steiner, 1972; Rohrbaugh, 1979) have suggested that when judgments require little depth of analysis (e.g., judging qualities such as weight or temperature) then statistical groups should prove an efficient aggregation approach, though when judgment requires a deeper analysis (perhaps involving some cognitive work, as in problem solving), then direct interactions may prove the most useful approach, over simple averaging. However, Hill (1982), reviewing research on group performance in which she divided studies according to the type of task the subjects were required to perform (since task demands may elicit performance strategies which interact with the characteristics of the group, e.g., Hoffman, 1965), showed that matters are somewhat more complex than this. For example, in tasks that she deemed of the "learning" and "abstract problem solving" type, she concluded that research has generally shown interacting groups to perform at least as well as statistical averaging (mathematical aggregation), though in the case of "complex problem solving" tasks (when more than one correct or sensible answer may be allowed) interacting groups were generally shown to be inferior to an averaging process.

Hence, Hill (1982) demonstrated the potential for groups to achieve process gain—and also their potential for process loss. In the case of "complex problem solving," much of the difficulty found in studies with the interacting groups (such as in Tuckman & Lorge, 1962), seemed to arise from information loss due to the groups ignoring key ideas generated by some of their members, though other problems were found in the areas of: aggregating/integrating information; error checking, and; the division of labor. Many of these problems, we might suggest, could be overcome through the application of more highly structured behavioral techniques (ensuring that all ideas are considered, etc.), or through the use of an appropriate "mixed" approach, which could remove aggregational difficulties and ensure the more rounded division of labor/contributions. It is notable that Hill's review was deficient in appropriate examples of applications of "mixed" approaches in this latter task category, demonstrating once more the lack of comprehensiveness of empirical research. However, sufficient studies were available for her to demonstrate the general utility of interacting groups in learning tasks, where resolutions of problems tended to be more rapid than when using noninteracting processes to attain judgments.

In most judgment tasks behavioral aggregation should be capable of outperforming mathematical aggregation, as long as the environment is so arranged as to allow the full and active participation of all group members, with mixed aggregation being superior when process loss might be expected. This is because most tasks will be of such a complexity that information exchange will be useful in leading to a more valid judgment; and hence it is where information exchange is not necessary that mathematical aggregation should be preeminent. This latter situation might occur in cases where the task requires only low levels of analysis (such as in judging temperature, as noted earlier, where knowing another's assessment should have little value in causing a rethink on one's own part), or when all judges are sufficiently knowledgeable about the judgment problem (with similar knowledge) that the main process whereby accuracy may be improved may be through the cancelling of random error.

However, like our "temperature" example, many apparently complex problem-solving tasks might prove suitable for mathematical aggregation because of the nature of the people employed to make the specified judgments. For example, if we consider the case where subjects are asked to estimate the tonnage of a particular material shipped from New York harbor in a certain year (an actual— and far from atypical—example of the sort of judgment task presented to subjects in early Delphi laboratory studies), we can imagine that a group of inexpert subjects will largely have to resort to guessing the appropriate order of magnitude, with little real causal theory behind their estimates. In such an interacting group, one can imagine information exchange to be highly limited with response along the lines of "well, I just think it should be a bit higher than that . . ."

If so, where the benefit of using an interacting group? And yet, to real experts on the topic the group may be useful in allowing true reasons and theories to be exchanged as to why the answer should be more like one figure than another ("I know 'x' tonnes was shipped in the year prior, since when timber demand abroad has increased due to the . . ."). Thus, we see the interaction between "task nature" and "attributes of the judges," where the nature of the latter will influence the former (and probably vice versa), and jointly determine which aggregation technique is liable to find most success.

Some pertinent work on group composition was carried out by Hogarth (1978) who developed an analytical model to help determine how many, and which, experts should be included to comprise a *statistical* group. His model yielded group validity as a function of the number of experts, their mean individual validity, and the mean intercorrelation of their judgments. The model went on to explore how "group" validity would change as a result of adding additional experts of differing qualities to the original aggregation, and provided some interesting results—such as demonstrating how judgment validity could, in certain circumstances, be improved to a greater degree by adding an expert with less individual validity than another expert (if, for example, that addition served to decrease the intercorrelation of the experts' judgments).

Hogarth's model further predicted that most improvement in "group" judgment validity would arise through the aggregation of the first few judgments—a prediction supported by subsequent experimental studies. For example, Libby and Blashfield (1978) showed that most of the improvement in validity of judgments in three different judgment tasks (predictions of future business failures; predictions of graduate admissions committee decisions; differentiations of neurotic from psychotic patients) could be obtained by aggregating just three judges (true experts in these studies). Further, Ashton and Ashton (1985) and Ashton (1986), reanalyzing the data from the Ashton (1982) study, found that the best gains in accuracy could be attained by aggregating the first two to five judges, and that adding on more judges up to a number of thirteen did little to enhance accuracy of judgments further. By and large, the number of judges required would seem to vary as a function of their actual individual validity or expertise.

The main recommendation we might draw from the above studies is that, if one intends to use a mathematical aggregation approach, one need only select a small number of experts, and these should preferably be possessed of a reasonable degree of individual validity/expertise. The generalizability of this assertion to interacting group composition, however, must be limited. Ferrell (personal communication, 1990) has noted that Hogarth's results are due to the properties of averages of random variables, and that if this is a good model of the group process then the results will hold, but, though it probably is a good model of the groups often used in research, it *shouldn't* be! Group size, as other group composition factors, will need to vary according to the detailed nature of the task (etc.).

For example, if the task is to recall an obscure synonym for a word, the more people, the more likely it will be recalled; but in many other cases additional voices may merely obscure the issue with a superabundance of information, leading to a kind of overload. The relative influence of the number of experts in a group, across the different aggregation approaches, is unknown, and hence we can make no recommendations as to whether, for example, a statistical group with five members may be better than an interacting group with eight members, and so on. With respect to the composition of the group in terms of the individuals selected, we can only be vague because of the difficulty which exists in identifying absolute and relative expertise a priori: we might suggest that, regardless of the specific technique employed, our overseer should simply choose reasonably competent experts who possess differences in knowledge or perspective.

As far as practical matters on implementation are concerned, mathematical aggregation seems to have advantages over other aggregation approaches in a number of ways, such as: the ease of use of statistical aggregation; the ability to conduct the technique whenever or wherever one wishes (for one's experts need not be in the same location at the same time); and the avoidance of potential process loss factors in regular groups. Hence, unless substantial gains may be derived using an alternative technique, economics may advocate the selection of a mathematical aggregation approach.

However, a number of other factors need to be borne in mind: Ferrell (1985) has warned of the deceptive simplicity of such approaches. For example, Ferrell notes that such aggregations may not represent the reality they are meant to summarize (e.g., two opposed zealots do not combine to bland indifference); interactions may occur between the axiom system of the measures being assessed (e.g., averaging probabilities destroys their multiplicative properties); and problems exist in the interpersonal comparison of values (a value of "five" will mean different things to different people).

Hence, Ferrell has warned that, if one selects a mathematical means for aggregation, then one must select an appropriate method for doing so (particularly in the case of probabilistic judgments). We have attempted to point to where and when such aggregation might be preferred to other approaches, rather than considering the subtleties of the mathematics.

SUMMARY

Throughout this work, we have attempted to make clear that our advice to our hypothetical "overseer" is necessarily vague, due to the limited number of judgmental scenarios considered in depth by experimental studies in this field. It is apparent that, of the large set which includes the entirety of all possible judgmental environments, only a small subset has been sampled, this subset largely consisting of atypical exemplars at that (atypical with respect to environments in the "real world"), such that our ability to generalize is limited. While it is true that a recognition of the importance of "ecological validity" seems to be increasingly considered in research in many areas, we might argue that, particularly in the case of "mixed" aggregation approaches, this realization has hardly effected the conduct of laboratory studies. This is important, as such "mixed" approaches possess great potential, theoretically, in that they seek to combine the best of their constituent approaches, letting human judges perform those tasks at which they are most capable, and interjecting mechanical manipulations where this is viable.

At least in the case of Delphi studies, these inadequacies are partly understandable due to the technique's past history: it began largely as a tool for forecasting long-term changes, and has since emerged as a judgment-aiding device—though forecasting tasks are still a favored area for the application of Delphi, and these are particularly difficult to study in a controlled yet ecological manner. If such approaches do have unobserved potential, it might be premature for us to recommend the implementation of alternative approaches in particular situations, when Delphi, NGT, or any similar procedure, might shortly be shown to do better.

Further, we have attempted to demonstrate the difficulty in identification of experts. On the basis of this we would largely recommend our overseer to leave well alone any differential mathematical weighting approach, for the added complexities do not seem justified by the method's potential. In one of the few studies which have shown any significant advantage for this approach, Larreche and Moinpour (1983) found a weighting based on objective assessment criteria to outperform a variety of other techniques, including Delphi and interacting groups. However, when they analyzed the Delphi groups after the study, they found that groups that contained more than one of these objectively identified experts proved even better—and the potential of groups initially constructed *entirely* of such identified individuals can only be guessed at.

Thus, if one can identify experts appropriately, then perhaps this information might find greatest use in helping to construct an interacting group (or a group for use in a "mixed" technique) rather than as a means for weighting individuals in a statistical aggregate. By choosing the appropriate individuals to make up an interacting group, we might thereby hope that improvement in group accuracy may be caused/accompanied by an increase in the expertise or knowledge of each of the individuals, leading to a generalizable gain which might be carried forward by those experts into other judgment situations—a gain which is certainly unavailable from any mathematical aggregation approach.

REFERENCES

Armstrong, J. S. (1986). Research on forecasting: A quarter-century review, 1960–1984. *Interfaces, 16*(11), 89–109.

Ashton, A. H. (1982). An empirical study of budget-related predictions of corporate executives. *Journal of Accounting Research, 20*(2), 440–449.

Ashton, A. H., & Ashton, R. H. (1985). Aggregating subjective forecasts: Some empirical results. *Management Science, 31,* 1499–1508.

Ashton, R. H. (1986). Combining the judgments of experts: How many and which ones? *Organizational Behavior and Human Decision Processes, 38,* 405–414.

Best, R. J. (1974). An experiment in Delphi estimation in marketing decision making. *Journal of Marketing Research, 11,* 448–452.

Bender, A. D., Strack, A. E., Ebright, G. W., & von Haunalter, G. (1969). Delphi study examines developments in medicine. *Futures, 1,* 289–303.

Brockhoff, K. (1975). The performance of forecasting groups in computer dialogue and face to face discussion. In H. Linstone & M. Turoff (Eds.), *The Delphi Method: Techniques and applications.* London: Addison-Wesley.

Bunn, D. (1989). Forecasting with more than one model. *Journal of Forecasting, 8*(3), 161–166.

Clemen, R. T. (1989). Combining forecasts: A review and annotated bibliography. *International Journal of Forecasting, 5,* 559–583.

Dalkey, N. C., & Brown, B. (1971). Comparison of group judgment techniques with short-range predictions and almanac questions. The RAND Corporation, R-678-ARPA.

Dalkey, N. C., Brown, B., & Cochran, S. W. (1970). The Delphi Method III: Use of self-ratings to improve group estimates. *Technological Forecasting, 1,* 283–291.

Dalkey, N. C., & Helmer, O. (1963). An experimental application of the Delphi Method to the use of experts. *Management Science, 9,* 458–467.

Dawes, R. (1988). *Rational choice in an uncertain world.* San Diego: Harcourt Brace, Jovanovich.

Dawes, R. M., & Corrigan, B. (1974). Linear models in decision making. *Psychological Bulletin, 81,* 95–106.

DeGroot, M. H. (1974). Reaching a consensus. *Journal of the American Statistical Association, 69,* 118–121.

Delbecq, A. L., Van de Ven, A. H., & Gustafson, D. H. (1975). *Group techniques for program planning.* Glenview, Ill.: Scott Foresman.

Deutsch, M., & Gerard, H. B. (1955). A study of normative and informational social influences upon individual judgment. *Journal of Abnormal and Social Psychology, 51,* 629–636.

Eils, L. C., & John, R. S. (1980). A criterion validation of multiattribute utility analysis and of group communication strategy. *Organizational Behavior and Human Performance, 25,* 268–288.

Einhorn, H. J. (1974). Expert judgment: some necessary conditions and an example. *Journal of Applied Psychology, 59*(5), 562–571.

Einhorn, H. J., & Hogarth, R. M. (1975). Unit weighting schemes for decision making. *Organizational Behavior and Human Performance, 13,* 171–192.

Einhorn, H. J., Hogarth, R. M., & Klempner, E. (1977). Quality of group judgment. *Psychological Bulletin, 84,* 158–172.

Ferrell, W. R. (1985). Combining individual judgments. In G. Wright (Ed.), *Behavioral decision making.* New York: Plenum.

Fischer, G. W. (1981). When oracles fail—A comparison of four procedures for aggregating subjective probability forecasts. *Organizational Behavior and Human Performance, 28,* 96–110.

Flores, B. E., & White, E. M. (1989). Subjective vs objective combining of forecasts: An experiment. *Journal of Forecasting, 8,* 331–341.

Fraser, C., & Foster, D. (1984). Social groups, nonsense groups and group polarization. In H. Tajfel (Ed.), *Group Processes,* New York: Academic Press.

Granger, C. W. J., & Newbold, P. (1975). Economic forecasting: The atheist's viewpoint. In Renton, G. A. (Ed.), *Modelling the economy.* London: Heineman.

Gustafson, D. H., Shukla, R. K., Delbecq, A., & Walster, G. W. (1973). A comparison study of differences in subjective likelihood estimates made by individuals, interacting groups, Delphi groups and nominal groups. *Organizational Behavior and Human Performance, 9,* 280–291.

Hackman, J. R., & Morris, C. G. (1975). Group tasks, group interaction process and group performance effectiveness: A review and proposed integration. *Advances in Experimental Social Psychology, 8,* 45–99.

Hall, J., & Watson, W. H. (1971). The effects of a normative intervention on group decision-making performance. *Human Relations, 23,* 299–317.

Hastie, R. (1986). Experimental evidence on group accuracy. In B. Grafman & G. Owen (Eds.), *Decision research* (Vol. 2), Greenwich, CT: JAI Press.

Hill, G. W. (1982). Group versus individual performance: Are N+1 heads better than one? *Psychological Bulletin, 91*(3), 517–539.

Hill, K. Q., & Fowles, J. (1975). The methodological worth of the Delphi forecasting technique. *Technological Forecasting and Social Change, 7,* 179–192.

Hoffman, L. R. (1965). Group problem solving. In L. Berkowitz (Ed.), *Advances in experimental social psychology* (Vol. 2). New York: Academic Press.

Hogarth, R. M. (1978). A note on aggregating opinions. *Organizational Behavior and Human Performance, 21,* 40–46.

Hogarth, R. M., & Makridakis, S. (1981). Forecasting and planning: An evaluation. *Management Science, 27,* 115–138.

Janis, I. (1972). *Victims of groupthink,* Boston: Houghton Mifflin.

Jenkins, G. M. (1974). Discussion of a paper by Newbold and Granger. *Journal of the Royal Statistical Society A, 137,* 148–150.

Jolson, M. A., & Rossow, G. (1971). The Delphi process in marketing decision making. *Journal of Marketing Research, 8,* 443–448.

Kleinmuntz, B. (1989). Why we still use our heads instead of formulas: Towards an integrative approach. *Psychological Bulletin,* in press.

Larreche, J. C., & Moinpour, R. (1983). Managerial judgment in marketing: The concept of expertise. *Journal of Marketing Research, 20,* 110–121.

Libby, R., & Blashfield, R. K. (1978). Performance of a compolite as a function of the number of judges. *Organizational Behavior and Human Performance, 21,* 121–129.

Lichtenstein, S., Fischhoff, B., & Phillips, L. D. (1982). Calibration of probabilities: The state of the art to 1980. In Kahneman, D., Slovic, P., & Tversky, A. (Eds.), *Judgment under uncertainty: Heuristics and biases,* New York: Cambridge University Press.

Linstone, H. A. (1978). The Delphi Technique. In R. B. Fowles (Ed.), *Handbook of futures research,* Westport, CT: Greenwood Press.

Linstone, H., & Turoff, M. (1975). *The Delphi Method: Techniques and applications,* London: Addison-Wesley.

Lock, A. (1987). Integrating group judgments in subjective forecasts. In G. Wright & P. Ayton (Eds.), *Judgmental forecasting,* Chichester: Wiley.

Lorge, I., Fox, D., Davitz, J., & Brenner, M. (1958). A survey of studies contrasting the quality of group performance and individual performance. *Psychological Bulletin, 55,* 337–372.

McKinnon, W. J. (1966). Development of the SPAN technique for making decisions in human groups. *American Behavioral Scientist, 9,* 9–13.

Martino, J. (1983). *Technological forecasting for decision-makers* (2nd ed.). New York: Elsevier.

Nisbett, R., & Ross, R. L. (1980). *Human inference: Strategies and shortcomings of social judgment.* Englewood Cliffs, N.J.: Prentice-Hall.

Northcroft, M. A., & Neale, G. B. (1987). Experts, amateurs and real-estate: An anchoring and adjust perspective in property pricing decisions. *Organizational Behavior and Human Decision Processes, 39,* 84–97.

Parente, F. J., & Anderson-Parente, J. K. (1987). Delphi inquiry systems. In G. Wright & P. Ayton (Eds.), *Judgmental forecasting,* Chichester: Wiley.

Riggs, W. E. (1983). The Delphi Method: An experimental evaluation. *Technological Forecasting and Social Change, 23,* 89–94.

Rohrbaugh, J. (1979). Improving the quality of group judgment: Social judgment analysis and the Delphi technique. *Organizational Behavior and Human Performance, 24,* 73–92.

Rowse, G. L., Gustafson, D. H., & Ludke, R. L. (1974). Comparison of rules of aggregating subjective likelihood ratios. *Organizational Behavior and Human Performance, 12,* 274–285.

Salancik, J. R., Wenger, W., & Helfer, E. (1971). The construction of delphi event statements. *Technological Forecasting and Social Change, 3,* 65–73.

Seaver, D. A. (1979). Assessing probability with multiple individuals, Unpublished doctoral dissertation, University of Southern California, Los Angeles.

Sniezek, J. A., & Henry, R. A. (1989). Accuracy and confidence in group judgment. *Organizational Behavior and Human Decision Processes, 43,* 1–28.

Steiner, I. D. (1972). *Group process and productivity.* New York: Academic Press.

Tuckman, J., & Lorge, I. (1962). Individual ability as a determinant of group superiority. *Human Relations, 15,* 45–51.

Tversky, A., & Kahneman, D. (1974). Judgment under uncertainty: Heuristics and biases. *Science, 185,* 1124–1131.

Uecker, W. L. (1982). The quality of group performance in simplified information evaluation. *Journal of Accounting Research, 20,* 388–402.

Van de Ven, A. H., & Delbecq, A. L. (1971). Nominal versus interacting group processes for committee decision making effectiveness. *Academic Management Journal, 14,* 203–213.

Winkler, R. L. (1971). Probablistic prediction: Some experimental results. *Journal of the American Statistical Association, 66,* 675–685.

CHAPTER 8

Decision Conferencing
A Unique Approach to the Behavioral Aggregation of Expert Judgment

Patricia Reagan-Cirincione and John Rohrbaugh

Judgment is an inferential cognitive process by which an individual draws conclusions about unknown quantities or qualities on the basis of available information. The flaws in an individual's cognitive process leading to inaccurate judgment have been explored widely (Hammond, Stewart, Brehmer, & Steinmann, 1986; Hogarth, 1987; Kahneman, Slovic, & Tversky, 1982; Simon, 1945, 1960). The earliest research on group judgment led to some confidence that the mathematical aggregation of judgments from several individuals (collected as a "statistized," "nominal," or "noninteracting" group) usually would be better than the accuracy expected by randomly selecting a single individual from the population of all prospective group members (Bruce, 1935; Gordon, 1924; Knight, 1921).

Kelley (1925) was the first statistician to note that the superiority of "statistized" group judgment over a selected individual's judgment (on simple tasks where individuals' errors are randomly distributed) is due to increased reliability provided by larger samples; experimental evidence was offered later by Stroop (1932) that supported Kelley's claim. Preston (1938) and Smith (1941), however, produced both theoretical and empirical work to demonstrate that, where tasks

Patricia Reagan-Cirincione • University Center for Policy Research, State University of New York at Albany, Albany, New York 12222.   **John Rohrbaugh** • Graduate School of Public Affairs, State University of New York at Albany, Albany, New York 12222.
Expertise and Decision Support, edited by George Wright and Fergus Bolger. Plenum Press, New York, 1992.

systematically mislead or confuse, "statistized" group judgment frequently may be worse than the accuracy expected by randomly selecting a single individual from the population of all prospective group members. This phenomenon is illustrated explicitly in the Appendix.

Under what circumstances should one depend on "statistized" group judgment? Where task properties are known and the lack of systematic errors in individual judgments can be assured (i.e., the task evokes unbiased estimates), mathematical aggregation clearly is preferable to the estimate of one randomly selected person (Einhorn, Hogarth, & Klempner, 1977). Such circumstances are rare. In many, if not most, situations, task properties are altogether unknowable. Historical data including the criterion to be estimated may not be available or, if accessible, may suggest an unstable flux. In either instance, there is good reason to be cautious about possible but unconfirmable systematic errors that may intrude on individual judgment making. Perhaps the best advice in such situations is to assume that any complex task evokes considerable bias, making it wise to avoid the mathematical aggregation of multiple judgments.

IMPROVING THE ACCURACY OF GROUP JUDGMENT ON COMPLEX TASKS

Since "statistized" groups may be quite poorly suited to the frequent conditions of potential individual bias on tasks with considerable complexity or "intentional depth" (Rohrbaugh, 1979), alternative methods have been sought to improve the accuracy of individual judgment. In the late 1930s, group judgment research moved forward to the study of interacting groups. Thorndike (1938) and Timmons (1942) demonstrated that interacting groups could reliably outperform "statistized" groups on more difficult judgment tasks that induce systematic errors from individuals, findings that have been replicated repeatedly over the last 40 years (Burleson, Levine, & Samter, 1984; Hall, Mouton, & Blake, 1963; Holloman & Hendrick, 1971, 1972; Uecker, 1982; Yetton & Bottger, 1982). Such behavioral aggregation in interacting groups, as contrasted to mathematical aggregation (Ferrell, 1985), appears to benefit from group members having an opportunity to pool relevant knowledge, check mistaken assumptions, and provoke new insights. Recent studies have reported similar advantages of group interaction for improving judgmental accuracy or, in other terms, "the subjective combining of subjective forecasts" on complex tasks (Flores & White, 1989; Sniezek & Henry, 1989).[1]

---

[1]It should be emphasized again that the conclusions drawn here pertain to complex tasks with considerable "intentional depth"; in situations involving easy tasks with little systematic error in individual judgments, the levels of accuracy produced by mathematical and behavioral aggregation appear to converge (Sniezek, 1990).

Research also has indicated, however, that, in an interacting group at work on a complex task, the final collective judgment achieved usually does not surpass the accuracy of one or two members' initial estimates: a substantial majority of interacting groups are outperformed by the individual judgments of their most capable members (Einhorn, Hogarth, & Klempner, 1977; Hall, Mouton, & Blake, 1963; Herbert & Yost, 1979; Holloman & Hendrick, 1971; Miner, 1984; Nemiroff, Pasmore, & Ford, 1976). Thus, although behavioral aggregation may be found to outperform mathematical aggregation in quality of judgment, interacting groups typically fail to use fully the best individual knowledge and insight available as resources during the discussion of a complex task.

To account for the apparent fact that untapped expertise exists in most groups, Steiner (1972) noted that process problems arise during group deliberations that reduce the potential of the group to perform optimally. As a result, the accuracy of group judgment on a complex task typically is worse than one or two proficient members are able to achieve independently. Since behavioral integration of individual judgment in freely interacting groups typically involves a wholly unstructured process, a variety of structured interventions in group processes have been proposed and tested to assess their incremental yield in the accuracy of the final group judgment.

Although one popular line of investigation has been to attempt to eliminate process losses through the elimination of all group discussion,[2] a less extreme proposal also has gained attention, the so-called "estimate-talk-estimate" group process (Gustafson, Shukla, Delbecq, & Walster, 1973). Fischer (1981) carefully reviewed a decade of research on "estimate-talk-estimate" (as well as "estimate-feedback-estimate") process interventions, and he concluded virtually no empirical evidence had accumulated to support either as a method to improve upon the level of accuracy expected from freely interacting groups; the study of Nemiroff, Pasmore, and Ford (1976) was excluded from Fischer's (1981) review but is consistent with his conclusion.

An alternative process intervention that has been tested infrequently but with quite promising results might be described simply as "estimate-feedback-talk," that is, group members independently make judgments that are then com-

---

[2]The Delphi technique is used to create "statistized" groups whose individual members independently make estimates and, then, re-estimate after receiving feedback about the central value and variability of the entire set of original judgments collected. Evidence suggests that such sequential mathematical aggregations will enable groups working on simple tasks (where individuals' errors are randomly distributed) to perform as well or better than their most capable members (Linstone & Turoff, 1975). However, on difficult tasks where systematic errors intrude, Delphi-like "estimate-feedback-estimate" procedures appear to perform as poorly as simpler forms of mathematical aggregation when compared to the accuracy of interacting groups (see, for example, Burleson, Levine, & Samter, 1984). Stewart (1987) provides an excellent, critical review of the Delphi literature.

pared and discussed. The distinguishing feature of this process is that, although the group receives feedback following an initial round of individual estimates, the final group judgment is consensually derived rather than based on mathematical aggregation. Holloman and Hendrick (1972) called this process "consensus after majority vote," Herbert and Yost (1979) somewhat mistakenly used the term "Nominal Group Technique," and Miner (1984) described two individual-group sequences (IGB and IBG conditions). All three studies documented that groups using "estimate-feedback-talk" procedures significantly outperformed conventionally interacting groups.

The "estimate-feedback-talk" intervention requires only a modest intrusion during the first phase of a conventional group interaction process: a few minutes set aside (1) for individuals to work on the task independently and (2) for the group to review systematically the judgments of every member. Several researchers also have focused on the potential advantages of enhancing the subsequent "talk" phase by attempting to improve the "group skills" of prospective members. Several studies (Hall & Watson, 1971; Hall & Williams, 1970; Nemiroff & King, 1975; Nemiroff, Pasmore, & Ford, 1976) have indicated that providing participants with six straightforward guidelines for effective meetings leads to significant improvement in judgment accuracy.[3] Where 5% to 35% of the uninstructed groups were found to outperform their most proficient members, 50% to 75% of the groups receiving process instructions were more accurate in their collective consensus than the best individual judgments.

The preponderance of empirical evidence concerning the superiority of behavioral aggregation over mathematical aggregation on complex tasks, especially in "estimate-feedback-talk" conditions with specially instructed groups, has led directly to the design and development of innovative, integrative methods for improving the accuracy of judgment in the 1980s. One of the first and now most widely used methods in this new generation of group process techniques is decision conferencing. Decision conferencing is distinguished by its reliance upon both (1) the support of information technology for individual judgment making, collective feedback, and consensus building; and (2) the assistance of an experienced facilitator to encourage continuously (far better than one-time-only instructions) the most effective patterns of communication within the group.

---

[3]The guidelines typically used to instruct group members strongly discourage (1) accepting initial agreement as good (since quick consensus breeds complacency about assumptions); (2) viewing differences of opinion as bad (since disagreement reflects a useful testing of a variety of ideas); (3) changing one's mind merely to avoid conflict (that is, mistaking unthinking capitulation for enlightened flexibility); (4) arguing at length for one's own priorities (rather than stating a position clearly and concisely); (5) harboring the notion that someone must win and someone must lose (when mutually acceptable alternatives can be created); and (6) reducing conflicts too efficiently with quick techniques such as votes and averages (instead of continuing to share relevant knowledge and insight). These group process guidelines are also an important element of decision conferencing, as described below.

DECISION CONFERENCING: AN OVERVIEW

Decision conferencing refers to intensive, computer-supported meetings, typically two days long, that include every person with a substantial stake in solving a pressing organizational problem. In a carefully selected conference room apart from daily interruptions and distractions, the group is offered an opportunity to develop a shared understanding of their problem and to create a clear plan of action. The central feature of decision conferencing is the on-the-spot development of a computer-based decision model. This model is constructed by the participants to incorporate their differing perspectives and priorities and allows interactive analysis of alternative estimates and assumptions. The group can examine the implications of the decision model, modify it, and test the effects of conflicting judgments, thereby ruling out ineffective strategies and focusing quickly on primary issues of major impact (McCartt & Rohrbaugh, 1989; Phillips, 1988a, 1988b).

Customizing the design of the meeting room and furnishings for the size and composition of each unique group is essential to enhance interpersonal interaction and creative thinking in decision conferences. Square spaces have been found to be more suitable than rectangular areas. In general, the arrangement includes several whiteboards and a large projection screen to provide ample workspace (both traditional and electronic) for organizing the many aspects of the problem and for building the decision model. Conference participants are seated in comfortable, executive-style chairs with casters, typically set in a semicircle, to permit a completely connected pattern of communication with a common group focus on the whiteboards and screen. A portion of the room (often to one side or to the back of the group) is set aside for conference support, including at least one microcomputer connected to an LCD panel for large screen projection and another microcomputer dedicated to maintaining a record of the key aspects of the group's deliberations.

A decision conference is supported by a team of at least three professionals who fill specific roles during the meeting: the primary facilitator, the decision analyst, and the correspondent. The primary facilitator, a specialist in the techniques of group dynamics and decision modeling, works directly with the group and takes responsibility for the interaction process by focusing discussion, managing disagreement, and enhancing the pattern of communication. By systematically integrating the various aspect of group discussion in a decision model that takes shape on the whiteboards, the facilitator helps the group achieve a shared framework for understanding the key elements of the problem. The facilitator must be especially skilled and experienced to productively handle the resulting conflict and tension and to keep the process moving efficiently without resorting to the shortcuts of final votes and averages. The decision analyst takes responsibility for the group's computer modeling support as the discussion unfolds, periodically providing the group with feedback from the computer analysis using the large screen projection system, and continuously updating the model as informed changes in group judgment occur. The correspondent monitors this process, as well, electronically recording the important details of the group's discussion, so that thorough documentation of their deliberation is immediately available at all times during the meeting and as a printed report by conference end.

As participants initially develop their decision model in the first morning of a decision conference, a representation of the group's collective thinking about the problem begins to emerge. Knowledge of the problem is integrated into the model through use of both available data and subjective judgment. Typically, the process of structuring the problem takes much of the first conference day. When the initial version of the model is complete, the computer is used to project its implications for decision making on the large screen so all participants can give them careful review. Group members can be expected to challenge these initial results, since analysis and intuition are frequently at considerable odds. A good portion of time on the second day of a decision conference is used to collect suggested modifications to the model and to test alternative assumptions. These sensitivity analyses continue until the group is satisfied that the model captures their best thinking about the problem, and consensus about a set of final judgments is obtained. These judgments then provide the basis for the wording of a detailed action plan of "next steps that must be taken," backed by a printed summary of the session produced by the correspondent.

While participants in past decision conferences have generally viewed the process as a highly participatory and goal-centered intervention (McCartt & Rohrbaugh, 1989), it must be recognized that decision conferencing is resource-intensive. The approach is most cost-effective, therefore, when an organization is wrestling with a crucial problem that must be solved expeditiously. Under these circumstances, a decision conference allows the group to resolve its problem more quickly and at a lower cost than other possible approaches that involve a large investment of staff time over many months. There are 14 organizations worldwide that provide decision conferencing as an integrative method for improving group judgment; the total number of decision conferences conducted is estimated to approach 500.

One of the most active centers of decision conferencing is the Decision Techtronics Group (DTG) of the State University of New York. Since its inception in 1981, DTG has hosted over 80 decision conferences for private and public sector organizations located throughout the United States. The majority of these conferences have been conducted for departments of the State of New York. For this reason, DTG is recognized particularly for its innovative work in decision support for senior executive teams in government. DTG also is noted for its application of a wide range of decision modeling technologies. DTG decision conferences have used such software packages as EQUITY for allocating scarce resources, POLICY for making experts' judgments explicit, HIVIEW for evaluating and selecting strategic options, STELLA for analyzing and forecasting the performance of dynamic systems, and LINDO for settling multiparty disputes.

The problems tackled by DTG through decision conferencing have been diverse. In Georgia, a decision conference for 30 community leaders was convened to develop a $100 million, 10-year strategic plan for their city. A national professional organization based in Washington, D.C., used a decision conference to support the work of a 10-member task force charged with the review of alternative revisions in its dues structure. Three AT&T executives in New Jersey arranged a small decision conference to plan the consolidation of regional offices. A Texas decision conference of 15 child welfare experts prioritized the urgency of response to individual abuse cases. A state regulatory agency in New York scheduled two decision conferences for senior executives to identify their common data base needs across divisions in preparation for their first integrated computer-based information system. In Michigan, a private foundation gathered 35 influential leaders in environmental policy from the private and public sectors statewide to prioritize and endorse a set of funding initiatives for legislative action.

The use of decision conferencing to improve the behavioral integration of expert judgment ("estimate-feedback-talk" with skilled facilitation for enhancement of the interaction process) is best illustrated through a specific case study. The application discussed below describes the use of decision conferencing to estimate parameters for a simulation model of a recently adopted alcoholism treatment system for New York State. Because the new treatment system was substantially different from the *status quo,* historical data were not altogether applicable to the judgments required. Where data might have been obtainable as a substitute for expert judgment, the costs of collection (in time and money) were viewed as prohibitive.

ESTIMATING DEMAND FOR ALCOHOLISM TREATMENT IN NEW YORK STATE: A CASE STUDY

Prior to 1984, alcoholism treatment services in New York State often were fragmented and lacked coordination. To improve service and ensure access to treatment within every community in the state, administrators in the New York State Division of Alcoholism and Alcohol Abuse developed a five-year comprehensive plan for the provision of alcoholism services. The successful development of this plan hinged on the accurate assessment of the level of need for various types of treatment programs. Assessment of need required (1) consensus on client eligibility criteria that defined entry into and movement through the various treatment components of the system, and (2) expert judgment to establish the rates of client movement from one type of facility to another. In response to these issues, two decision conferences were hosted by the Decision Techtronics Group at the request of the New York State Division of Alcoholism and Alcohol Abuse.

Participants in the decision conferences were selected on the basis of professional background and experience. Each conference brought together a representative group of experts drawn from the ranks of service providers, payors (insurance companies), planners, and government representatives. The first conference, focusing on systemwide issues, included 13 persons who had experience in planning, policy development, and systems design. During this decision conference, a system dynamics simulation model of the alcoholism treatment system was constructed. Participants focused on carefully defining the types of treatment programs in the model alcoholism service delivery system. Seven types of treatment components were distinguished, points of entry into and exist from treatment facilities were clarified, and alternative paths of client flow through the system were established. The basic outline of the system model as shown in Figure 1 was completed by the end of the first day of the conference. Next, the group identified client eligibility criteria and specified indicators of need for each of the seven types of alcoholism services. Brainstorming techniques (Diehl & Stroebe, 1987) that rely on the initial generation of individual lists of ideas (where group members work independently) were used to identify the most salient characteristics that might be associated with an individual's entry into and movement through the model alcoholism service delivery system; a total of 34 key attributes were generated.

The second conference, which focused on the flow of clients through the system and length-of-stay issues, included 17 individuals with clinical backgrounds and expertise in the operation of alcoholism treatment programs. During this decision conference, rates at which patients move from one type of treatment program to another, as well as the expected length of stay in each type of treatment program, were established. This task was accomplished by dividing the larger group of experts into three subgroups. Working with a facilitator, each subgroup was asked to make judgments regarding the proportion of clients in a particular treatment facility who would move to another type of facility or out of the system during a three-month period. In order to obtain as accurate collective judgments as possible, participants first were asked to make individual estimates of the rates of flow into and out of all seven types of facilities. These individual estimates were recorded electronically by the analyst, presented to the group, and thoroughly discussed. Individual estimates again were made, recorded, and presented to the group. Open discussion then commenced as the subgroups worked toward reaching consensus on each of the estimates. As necessary, the facilitator would intervene in the discussion to ensure that all points of view were acknowledged, assumptions were challenged, and fresh insights explored. Discussion proceeded until consensus estimates were established for the movement of clients

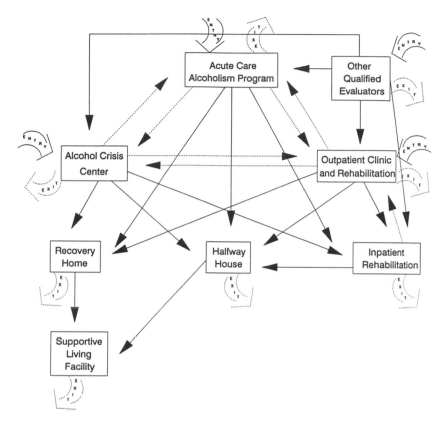

Figure 1. Diagram of treatment and flow within system model.

to and from each type of program. A representative example of the estimated flow rates for two program components (acute care and inpatient rehabilitation) is shown in Figure 2. Estimated lengths of both short-term and long-term stay in each type of treatment program also were determined through this "estimate-feedback-talk" process.

The entire group was then assembled to review and refine both sets of estimates. The estimates generated by each of the subgroups reflected differences in the assumptions underlying movement of clients in the system. Discussion of these differences was initiated by the facilitator. As the estimates for different facilities were debated, the analyst was able to incorporate proposed figures into the simulation model. In real time, the implications of different flow rates and lengths of stay on the number of clients in a treatment facility at any given time were then displayed to the group. This feedback enabled group members to recognize miscalculations and errors in judgment. By the end of the second

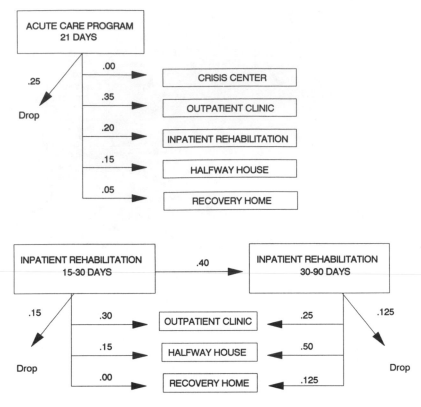

Figure 2. Selected estimates of flow rates.

conference, consensus was reached on the flow rates and lengths of stay for each treatment program, and final trajectories of client loads on the various treatment programs could be projected as shown in Figure 3.

Decision conferencing was a particularly beneficial approach to the aggregation of individual judgment because, through the construction of a simulation model, the participating experts were expected to clarify and define the nature of different types of treatment programs. Prior to these conferences, no single expert could be relied upon to make accurate forecasts of alcoholism treatment needs, nor did any pertinent data bases exist. As a result of the decision conferences, it was possible to increase confidence in estimates of the need for various alcoholism treatment facilities within the state. Perhaps more importantly, the participating experts left the decision conferences with far greater support of and commitment to the eventual implementation of the new treatment system. The results of these two decision conferences were incorporated in the Division's response to a request by the Governor for a full report, *Five-Year Comprehensive Plan for Alcoholism Services in New York State 1984–1989.* Since the decision

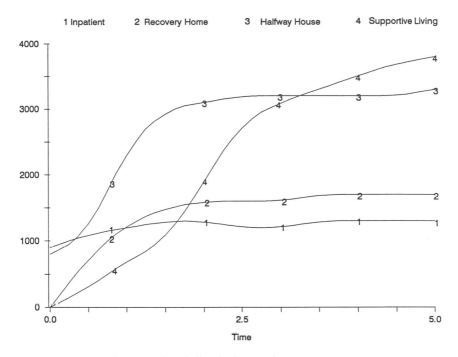

Figure 3. Trajectories of client loads on various treatment programs.

conferences, the plan has been implemented and provides a blueprint for the current alcoholism delivery system. Recognizing the benefits provided by decision conferencing, staff members at the Division of Alcoholism and Alcohol Abuse recently held another decision conference to address the issue of meeting the alcoholism service needs of the indigent.

In this case study of decision conferencing, experts discussed the apparent differences in their estimates, noted the implications of these differences in the systems model, and consensually agreed on a final set of parameters to use. It is important to note, however, that the differences in judgment which occur among experts may reflect in large part the existence of cognitive conflict. Where such disagreements can be identified explicitly as cognitive conflict, the focus of group work productively shifts from merely reconciling specific, individual estimates to conducting a thorough analysis of the *reasons* for judgmental discrepancies.

BEYOND ESTIMATION: THE STUDY OF COGNITIVE CONFLICT

According to McGrath (1984, p. 64), cognitive conflict tasks should be distinguished from other types of group work where "members of the group do not just have different preferences, but have systematically different preference structures. They may interpret information differently, may give different weights to different dimensions, and/or may relate dimensions to preferences via different functional forms." In principle, all judgment-making tasks can be studied with respect to the cognitive conflict inherent in the process of group task performance. Eils and John (1980) made this point clear when they used a "decomposition" procedure to study group evaluations of customer creditworthiness. Rather than merely focus on the differences in individuals' evaluations of each credit applicant, experimental groups worked collectively to formulate a uniform policy or system that would best integrate available information as a means to make specific judgments. This approach allowed the groups to discuss explicitly the differences in their personal methods for weighing and aggregating information. When a group reached agreement on an explicit review policy, they had overcome their cognitive conflict; as a result, the review policy reflected the collective expertise of the group and could be used to make repeated, consistent evaluations.

It should be noted that the redefinition of group judgment making as a cognitive conflict task gives additional structure to "estimate-feedback-talk" interventions. In cognitive conflict, group members must estimate their individual weights and function forms, receive feedback about the weights and function forms of the other members, and discuss clearly apparent differences. Although the customary "estimate-feedback-talk" intervention (Herbert & Yost, 1979; Holloman & Hendrick, 1972; Miner, 1984) attempts to provide group members with the opportunity to discuss their cognitive differences as a method for resolving conflicting estimates, such interventions are not designed to formally decompose the problem as Eils and John (1980) described. Cognitive feedback (Harmon & Rohrbaugh, 1990; Rohrbaugh, 1979, 1981) also has been used successfully to direct a group's attention to the *implicit* differences in judgment policies that produce *explicit* differences in observed judgments.

When time is available, decomposition of a problem may be extremely useful as a means of better articulating the reasons for systematic differences between expert estimates. Decision conferences have been used repeatedly as the forum for revealing and managing cognitive conflict. When child welfare experts disagreed about assessing the urgency of response to individual abuse cases, a decision conference was hosted to identify the key criteria that should influence such judgments (Rohrbaugh, 1988). By comparing and contrasting alternative judgment policies specified with weights and function forms, the group was able to discuss the merits of alternative models. Computer software at the decision conference allowed these experts to "test-run" several versions of a final review policy as a way of explicitly checking how specific abuse cases would be prioritized. Milter and Rohrbaugh (1988) also have described in detail how cognitive conflict embedded in a controversy about the appropriate timing of utilization reviews for psychiatric outpatients was managed in the context of a decision conference hosted for the New York State Office of Mental Health.

Is there any empirical evidence that changing the nature of the group conflict from "surface" disagreements about specific estimates to "depth" discussions about judgment policies (i.e., decomposition of the problem) improves the level of accuracy achieved through behavioral aggregation? No comparative studies of decision conferencing and other approaches have been undertaken as yet. An experimental study has been conducted recently by Reagan-Cirincione (1991) to determine the potential of decision conferencing in enabling groups to make more accurate judgments than their most proficient group members on complex judgment tasks with substantial bias. Individuals were asked to either establish a policy predicting the success of baseball teams based on selected team statistics or to establish a policy predicting average teachers' salaries on selected economic and demographic characteristics of states. These tasks were chosen because the correct answers were known to the researchers but were not intuitively obvious to the population of experimental participants. Four- and five-member groups then developed a collective judgment policy in a simulated decision conference environment which included a process facilitator and decision modeling techniques supported by computer. Over 80% of the groups in the study performed more accurately than their most capable members.

Decision conferencing appears to allow groups to consistently outperform even the best individual members because it is a highly developed method of behavioral aggregation that is well suited to the resolution of cognitive conflict. Not only is the "estimate-feedback-talk" method employed, but it is used to explore differences in judgment policies, not merely the differences in judgments. Improvement in the group interaction process is provided, not merely by a one-time-only set of instructions, but by the continual attention and support of a highly skilled facilitation team. The appropriate use of information technology and decision modeling in decision conference provides the most contemporary form of group decision support system for expert teams (McCartt & Rohrbaugh, 1989). In short, decision conferencing offers an ideal environment for expert teams who are prepared to build models, make explicit judgments, work with computer-generated displays, and test alternative policies, that is, for expert teams that expect not only to uncover their cognitive conflicts but also to resolve them during the two-day meeting.

APPENDIX

The relative superiority of "statistized" group judgment over the judgment of an individual randomly selected from the population of all prospective group members depends upon the properties of the task. Where the task evokes un-

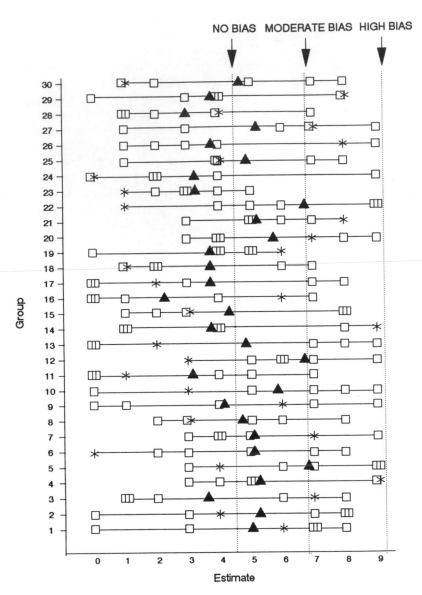

Figure A1. Individual estimates and group averages.

Table 1. Errors of Estimates for Individuals and Groups—No-Bias Condition
(True Value = 4.5)

Group	Most capable	More capable	Average member	Less capable	Least capable	Average error
1	1.5	2.5	2.5	3.5	4.5	0.5
2	1.5	2.5	3.5	3.5	4.5	0.7
3	1.5	2.5	3.5	3.5	3.5	0.9
4	0.5	0.5	0.5	1.5	4.5	0.7
5	1.5	1.5	2.5	4.5	4.5	2.3
6	0.5	1.5	2.5	2.5	3.5	0.5
7	0.5	0.5	0.5	1.5	4.5	0.5
8	0.5	1.5	1.5	2.5	3.5	0.3
9	0.5	2.5	3.5	4.5	4.5	0.3
10	0.5	2.5	3.5	4.5	4.5	1.3
11	0.5	0.5	2.5	4.5	4.5	1.3
12	0.5	1.5	1.5	2.5	4.5	2.1
13	2.5	3.5	4.5	4.5	4.5	0.3
14	0.5	0.5	3.5	3.5	3.5	0.9
15	1.5	2.5	3.5	3.5	3.5	0.1
16	0.5	2.5	3.5	4.5	4.5	2.1
17	1.5	2.5	3.5	4.5	4.5	0.9
18	1.5	2.5	2.5	2.5	3.5	0.9
19	0.5	0.5	0.5	0.5	4.5	0.9
20	0.5	0.5	1.5	3.5	4.5	1.1
21	0.5	0.5	1.5	1.5	2.5	0.7
22	0.5	0.5	1.5	4.5	4.5	2.1
23	0.5	0.5	1.5	1.5	2.5	1.1
24	0.5	2.5	2.5	4.5	4.5	1.1
25	0.5	0.5	2.5	3.5	3.5	0.3
26	0.5	1.5	2.5	3.5	4.5	0.7
27	1.5	1.5	2.5	3.5	4.5	0.7
28	0.5	2.5	2.5	3.5	3.5	1.5
29	0.5	0.5	1.5	3.5	4.5	0.7
30	0.5	2.5	2.5	3.5	3.5	0.1

biased estimates (i.e., the errors in individuals' judgments are distributed randomly around the true value), mathematical aggregation will often outperform even the most capable group member. However, where the task evokes biased estimates, mathematical aggregation does not perform so well. In fact, in such situations "statistized" group judgment frequently may be worse than the accuracy expected by randomly selecting a single individual to make an estimate.

To illustrate this phenomenon, 30 five-member groups were selected randomly from a population of prospective members. The population parameters of the individual estimates were known: a mean of 4.5 and a standard deviation of 2.8. No individual estimate was less than 0.0 or greater than 9.0. Three distinct

Table 2. Errors of Estimates for Individuals and Groups—Moderate-Bias Condition (True Value = 6.8)

Group	Most capable	More capable	Average member	Less capable	Least capable	Average error
1	0.2	0.2	1.2	3.8	6.8	1.8
2	0.2	1.2	1.2	3.8	6.8	1.6
3	0.8	1.2	4.8	5.8	5.8	3.2
4	1.8	1.8	2.2	2.8	3.8	1.6
5	0.2	0.8	2.2	2.2	3.8	0.0
6	0.2	1.2	1.8	3.8	4.8	1.8
7	1.8	2.2	2.8	2.8	3.8	1.8
8	0.8	1.2	1.8	3.8	4.8	2.0
9	0.2	2.2	2.8	5.8	6.8	2.6
10	0.2	1.2	1.8	2.2	6.8	1.0
11	0.2	1.8	2.8	6.8	6.8	3.6
12	0.2	0.8	0.8	1.8	2.2	0.2
13	0.2	1.2	2.2	6.8	6.8	2.0
14	1.2	2.8	2.8	5.8	5.8	3.2
15	1.2	1.2	3.8	4.8	5.8	2.4
16	0.2	2.8	5.8	6.8	6.8	4.4
17	0.2	1.2	3.8	6.8	6.8	3.2
18	0.2	0.8	4.8	4.8	5.8	3.2
19	1.8	1.8	2.8	2.8	6.8	3.2
20	1.2	2.2	2.8	2.8	3.8	1.2
21	0.2	0.8	1.8	1.8	3.8	1.6
22	0.8	1.8	2.2	2.2	2.8	0.2
23	1.8	2.8	3.8	3.8	4.8	3.4
24	2.2	2.8	4.8	4.8	6.8	3.4
25	0.2	1.2	2.8	2.8	5.8	2.0
26	2.2	2.8	3.8	4.8	5.8	3.0
27	0.2	0.8	2.2	3.8	5.8	1.6
28	0.2	2.8	4.8	5.8	5.8	3.8
29	1.2	2.8	2.8	3.8	6.8	3.0
30	0.2	1.2	1.8	4.8	5.8	2.2

circumstances were considered. In a "no bias" condition, the individual estimates were positioned so that they were distributed randomly around a true value of 4.5, that is, the population parameter of central value and the true value were identical. In a "moderate bias" condition, the individual estimates were repositioned so that they systematically underestimated the true value of 6.8; the bias in this condition was approximately .8 standard deviation unit (see Einhorn, Hogarth, & Klempner, 1977). In a "high bias" condition, the individual estimates again were repositioned so that *not a single person* overestimated the true value of 9.1; the bias in this condition was approximately 1.6 standard deviation units.

Table 3. Errors of Estimates for Individuals and Groups—High-Bias Condition
(True Value = 9.1)

Group	Most capable	More capable	Average member	Less capable	Least capable	Average error
1	1.1	2.1	2.1	6.1	9.1	4.1
2	1.1	1.1	2.1	6.1	9.1	3.9
3	1.1	3.1	7.1	8.1	8.1	5.5
4	0.1	4.1	4.1	5.1	6.1	3.9
5	0.1	0.1	2.1	3.1	6.1	2.3
6	1.1	2.1	4.1	6.1	7.1	4.1
7	0.1	4.1	5.1	5.1	6.1	4.1
8	1.1	3.1	4.1	6.1	7.1	4.3
9	0.1	2.1	5.1	8.1	9.1	4.9
10	0.1	1.1	2.1	4.1	9.1	3.3
11	2.1	4.1	5.1	9.1	9.1	5.9
12	0.1	2.1	3.1	3.1	4.1	2.5
13	0.1	1.1	2.1	9.1	9.1	4.3
14	1.1	5.1	5.1	8.1	8.1	5.5
15	1.1	1.1	6.1	7.1	8.1	4.7
16	2.1	5.1	8.1	9.1	9.1	6.7
17	1.1	2.1	6.1	9.1	9.1	5.5
18	2.1	3.1	7.1	7.1	8.1	5.5
19	4.1	4.1	5.1	5.1	9.1	5.5
20	0.1	1.1	5.1	5.1	6.1	3.5
21	2.1	3.1	4.1	4.1	6.1	3.9
22	0.1	0.1	3.1	4.1	5.1	2.5
23	4.1	5.1	6.1	6.1	7.1	5.7
24	0.1	5.1	7.1	7.1	9.1	5.7
25	1.1	2.1	5.1	5.1	8.1	4.3
26	0.1	5.1	6.1	7.1	8.1	5.3
27	0.1	2.1	3.1	6.1	8.1	3.9
28	2.1	5.1	7.1	8.1	8.1	6.1
29	1.1	5.1	5.1	6.1	9.1	5.3
30	1.1	2.1	4.1	7.1	8.1	4.5

Figure A1 graphically illustrates the resulting distributions of estimates for each of the 30 five-member groups. The three task conditions are superimposed on this figure merely by progressively moving the dotted line denoting the true value to the right: from 4.5 ("no bias") to 6.8 ("moderate bias") to 9.1 ("high bias"). Each of the "statistized" group estimates is marked by a solid triangle. In addition, one more individual was selected randomly from the population and paired with each group to provide 30 "independent" estimates, marked by large asterisks. This allows for a direct comparison between accuracies of the group average estimate and a randomly selected individual estimate relative to the true value in each of the three conditions.

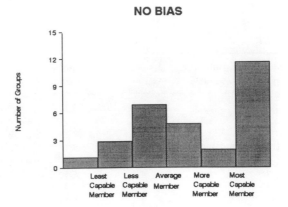

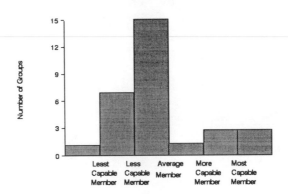

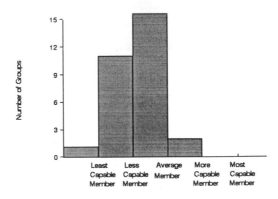

Figure A2. Group performance under varying conditions of bias.

A careful review of the results shown in Figure A1 indicates that in the "no bias" condition the average estimate of 25 groups is more accurate than a randomly selected individual estimate (a proportion of .83). In the "moderate bias" and "high bias" conditions, this proportion drops markedly to .57 and .53, respectively. It is apparent from Figure A1 that tasks evoking systematic individual errors in estimate substantially reduce the relative superiority of "statistized" groups.

Tables 1–3 depict the individual errors in estimate (i.e., the absolute differences between the individual estimates and the true value) for the five members of each of the 30 groups, as well as the error for the group average. For each of the three task conditions, these errors have been recomputed (since the true value shifts) and reordered from smallest individual error ("most capable" member) to greatest individual error ("least capable" member). For each group under each task condition, the error for the group average can be compared to the error for each group member from "most capable" to "least capable."

As shown in Figure A2, when individual errors are distributed randomly around the true value ("no bias" condition), mathematical aggregation performs quite well. The average estimate of 12 of the groups is more accurate than their most capable members (a proportion of .40). However, when individuals are systematically biased in their estimates, "statistized" groups fare more poorly. In the "moderate bias" condition, only 3 of the average estimates exceed the accuracy of their most capable members (a proportion of .10). When bias is high, 28 of the groups perform no better than their average member.

REFERENCES

Bruce, R. S. (1935). Group judgments in the fields of lifted weights and visual discrimination. *The Journal of Psychology, 1*, 117–121.

Burleson, B. R., Levine, B. J., & Samter, W. (1984). Decision-making procedure and decision quality. *Human Communication Research, 10*, 557–574.

Diehl, M., & Stroebe, W. (1987). Productivity loss in brainstorming groups: Toward the solution of a riddle. *Journal of Personality and Social Psychology, 53*, 497–509.

Eils, L. C., & John, R. S. (1980). A criterion validation of multiattribute utility analysis and of group communication strategy. *Organizational Behavior and Human Performance, 25*, 268–288.

Einhorn, H. J., Hogarth, R. M., & Klempner, E. (1977). Quality of group judgment. *Psychological Bulletin, 84*, 158–172.

Ferrell, W. R. (1985). Combining individual judgments. In G. Wright (Ed.), *Behavioral decision making*. New York: Plenum.

Fischer, G. W. (1981). When oracles fail—A comparison of four procedures for aggregating subjective probability forecasts. *Organizational Behavior and Human Performance, 28*, 96–110.

Flores, B. E., & White, E. M. (1989). Subjective versus objective combining of forecasts: An experiment. *Journal of Forecasting, 8*, 331–341.

Gordon, K. (1924). Group judgments in the field of lifted weights. *Journal of Experimental Psychology, 7*, 398–400.

Gustafson, D. H., Shukla, R. M., Delbecq, A. L., & Walster, G. W. (1973). A comparative study of differences in subjective estimation made by individuals, interacting groups, delphi groups and nominal groups. *Organizational Behavior and Human Performance, 9,* 280–291.

Hall, E. J., Mouton, J. S., & Blake, R. R. (1963). Group problem solving effectiveness under conditions of pooling vs. interaction. *The Journal of Social Psychology, 59,* 147–157.

Hall, J., & Watson, W. H. (1971). The effects of a normative intervention on group decision-making performance. *Human Relations, 23,* 299–317.

Hall, J., & Williams, M. S. (1970). Group dynamics training and improved decision making. *The Journal of Applied Behavioral Science, 6,* 39–68.

Hammond, K. R., Stewart, T. R., Brehmer, B., & Steinmann, D. O. (1986). Social judgment theory. In H. R. Arkes & K. R. Hammond (Eds.), *Judgment and decision making: An interdisciplinary reader.* London: Cambridge University Press.

Harmon, J., & Rohrbaugh, J. (1990). Social judgment analysis and small group decision making: Cognitive feedback effects on individual and collective performance. *Organizational Behavior and Human Decision Processes, 46,* 34–54.

Herbert, T. T., & Yost, E. B. (1979). A comparison of decision quality under nominal interacting consensus group formats: The case of the structured problem. *Decision Sciences, 10,* 358–367.

Hogarth, R. M. (1987). *Judgment and choice.* New York: Wiley.

Holloman, C. R., & Hendrick, H. W. (1972). Adequacy of group decisions as a function of the decision-making process. *Academy of Management Journal, 8,* 175–184.

Holloman, C. R., & Hendrick, H. W. (1971). Problem solving in different sized groups. *Personnel Psychology, 24,* 489–500.

Kahneman, D., Slovic, P., & Tversky, A. (1982). *Judgment under uncertainty: Heuristics and biases.* Cambridge: Cambridge University Press.

Kelley, T. L. (1925). The applicability of the Spearman-Brown formula for the measurement of reliability. *Journal of Educational Psychology, 16,* 300–303.

Knight, H. C. (1921). *A comparison of the reliability of group and individual judgments.* Unpublished master's thesis, Columbia University.

Linstone, H. A., & Turoff, M. (1975). *The Delphi method: Techniques and applications.* Reading, MA: Addison-Wesley.

McCartt, A. T., & Rohrbaugh, J. (1989). Evaluating group decision support system effectiveness: A performance study of decision conferencing. *Decision Support Systems, 5,* 243–253.

McGrath, J. E. (1984). *Groups: Interaction and performance.* Englewood Cliffs, N.J.: Prentice-Hall.

Milter, R. G., & Rohrbaugh, J. (1988). Judgment analysis and decision conferencing for administrative review: A case study of innovative policy making in government. In R. L. Cardy, S. M. Puffer, & J. M. Newman (Eds.), *Advances in information processing in organizations* (Vol. 3). Greenwich, Ct.: JAI Press.

Miner, F. C. (1984). Group versus individual decision making: An investigation of performance measures, decision strategies, and process losses/gains. *Organizational Behavior and Human Performance, 33,* 112–124.

Nemiroff, P. M., & King, D. C. (1975). Group decision-making performance as influenced by consensus and self-orientation. *Human Relations, 28,* 1–21.

Nemiroff, P. M., Pasmore, W. A., & Ford, D. L. (1976). The effects of two normative structural interventions on establishes and ad hoc groups: Implications for improving decision making effectiveness. *Decision Sciences, 7,* 841–855.

Phillips, L. D. (1988a). Requisite decision modeling for technological projects. In C. Vlek & G. Cvetkovitch (Eds.), *Social decision methodology for technological projects.* Amsterdam: North Holland.

Phillips, L. D. (1988b). People-centered group decision support. In G. Doukidis, F. Land, & G. Miller (Eds.), *Knowledge based management support systems.* Chichester: Harwood.

Preston, M. G. (1938). Note on the reliability and validity of the group judgment. *Journal of Experimental Psychology, 22*, 462–471.

Reagan-Cirincione, P. (1991). Improving the accuracy of forecasts: A process intervention combining social judgment analysis and group facilitation. Unpublished doctoral dissertation. The University at Albany, State University of New York.

Rohrbaugh, J. (1988). Cognitive conflict tasks and small group processes. In B. Brehmer & C. R. B. Joyce (Eds.), *Human judgment: The SJT approach.* Amsterdam: North-Holland Elsevier.

Rohrbaugh, J. (1981). Improving the quality of group judgment: Social judgment analysis and the Nominal Group Technique. *Organizational Behavior and Human Performance, 28*, 272–288.

Rohrbaugh, J. (1979). Improving the quality of group judgment: Social judgment analysis and the Delphi technique. *Organizational Behavior and Human Performance, 24*, 73–92.

Simon, H. A. (1945). *Administrative behavior.* New York: Free Press.

Simon, H. A. (1980). *The new science of management decision.* New York: Harper and Row.

Smith, B. B. (1941). The validity and reliability of group judgments. *Journal of Experimental Psychology, 29*, 420–434.

Sniezek, J. A. (1990). A comparison of techniques for judgmental forecasting by groups with common information. *Group and Organizational Studies, 15*, 5–19.

Sniezek, J. A., & Henry, R. A. (1989). Accuracy and confidence in group judgment. *Organizational Behavior and Human Decision Processes, 43*, 1–28.

Steiner, I. D. (1972). *Group processes and productivity.* New York: Academic Press.

Stewart, T. R. (1987). The Delphi technique and judgmental forecasting. *Climatic Change, 11*, 97–113.

Stroop, J. R. (1932). Is the judgment of the group better than that of the average member of the group? *Journal of Experimental Psychology, 15*, 550–562.

Thorndike, R. L. (1938). On what type of tasks will a group do well? *Journal of Abnormal and Social Psychology, 33*, 409–413.

Timmons, W. M. (1942). Can the product superiority of discussors be attributed to averaging or majority influences? *Journal of Social Psychology, 15*, 23–32.

Uecker, W. C. (1982). The quality of group performance in simplified information evaluation. *Journal of Accounting Research, 20*, 388–402.

Yetton, P. W., & Bottger, P. C. (1982). Individual versus group problem solving: An empirical test of a best-member strategy. *Organizational Behavior and Human Performance, 29*, 307–321.

CHAPTER 9

Knowledge Engineering Issues for Decision Support

John Gammack

INTRODUCTION

Decision support systems (DSS) are widely used throughout the financial services industry. Unlike expert systems, which aim to replace expert decision making in narrow domains, decision support systems allow cooperation between user and system to improve the quality of decision making. In DSS a machine's number-crunching and memory capability is coupled with human common sense, subjective judgment, and sensitivity to context. The areas in which humans are strong are generally those areas where experts systems are weak; so it seems appropriate to design cooperative systems recognizing this. Although expert systems and decision support systems have much in common, important differences between them mean that knowledge acquisition for DSS must be considered in its own right.

This chapter describes some case studies from our project on life insurance underwriting (Bolger et al., 1989), concentrating on the knowledge acquisition involved in building both an expert system for use in training underwriters, and a decision support system intended for use in everyday operation. By reference to the actual way in which expert underwriting decisions are made, the requirement for a design based on user/system cooperation will be made clear.

Firstly, some general issues in knowledge acquisition are considered, and

John Gammack • Bristol Business School, Coldharbour Lane, Frenchay, Bristol BS16 1QY, England.

Expertise and Decision Support, edited by George Wright and Fergus Bolger. Plenum Press, New York, 1992.

then, by way of three case studies, the different approaches to knowledge acquisition in the life underwriting domain are described.

ISSUES IN KNOWLEDGE ENGINEERING

Expert systems may be defined as computer programs which reproduce the decisions a knowledgeable, intelligent expert would make in a particular domain of interest. Thus in the present example, given an application form as input, the system should be able to make recommendations such as "Reject this proposal," or "Send for a doctor's report regarding (particular medical) details." Decision support systems (DSS) are not synonymous with expert systems, and comprise a broader class of software. DSS evolved from management information systems, and often have a distinctive architecture of their own (Turban, 1988). However, because it is common to use both expert systems and DSS in advisory support to decision makers, there is sometimes confusion as to where the boundaries are. However, as the chapter progresses, the critical distinctions I am drawing between them will become clearer.

For the moment, it is true to say that both types of software require the knowledge (and reasoning) of a domain expert to be formalized and coded in, and this involves *knowledge acquisition,* which is done by a *knowledge engineer.*

It is not my intention to give a detailed review of knowledge acquisition methods here, since these are adequately covered elsewhere (Welbank, 1983; Neale, 1988). However, in describing some typically used techniques I will point out some fundamental inadequacies relating to the limitations of expert systems. Following a consideration of some validation issues, I hope to show why it is more appropriate to consider knowledge acquisition for DSS instead.

KNOWLEDGE ACQUISITION TECHNIQUES

Probably the most common technique used in knowledge acquisition is the interview. As the name implies this technique broadly covers question and answer sessions between the knowledge engineer (or system designer), and the domain expert. In knowledge engineering interviews can take various forms, from an unstructured discussion between domain expert and knowledge engineer, to a structured series of questions, designed to probe specific areas in depth. The discussion is typically recorded, and the transcript used as source material for identifying rules or facts in the domain. This notion of interview is more akin to taking cranial measurements than negotiating a shared representation of a domain. An inherently interactive conception of the interview, teach-back interviewing, is described by Johnson and Johnson (1987), and aims to ensure common perception of the verbal material.

This latter conception recognizes one of the basic philosophical issues with expert systems: a reliance on expressing knowledge symbolically in language. Different perceptions of verbal material are possible, since language is not sufficient to specify adequately the fullness of knowledge itself. Unlike the ideal of the classical physical sciences, where unambiguous correspondence between the measurement and the measured may be assumed, the expression of knowledge is not the actual knowledge, and the problems of interpretation pertain. For more on this issue see Gammack and Anderson (1990) and Farr (1987). An expert system acting on a single, possibly erroneous, interpretation of verbal material is one possible undesirable consequence of this tradition.

Other, more formal techniques derive from experimental psychology, and have been successfully used in establishing conceptual models of expert domains. These techniques include repertory grid (Boose, 1986), protocol analysis (Fox et al., 1984; Breuker & Wielinga, 1987), and card sorting (Gammack, 1987a, 1987b).

Briefly, *repertory grid* involves picking three concepts from the domain (e.g., apples, oranges, and bananas in the domain of fruit), and asking the expert to identify a dimension which discriminates one item from the other two. Thus the 5-point scalar dimension (or construct):

(1) round—elongated (5)

may be identified. Other domain items are placed along this continuum, so that "pear," for example, may be given a value of 3. This process is repeated until a grid discriminating and relating the concepts is built up.

Protocol analysis essentially involves keeping a detailed record of an expert's problem solving process (usually the expert verbalizes throughout and this "think-aloud" is recorded). Subsequently, the knowledge engineer attempts to infer the reasoning and knowledge involved.

Card sorting involves noting a number of domain concepts on index cards, and asking the expert to provide a meaningful organization for them. Often this is restricted to groupings in a hierarchy, but not necessarily.

Some of these techniques lead directly to rules, while others provide descriptions of domain entities and relationships among them seen by the expert as important, which can be used in producing a conceptual model. Producing such models is a stage in the life cycle of system development, and is an integral part of the KADS methodology (e.g., Breuker & Wielinga, 1987).

These approaches to a greater or lesser extent embrace a number of assumptions which imply other epistemological problems for expert systems. These may not matter in practice, for simple systems doing a well-defined job in a relatively static environment, but they remain an essential limitation on the viability of expert system technology. One of the assumptions is that objects relate to one another in a lawful way which the expert knows. This arrangement corresponds to the way things are in the "real world," and has a structured counterpart in the expert's head. Once this view is adopted, consciously or otherwise, it is natural to try to discover the true structure by formal methods. Although compelling to those inculcated in an atomist or scientific tradition, such endeavors rest on an arbitrary view, which is not always helpful. Gregory (1986, 1987) contrasts this "realist" view with an equally ancient philosophical tradition which sees knowledge as a process, whose expression is constructed in specific contexts for specific purposes. Because knowledge supports construction, without being limited to a uniquely specific fixed structure, the manifestation of any static conception is not confused with the underlying knowledge itself.

It is only common sense that objects may relate to one another in various ways, and that the importance, and indeed relevance, of these relationships will vary across circumstances. This applies to rules as well as simple relationships between entities, and is sometimes known as the problem of applicability. The rules themselves may specify what to do, but do not themselves know when they apply. Thus in the example of the fruit concepts, pears may be similar to avocados in size and shape, which may be relevant in figuring out how best to stack a fruit bowl; but this similarity is less relevant than their other properties in the case of planning which fruit to pack for a 4-day backpacking trip. The "tendency to go mushy after a couple of hot days and make a mess" property of avocados puts them in the same category as bananas. As for rules—Collins (1987) points out that it is hard to mechanize (say) legal advice systems, even though the rules are already codified, due to the possibility of novel interpretation, and the continual creation and recreation of the rules' meaning in the courts. The scope for this lies in the privileged possibility of standing back from the rule, and assessing its value in current context. Those legendary car-spraying robots which continue to spray determinedly even when the car has fallen from its hook have no such essential possibility. As automata, expert systems may contain rules that are ideal in one context, and inappropriate if that context changes.

Expert systems have been plagued with this problem in one form or another, and attempts to get round it have included adding extra qualifiers to the left-hand side of a rule, leading to cumbersome reasoning, and having metaknowledge or metarules operate to resolve rule conflicts. For example, extra conditions could be built into the paint-spraying robot's routine, such as:

> "If car on hook, then (continue)," and, upon realizing the insufficiency of this alone:
> "If car on hook AND car in right orientation, then (continue)."

Such solutions elaborate the existing paradigm, but do not solve the essential problem. The decision as to when a relationship or a rule applies is a judgmental problem, best done by a (human) agent with sensitivity to the environmental context. Even a paint-spraying robot's behavior is governed by wider economic rules, which in turn are governed by. . . . This is one of the arguments for designing knowledge bases within a decision-support paradigm, and one approach to this is discussed below.

A second assumption is that the elicited knowledge is reliable, representing a stable domain conception. Since it is known that questions provide a context for their answers (Loftus & Palmer, 1974), an uninformed knowledge engineer may unwittingly constrain the quality and form of the answer given by the expert. I (Gammack, 1988) attempted to get round this problem by minimizing such contextual demands and eliciting information indirectly using a series of converging techniques. The idea was that a core structure of context-free information would emerge that remained common across elicitation tasks, representing a stable underlying knowledge base. However, this did not happen, and it appeared that the particular relationships elicited were contingent on the properties of the elicitation task, and there was no evidence of any long-term stabilized structure of this form. I chose to conclude from this that explicated conceptual models emerge largely from processing knowledge in a context, even as minimal a context as an experimental task and the analysis of its data.

Accordingly, since the same knowledge must be used to support the many different questions that may be asked of it, it makes sense to have a representation that has minimal commitment to formality, and which can support construction of the specific answers demanded by specific contexts. Rules are generally too high-level to serve as an underlying representation of knowledge, and an alternative is required. The second case study describes one such alternative, which makes use of a more flexible underlying representation than a decision tree of rules. This suggests that any fixed conception of a domain, rather than embodying the "truth," instead has undesirable properties, such as inflexibility, and the capacity to be quite, quite wrong at times. The two associated problems behind this are (1) lack of awareness of the wider context within which the rules apply, and (2) the fixing of flux. If a domain conception is dynamically constructed, and may be actively reconstructed as contextual factors change, this raises special problems for the validation of systems, as it is unclear what the "gold standard" should be. Both for decision support and for expert systems however, the validity of the knowledge must be addressed at some point in development, so this is discussed next.

VALIDATION OF KNOWLEDGE-BASED SYSTEMS

To date, very little specific work has been done on validation of knowledge-based systems, and, rarely any of that has been before the late 1980s. It is worth considering what is meant by validation in this context. Validation is a general term that embraces verification (i.e., testing that an implemented program meets its specification), but also is concerned with accuracy of advice, quality of recommendation, soundness of underlying model, and even user acceptability. In fact, validation covers everything involved in assessing that the system meets its goals.

Validation of KBS or DSS may be considered in different ways—either as a software verification task, or in terms of system performance with respect to other measures of decision-making quality. The criteria for validating systems will differ depending on which emphasis is applied—formal computational criteria will apply when the emphasis is on software verification, psychological and performance criteria will pertain with an emphasis on decision quality.

Issues of completeness and consistency arise with any system, and to the extent that a KBS or a DSS is rule-based, issues of rule subsumption and conflict play a part in these wider problems. For instance, the two rules:

"If salary < 10000 then reject proposal" and
"If salary < 10000 and age < 20 then reject proposal"

provide an example where one rule subsumes another. In this case the first rule is enough, and subsumes the second, which can be discarded. If the second rule recommended acceptance rather than rejection, there would be a potential conflict requiring resolution at a higher level. Furthermore, although generally desirable, consistency and completeness are no guarantee of the correctness of individual rules (Chignell & Peterson, 1988, noted in Long & Neale, 1989). Rules may satisfy the formal properties implied above, and yet misrepresent the expert's intention. Accordingly, these formal "syntactic" aspects of validation should be separated from the practical "semantic" aspects.

Nazareth (1989) has considered the issue of verification of knowledge in rule-based systems, and specifically addresses these formal aspects. He provides a taxonomy for identifying errors such as redundancy, subsumption, circularity, and conflict in sets of rules. KBS system developers have found these issues a "headache" (e.g., Alvey, 1985); however, the reasons for this go deeper than mere sloppy programming.

For instance, it may not always be appropriate to simplify knowledge into logical rules in the categorical way typified by expert systems. Since humans often appear to behave "inconsistently" inasmuch as they do one thing in one context, and the opposite in another, guided perhaps by current circumstances which are unrepresented in the rule base, it is quite conceivable that formally inconsistent rules will be elicited, and possibly represented by an observer. Resolution implies extending the rule base to specify contextual conditions under which rules apply, which is not merely a non-trivial problem, but an essential problem for all systems. In many domains, specifying such rules will be impossible (Collins, 1987), and no matter how many rules and conditions are included, there is always the possibility of unforeseen circumstances which qualify the utility of a rule. The domain of legal reasoning is one example, where up-to-date judgment is required to establish whether something constitutes "reasonable behavior" or not. In order to support a flexible range of intelligent behaviors, it may be desirable to retain formally inconsistent rules, given that decision on their applicability in a DSS will rest with the end user. Better still, by avoiding a representation based on rules, and instead providing a flexible facility to construct behaviors which can be seen to be consistent with the current context, formal conflicts of rules do not arise.

Likewise, detecting redundancy to improve computational efficiency is an admirable application of the parsimony principle, however this may not be the most important priority for an operational system. In humans, redundancy serves numerous psychological purposes (e.g., repetition in effective oral communication, duplication of brain functionality, etc.) and indeed redundancy due to such overdesign may be positively desirable in some systems.

Finally, cases where the whole is different from the sum of the parts defy simple formal verification. One example from the underwriting domain is the case of the Zimbabwe farmer. Our expert assessed at different times, "Zimbabwe as a country is a low risk, thus is OK to insure," and also "The occupation farmer is low risk, thus is OK to insure." However a farmer in Zimbabwe may be a high risk since they are likely to fly single-engined planes and land on rough airstrips. The formal combination of the two assertions using inclusive OR:

if Zimbabwe or farmer then OK to insure

would be invalid. The concept of Zimbabwe in the context of farmer (and vice versa) is modified through a general knowledge of its other attributes which are generally irrelevant to insurers. Nonetheless, such "interactions" produce emergent properties which require explicit consideration. Such problems do not tend to arise in the well-defined "platonic" domains where verification algebras apply. Case Study Three discusses this further.

Thus formal verification procedures would appear to be only part of the validation of DSS, which supports Long and Neale's (1989) general conclusion from this literature; namely that because the problem domains of KBS and software engineering are fundamentally different, verification techniques from software engineering have limited use for KBS builders. Something about knowledge eludes the system.

A formal system may still be able to provide useful work though, and, of more interest to managers is the quality of the recommendations from a DSS. For validating decision quality, performance measures are more relevant. Thus a DSS's performance may be compared with that of an expert or group of experts, or alternatively with the performance of other systems or models in the same domain.

Long and Neale have proposed one scheme for validating and testing a KBS which takes place within a model-driven system development strategy. Their system advised on underwriting life insurance proposals which disclosed the presence of ischemic heart disease. Since underwriters routinely disagree among themselves, the performance goal they used was that the system should produce a quantitative rating within the range produced by four expert underwriters using the same input data. A system value outside this range did not imply the system was necessarily wrong, but was reviewed by the experts to check if modification was required. This shows one pragmatic approach to validation: peer comparison and review. In addition, Long and Neale propose further validation through examining specific correlations and mappings between elements of the KBS's conceptual model and its implementational counterpart.

In general, with this sort of approach, the system and an expert or experts are given some cases for which normative answers or classifications exist, and performance is directly compared. This approach has been used by various expert system developers, and is usually summarized by a simple statistic or percentage.

Other validation schemes compare the outputs from a DSS with other systems. For instance, Collopy and Armstrong (1989) compared performance on their system with a variety of standard techniques (e.g., random walk, linear models), while Bounds et al. (1989) compared their (multilayer perceptron) computer-aided diagnosis system with another state-of-the-art system based on fuzzy logic. Such studies usually also include comparison with human experts.

Validation procedures may take the form of gross performance measures, or the relatively precise mappings proposed by Long and Neale. They may be as informal as looking at user satisfaction and managerial take-up, or as formal as logical program verification. Where the system is performing poorly, validation procedures can indicate where further knowledge acquisition should be done, or the system redesigned extensively. Validation is likely to be an increasingly important issue within KBS development, but is probably more tractable within a DSS framework. This is because the critical decisions are left to the human, supported by the results of running models on the machine. It has been routine since the early days of management information systems for managers to run computer models (statistical or econometric), and then adjust or attune their decision from that output (see Wright & Ayton, 1989). Acceptance of the supporting but fallible role of the system means that the validity requirement is less onerous for a DSS than for a "stand-alone" decision-making expert system. Other roles played by systems within organizations imply that validity is not a necessary requirement. For instance, if a system is used as a scapegoat to justify, or to defer responsibility for a decision, its validity will be of secondary interest.

REPRESENTING KNOWLEDGE WITHIN DECISION SUPPORT ENVIRONMENTS

Evidently, acquiring knowledge for rule-based systems is fraught with problems. Not only are rules too high-level to provide a flexible basis for decision making, but they do not naturally cope with inconsistency. Yet this "inconsisten-cy" may reflect intelligent, adaptable thinking. An expert system with no sen-sitivity to context will produce predictable answers, which may no longer be relevant in current circumstances, and does not have the functionality to adapt to other modes. Validation is a general problem, but its formal aspects are probably less important with DSS than with expert systems, due to the explicit emphasis on reporting relevant information, rather than taking categorical decisions.

One argument for designing knowledge bases within a decision support framework concerns who is in control. Typically, the manager or decision maker will have a specific question to be answered, and will want to make use of existing "knowledge" to support an informed decision. An expert system, though, takes the initiative, asking questions of the user, reducing the manager to little more than a data entry mechanism. The manager may also want to explore alternative scenarios, using different configurations of information, the "what-if" option of a decision support system. However, the highly deterministic flow of control in expert systems does not readily support this functionality.

Another issue concerns the role of judgment, which is inherently variable and uncertain. It is unrealistic to expect judgment to be quantified once and for all at elicitation, and then the figure used as a shibboleth thereafter. Combining these figures (certainty factors) in a simplistic Bayesian or similar manner com-pounds the problem, and this is well known to practitioners, who rarely report finding this facility of expert systems useful. Human judgment depends too much on subjective perception of circumstances and other unforeseeable factors to be predetermined in this manner, yet clearly judgment is a critical aspect of decision making. It would be premature to suggest anything other than that judgment is best left to the human, although other chapters in this volume question the quality of human judgment.

The final issues I want to consider concern psychological plausibility. There is of course no necessity for a computer system for decision support or anything else to mimic human behavior or thought processes. Apart from psychologists who may be interested in expert systems as cognitive models of decision making in their own right, there are other motivations for considering the psychological plausibility of a decision support system. These concern the ways in which intelligent decisions are reached, and the human-computer communication as-pects of the system.

If user and knowledge-based system are cooperating to reach a decision, an explanatory justification of the system's contribution should be available in psy-chologically meaningful terms, rather than mere computational history (see also Gammack, 1987b). If the system's processing reflects human thought processes, such communication should be enhanced, and mutual understanding achieved (if "understanding" can apply to such systems). The importance of having explica-ble models is seen in Michalski and Chilausky's (1981) soybean disease classi-fier, which used statistically determined predictors to produce expert-level classification. Unfortunately, the statistical combinations of attributes did not map on to expert concepts, so explanation was stymied. If the system can explain its reasoning assumptions using units that are meaningful to its user, communication breakdowns and mismatches of understanding may be avoided (see Suchman, 1987, for an elegant treatment of this issue). Statistical predictors are not necessarily causal predictors, and are highly sensitive to the sampling process. Take, for example, the famous discovery that the best predictor of a high-impact psychology paper was the presence of a colon in its title. Reasoning based on such discoveries may have disappointing consequences. Because in DSS humans have the facility to override system recommendations, the reasoning behind such recommendations should be transparent to the manager. An opaque system with incomprehensible explanation capability can be expected to affect management take-up. Both human reasoning processes and human computer interaction are psychological issues of concern here, and the second case study below addresses these.

Summarizing the first part of this chapter: various problems with traditional rule-based expert systems imply a problem of knowledge acquisition. Some of these will be evident from Case Study One, which describes a typical expert system development. By targeting knowledge acquisition towards DSS instead, many of these problems can be obviated, as the second case study illustrates. Finally, a different approach aiming to understand the nature of expert judgments in the domain is described.

CASE STUDY ONE—A MODULAR EXPERT SYSTEM DEVELOPMENT

The underwriter's first task, faced with an insurance proposal form, is to decide whether it contains sufficient information to make a recommendation, or to request more information before approving or rejecting the proposal. The first system we built was intended to show new underwriters the conditions for which more information on an applicant should be requested.

The form contains a certain amount of information on medical history, financial standing, and other aspects of personal life, but sometimes more detail is required if the underwriter sees cause for suspicion. For example, certain diseases in the recent past would imply sending for a doctor's report, or a hobby of "mountaineering" would incur a detailed questionnaire. Trainee underwriters have to learn what things to look for, and what the Society's philosophy on their riskworthiness is, when to send for more information, and when to accept on the basis of the information already given on the form.

The expert system built to incorporate this information consisted of six modules, one for each area of risk covered by the form (medical, financial, geographical, occupation, hobbies, and life-style [AIDS]). With the current scare about AIDS, it was considered worthwhile treating it separately. Knowledge acquisition for most of these modules followed a traditional pattern: the geographical module is typical and illustrative.

Eliciting the knowledge for the geographical module took about a morning of the expert's time, and used a mixture of interview, card sorting, repertory grid, and context focusing (Wright & Ayton, 1987). The expert began by listing a representative set of countries and occupations related to geographical risk (TV reporter, armed forces, etc.) which he would be concerned to see on a form. These were put on index cards, and sorted hierarchically to yield typical considerations that differentiated one country from another in the underwriting context. Triadic comparison of random subsets of the cards followed to yield further distinctions among the set. Detailed procedures for conducting these techniques are given in Gammack (1987a). Having established a set of criteria in this way, the context-focusing technique was applied to produce a decision tree of questions leading to a recommendation, part of which is shown in Figure 1.

In the context focusing, the expert and knowledge-engineer role played a situation in which the knowledge engineer pretended to phone from a branch office, asking the expert if there was a geographical risk associated with the form he had in front of him. The expert was thus required to ask explicit questions about the caller's form, starting from a no-knowledge position. The order of

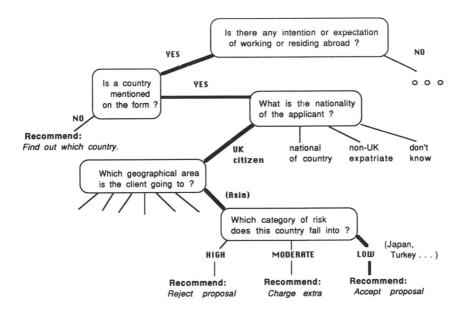

Figure 1. Part of decision tree for establishing geographical risk.

questions was noted, and each different branch was explored systematically by using hypothetical cases. In this way was the decision tree produced, and subsequent implementation as a rule-based production system was straightforward.

Similar procedures were followed for most of the other knowledge bases, but it soon became clear that such an approach would not work for the financial module. This was because (1) there was no preferred order of questions; (2) relevant information could come from any part of the form, and it could only loosely be determined in advance which parts these would be; and (3) many combinations of conditionally interdependent information were possible, and to encode this in a decision tree would prove intractable. Even with the relatively small geographical module, the decision tree contained much redundancy and repetition of structure, which the fully expanded version of Figure 1 would show.

In response to this problem, a novel scheme for knowledge acquisition was developed, described in detail in Gammack, Battle, and Stephens (1989). This scheme has several advantages, apart from making the acquisition of relevant knowledge tractable and fast. The scheme is primarily conceived within the philosophy of decision support systems, and has a non-rule-based knowledge representation while also supporting a variety of rule-based implementations. Technical properties include the representation's formal suitability for newer forms of computing, such as constraint-based and concurrent implementations, and straightforward extendability within its own framework, making modification a very simple matter indeed. Issues of psychological plausibility are discussed in the next section, following an exposition of the scheme itself.

CASE STUDY TWO—A KNOWLEDGE ACQUISITION SCHEME FOR DECISION SUPPORT

As an underwriter scans the information on a proposal form, many criteria are being simultaneously assessed, with relevant interactions among items of information being noted to provide support to the final decision. Since these particulars vary from case to case, an intelligent strategy for the expert to adopt is to reason forwards from the circumstances of the particular case, combining bits of information and being alert to combinations that seem suspicious in some way. For example, one obvious inconsistency would be if a client put her age as 15, and her marital status as divorcée. This much is general knowledge, but more specialized combinations are likely to be known to the underwriter which, once detected, should lead to an informed decision about a proposal's suitability. This is particularly true in the present domain of assessing financial risk and policy suitability in relation to personal circumstances. If there are no problematic combinations in a proposal, its suitability may be assumed.

Using conventional techniques, however, eliciting the knowledge supporting such decision making may be a problem when expertise consists in rapid combinatorial assessment of relevant information. Using hypothetical cases with context focusing becomes too expansive, and the decision criteria are anyway case-specific. Observation is little help—the expert (perhaps subconsciously) simply arrives at decisions too fast to provide detailed information. Interviews tend to give only patchy coverage of the possible considerations concerning a proposal, and without recording a substantial number of critical cases, protocol analysis is unlikely to yield much more. Other techniques such as card sorting and repertory grid would likewise appear to have only limited value here. Expert underwriter's judgment is based on experience of many cases, where a vast number of combinations of information have been seen, and similar problematic combinations are recognized again. Eliciting the knowledge for a decision tree representation would be a daunting task, let alone establishing the exceptions and threshold values associated with decision criteria. However, this model, and the knowledge elicitation it implies need not underlie a system for decision support, and our acquisition method was aimed at establishing this information systematically using a chart, or interaction matrix.

Our approach to acquiring the relevant knowledge supporting expert assessment of financial standing made use of a chart, resembling both decision tables, and the box diagrams used to solve logic problems. Certain general categories of information given on the insurance application form bear on the decision about an applicant's financial standing: these include *sum assured, reason for policy, occupation, age,* etc. Accordingly the set of such categories was first established through discussion of the form with the expert. Then, for each category, the expert directly generated a set of critical values, representative values, and extreme values. These included both point values and ranges. Thus the AGE category comprised ranges from "under 16s" to "over 79s" (80 being an upper limit on acceptable clients), with 65 a particularly critical value since it implies imminent retirement (in males), with associated problems of ability to pay. All the possible values for *finance plan* were considered, along with various critical levels of *sum assured. Occupations* were usually bracketed by status, though some were selected as special cases due to their interaction potential.

The complete chart was drawn up following this phase, and Figure 2 represents a reduced version, omitting many values of categories. Certain combinations of category values are alarming in some way to an underwriter making a decision, so for each pairwise combination of pieces of information the expert was asked to indicate this. An "A" in a cell indicates which combinations are abnormal or alarming, although some details have been changed to preserve confidentiality.

Some cells detect legal inconsistencies (divorcées under 16, teenage HGV drivers, etc.), while others embody expertly set underwriting limits (no one in a low-status occupation is likely to be able to afford a premium of $50 a week); still

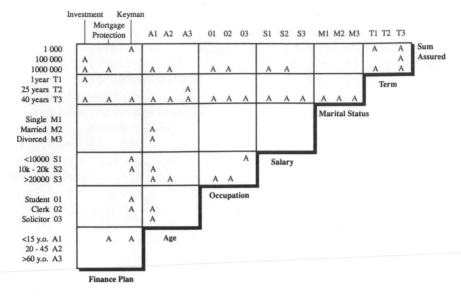

Figure 2. Part of chart used to assess financial riskworthiness. An "A" in the chart implies an abnormal combination of attribute values.

others embody general knowledge or expert opinion (someone under 20 with a salary above $20,000 is suspect). Each cell implies a textual explanation of why it is alarming, which the decision maker is alerted to from the system's output, and can then use discretion to make an informed decision.

Although it might appear that the combinatorics are prohibitive for anything other than a smallish chart, this is not necessarily the case. For instance a comment such as, "A forty-year term is always suspicious regardless" fills a whole row of entries at once. Similarly, a comment to the effect that "Any combination of marital status and job is possible and unproblematic (priests notwithstanding)" fills an entire block. In addition, many of the entries are not specialized knowledge, and can be filled in by a junior or, indeed, the knowledge engineer.

Several things are immediately apparent from Figure 2. For example, the "real-world" semantics are evident—a 40-year term in itself is always suspicious; a 25-year term rarely is. Similarly, any combination of marital status and occupation is normal, although in an extended chart, married priests (say) would be anomalous. Unsuitable policies are implicit in the chart, for instance a Keyman policy (covering "indispensable" personnel) on a student or for a low sum assured is represented by an entry in the appropriate cells.

The thresholds that discriminate problematic from unproblematic values are implied by the boundary between cells with and without an "A." Rules and their exceptions are likewise directly derivable from the chart, thus a 25-year term is generally acceptable, unless the client is of sufficiently advanced age that the policy will mature later than their 80th birthday, or the finance plan is a Keyman. Furthermore, "all possible" rules are implicit in the chart structure, which can be partitioned into any arbitrary rule set. This may be done using computational criteria (e.g., from information theory, which could provide an optimally efficient partitioning), or using psychological criteria from behavioral decision making, reflecting the qualitative considerations of the human.

This interaction matrix, augmented with the textual explanations, is held to constitute a qualitative model of the knowledge supporting expert underwriter's decision making.

IMPLEMENTATION

The elicited knowledge represented in the chart was the *intermediate representation* (Young & Gammack, 1987) used in system development. Intermediate representations are descriptions of the expert's knowledge lying between the two notional extremes of the expert's mind and the machine code, hence the name. Often they are the paper-based product of an elicitation session and may take the form of diagrams such as concept hierarchies or networks, rich pictures (Checkland, 1981), or systemic grammar networks (Bliss et al., 1983). They simultaneously provide a record of the elicitation, and a more or less formal specification useful in subsequent coding. Some of the advantages such an approach confers include:

1. the portability of the elicited knowledge across both machines and programming languages;
2. the relative ease of modification compared to written code;
3. the flexibility of notations compared with machine-executable representations;
4. the human (especially expert) readability of the elicited knowledge, and their likely intuitive familiarity to nonprogrammers;
5. the use of the (annotated) representation in documentation;
6. avoidance of the problems identified by Kidd and Cooper (1985), i.e., too-early commitment to an unsuitable representation language and participant's knowledge of the target language biasing elicitation towards rules which fitted that form; and
7. the provision of a model of the knowledge as a "conversation piece."

This latter point illustrates a specialized use of intermediate representations: namely as a communication artifact useful in further knowledge acquisition, and has much in common with what Johnson (1989) calls a *mediating* representation, which she defines as a "computer language independent notation used as a conceptual aid in synthesizing knowledge from talk with experts. It 'mediates' between verbal data and (knowledge representation schemes)" (Johnson, 1989, p. 181). Both Johnson and I are at pains to dissociate this conception from the formal linguists' notion of an intermediate representation as a representation flanked by its formal transformations according to clearly specific mapping rules. The use of intermediate representations as a conversation piece for further knowledge acquisition is illustrated in Gammack and Anderson (1990).

As an example of an intermediate representation, the chart acted as the specification for two separate implementations. Firstly, it provided the detail necessary for building a rule-based system (one of the training system modules of Case Study One) and, secondly, as a constraint-based system evaluated concurrently. This latter implementation is more in keeping with the philosophy of decision support, where the model of the system is available for the user to control in different modes of operation.

The first implementation followed the familiar cycle of expert system development, prototyping the chart directly as a rule-based system, and returned to the expert for fine-tuning. Because of the direct relationship between entries in the chart and single production rules, particular values were very easily modified. For instance, the rule:

IF sum assured > 100 000 and salary < 10000
    THEN print message "Client may not be able to afford payments"

was later amended by the expert to a value of 15,000 for salary. When each rule had been approved and changes made where necessary, the system was subjected to thorough evaluation by a team of underwriters, and only minor modifications were required before the production system was ready for use in training programs.

Independently, the chart was used to build a prototype DSS, using a constraint-based paradigm rather than a rule-based one. Traditional DSS architectures (Turban, 1988) include both data management and model management subsystems. In the underwriting domain, data consists of the known details about a client, which can be typed in by an underwriter, a clerk in a branch office, or possibly a scanner of some sort. The model of the underwriting domain, however, is not so much quantitative and numerical, but is rather qualitative and knowledge-based, embodying a set of assumptions corresponding to the Society's underwriting philosophy. It is this knowledge that the expert draws on when making a decision about an applicant, but there is an element of subjective judgment involved which allows discretion in application of the guidelines. Expert system rules tend not to have scope for this sensitivity to cases, and neither certainty factors nor fuzzy logic really substitutes for this discretion. For instance, a rule such as:

IF sum assured > $100 000 and occupation = student THEN decline

is setting an arbitrary limit where applications will founder. However, there may be indications elsewhere on the form that the applicant is a rich, retired person, studying for pleasure, and the guidelines can be waived in this case. Obviously, intermediaries running the model in the client's presence are in a position to establish such information at once. Although expert systems' recommendations can be treated as advisory, such inferences may form an integral and invisible part of their reasoning. Incorporating the guidelines in a DSS domain model allows effective use of expert-provided information, leaving the discretionary part of the decision to the human user.

In the expert system of Case Study One, inefficiency was caused by asking questions whose answers were unnecessary to the final decision, but required by the sequential structuring of the knowledge base, and the predetermined flow of control. In the constraint-based implementation, the user can input the value of *any* variable to the system (so is not reduced to passive data-entering in the order predetermined by the system), and the system will return a list of the categories and values which that information constrains. For instance, the user may enter an *age* of 79, to be told that a one-year investment policy would be the only possible policy that could be offered. More usefully, typical persons in their thirties on a high wage might be eligible for "any" length of term they liked, under any finance plan, since their age and salary do not constrain the acceptable values of these categories. The user, informed by this set, can then enter the value of another category to further constrain the set of values. If there is any problem caused by the interaction of particular category values, the user will be immediately informed, with a message. For example, one message is: "This applicant is applying for an inheritance tax mitigation policy, yet is 16 years old," which alerts the underwriter to check for (trivially) typing errors, or a mismatch of policy to client's circumstance, and (in extreme cases) some sort of swindle. This system allows the user to be informed at once about the inadmissibility of an application, without having to answer questions irrelevant to the outcome. Equally, the scheme is amendable to running in "what-if" mode. For instance, if the only problem with accepting a client for a policy is that the sum assured is too high (taking everything else into account), it is straightforward to enter a lower value and rerun the model to produce an acceptable configuration, which can then be mooted to the client. Providing the optimal configuration of policy, sum assured, term, and premium for a client may also be possible by extending this scheme.

PSYCHOLOGICAL PLAUSIBILITY

Because the decision made on a particular proposal will result from combining the particular values of the different categories, an expert is likely to reason forward from the "input" data on salary, age, and so on. Since which of these attributes is relevant will vary from case to case, and the acceptability of a proposal may rest on only one unusual combination, the most efficient order of appraising combinations will correspondingly vary from case to case. These two properties together suggest that a set of processes looking simultaneously at the different combinations of categories, and propagating their results to one another will lead to a realistic model of expert decision making.

In terms of the phenomenology of human reasoning, experts in many domains use data or event-driven strategies, forward-chaining from the givens of a situation, and using constraints to narrow down the search space (Patel & Groen, 1987). Later in the reasoning they may switch to a backward-chaining strategy to test specific hypotheses. During the reasoning process, an expert may ask for specific pieces of information, which may not appear relevant to an outside observer, who requires an explanation. This explanation will be contingent on the sequence of reasoning being followed: perhaps the expert is trying to establish an extra constraint to narrow the search space during forward-chaining, or possibly instead looking for a decisive fact that disconfirms a hypothesis, or eliminates a class of hypotheses. In a typical decision-making expert system, the explanation is frequently bound to a predetermined reasoning strategy, and the reasoning path follows a fixed order, whether the questions asked of the user are relevant to the answer or not. In a decision support system, however, designed along the lines suggested in the second case study, flexible reasoning strategies can be modeled in the way that experts clearly behave, asking questions in an intelligent order, not asking irrelevant or low information questions when it can be determined they are unnecessary, asking for, and making use of information input at any time, and jumping intelligently to a solution when decisive information is given. The flexibility of reasoning exhibited by experts is supported by a constraint-based system as already described, and whose explanation can explicitly be tied to particular reasoning paths.

Another aspect of the psychological plausibility concerns the evident rapidity with which underwriters make assessments. Our underwriter took seconds to conclude on a case that took an expert system minutes due to serially typing answers to the many questions the system required (see Bolger et al., 1989). Clearly, such a system is no realistic cognitive model. Intuitively, it seems more likely that experts notice critical information on any part of the form, judging relatedness to other aspects of the applicant's circumstances, ignoring or postponing information that does not impact on their decision. Case Study Three begins to examine the judgment process in underwriting.

CASE STUDY THREE—PARTICIPATIVE ELICITATION OF UNDERWRITING EXPERTISE

The system described in Case Study One, although adequate for its intended purpose of introducing some basic concepts to novice trainees, was insufficient for realistic decision support. It considered six modularized factors in isolation, and did not take into account subtle interactions among them as an expert would. The DSS of Case Study Two is designed to detect some interactions affecting decision making within a module, but presupposes that these have been identified at elicitation, and is anyway restricted to pairwise combinations. "Gestalts" remain beyond the scope of these systems. As acquisition progressed, the crucial importance of this in expertise became clear revealing a basic limitation of the modular design. The inadequacy of the elicitation techniques to detect such gestalts was also apparent.

Looked at from a humanistic perspective, much knowledge elicitation and system design has little ecological validity. The knowledge engineer interviews the expert attempting to formalize knowledge in an undistorting way, and without contributing to the explication of that knowledge in any dynamic sense. This formality is inherently unnatural. Furthermore, knowledge engineering rarely involves the expert in doing their daily task or, if it does, consists largely of passive observation supplemented by a subsequently rationalized interpretation, rather than one mutually agreed at the time. This final section illustrates the approach taken by S. P. Gill (1989, 1990) which is based around *exemplary* work materials of the expert as they are utilized in their daily practice, using these materials as the basis for comprehending expert working modes. Because of this close affinity with practice and working materials, the approach gives a more ecologically valid basis for establishing the expert's own decision making or judgmental procedures.

Instead of fabricating a formal domain conception from theoretical concepts describing the domain, the domain understanding emerges from its praxis. Through cases, the assumptions underlying judgment become explicated and recognized. However, working with exemplars is not merely another objectifying technology to be used like card sorting, it is instead closely allied to a human-centered methodology (Cooley, 1987; Gill, 1988) in which the system designer participates in understanding the practice. By working collaboratively with the expert and the work materials, problems of retrospective rationalization and misguided interpretation are avoided, since the meaning is established dynamically by both parties through both use and dialogue.

To discover how expert underwriters make decisions in practice, Gill adopted an ethnographic approach to knowledge acquisition, where the knowledge engineer is an active participant in the dialogue, rather than some kind of passive observation and measurement device. In contrast to earlier elicitation sessions where a previous knowledge engineer had treated the expert largely as a resource, this approach helped to establish the role of the expert as part of a process of constructive design. Accordingly, the project became recast as one of cooperatively establishing a suitable systems design based on ideas in keeping with the expert's working practice, as opposed to some form of conceptual engineering. Thus, an untried combination of "system designer" (not "knowledge engineer") and experts took part in the elicitation. The following is based on Gill's own report (Gill, 1989).

The session started informally, with general conversation to establish empathy and enough trust to enable relaxed communication. As tension inhibits good dialogue this was considered essential to an inherently participative process.

This dialogue involved the "system designer" (Gill) talking about herself and her interests, with two experts, Robert and Kath, who talked about their roles in the company. The experts were also asked questions on company structure and how the underwriters communicate among themselves in the work setting. Accordingly, both parties formed a picture of the other's professional context. In addition, this dialogue started to indicate the extent to which the underwriters' personal beliefs and values come into making a judgment.

After about ten minutes the experts were given a sample life insurance proposal form for reflection and the general objective was stated to the experts, namely to establish how information on a form was used to contribute to an assessment of the applicant's riskworthiness. Through the ensuing dialogue this purpose became clarified as mutual understanding was negotiated.

The task itself involved a number of dummy application forms prepared by previous experts, one of whom in an earlier session had identified "interactions" in the forms, i.e., pieces of information which combined significantly to produce an impression of the applicant.

It was mutually agreed that Robert and Kath consider each form to identify those aspects affecting their judgments and decisions both for pieces of information in isolation, and in combination. For instance, "vertigo" would indicate a mild medical risk in itself, as would the occupation of "window cleaner," but both on the same form would indicate a highly risky applicant. Although such an example may seem contrived, instances of epileptic professional drivers have been known in practice.

A previous expert, no longer involved in the project, had circled possibly relevant factors on the forms. Robert and Kath considered these in addition to providing their own views. Due to their own experience, however, they were not unduly influenced by the previous suggestions, and indeed were often in disagreement with them!

Robert and Kath talked through each form. Robert was more verbally active than Kath (his junior) who accepted Robert's judgment and apparently followed a similar style of analysis and description. This may be due to Robert's relative seniority, personality factors, or because juniors learn by emulating seniors in the company.

Robert characterized the task as building up an overall picture of the "person" being dealt with. Rather than merely appraising an application form per se, crucially, the applicant's motives and life-style are being analyzed, since the applicant's chances of living until a policy matures is critical. He observed that the general rule of thumb is to see things individually but to recognize they are only meaningful as a complete picture.

For example, the first hypothetical case concerned a (single) 60-year-old professional ballet dancer. To the experts, this implied the common-belief connotations that artistic and theatrical people as a group tend to have a large number of homosexuals; with obvious relevance to the AIDS problem. Age must then also be taken into account to determine how long the person has been sexually active, as the likelihood of AIDS increases with age. A minor medical condition, indicated on the form, although in itself not necessarily significant, in combination with the other factors triggered alarm bells. Taking these together, this client's medical circumstances implied further investigation, although none of these indications taken in isolation were, in themselves, serious. Whether valid or not, the various contrived cases highlighted other world-knowledge or popular beliefs. These included risks on grounds of geographical locations, whether political (e.g., Nicaragua), drugs (Edinburgh), or sexuality (San Francisco, Brighton), and various combinations of medical risk.

There is an issue here as to whether the system designer should intervene upon detecting suspected biases which is as much philosophical as methodological. Is the expert to be considered as infallible authority, or merely opinionated? Should the knowledge engineer keep quiet and listen, or question pronouncements and negotiate agreement, possibly compromising the expert inappropriately? For instance, the stereotype of Edinburgh youth as injecting drug users may be widely seen as unfair to the majority of young applicants from Edinburgh, yet it may provide a valid piece of general knowledge in helping an underwriter make a decision. Viewing the knowledge engineer as passive recipient of authentic fact can be dangerous if the expert's judgment really is biased, and there is much to be said for the positive alternative of having an active, negotiating approach to knowledge engineering. This is discussed more fully in Gammack and Anderson (1990).

Robert explained that often underwriters can ascertain suspicious cases from what is missing on a form. For instance, one applicant had admitted having an AIDS test, but had not given the result. However, elsewhere he claimed to be seeing a specialist regarding something which he had not specified. Thus even with straightforward, unambiguous answers to the questions, the expert must infer or investigate what is being left out.

Apart from using information from the media, friends, and professional connections in their decision making, there are other subtleties of expertise that elude easy reduction to an expert system. One such was noted by Robert who commented on one applicant's handwriting having a steady and clear flow. An arthritic applicant may well have shaky handwriting, but underwriters will generally be suspicious of shaky handwriting which may indicate alcoholism, undeclared drug use or diseases, as well as independently indicating the applicant's age. Graphonomic skill develops incidentally with underwriting expertise, conferring some subtle ability to detect various illnesses or physical problems.

Robert pointed out a problem with representing knowledge in a static knowledge base. Static systems cannot keep up with the vagaries of world affairs—in particular the changing political climate within and between nations. This does not involve only isolated changes to particular rules, but unforeseeable interactions are also implicated. For instance, a prison officer may have a fairly stable risk rating, but if the prison officer is restationed in Northern Ireland, added risk must be taken into account.

Gill (1989) has made a general observation concerning how "pictures get built up" in underwriting decision making.

It appeared that both Robert and Kath scan the forms first, but not in a procedural manner—the eyes wander over the pages gleaning some general sense or feeling for the basis of the picture, which seems an inescapable product of experience. It is hard to imagine how this could be trained in a novice or captured as a technical property of a system, since not only information, but also judgment is implicated. Not all underwriters will see the same form in the same way: the particular way in which that underwriter has lived and sees the world is likely to affect which "interactions" are noticed. In some sense interactions are not there until they are perceived to be there, and, ultimately, what is the basis for decision?

CONCLUSION

Three case studies have illustrated several issues in expert knowledge acquisition for automated decision making. The traditional decision tree most closely approximates the production system modules of Case Study One, but is severely limited for various reasons. An argument was made for acquiring knowledge within a decision support philosophy. Case Study Two illustrated one approach and its associated knowledge acquisition technique, where the dynamics of information input and running the domain model is put under user control. The elusive element of judgment in decision making was addressed in Case Study Three, where experts in practice seemed to follow a "holistic" strategy of building up a stereotypic impression, underscoring the demerits of the serial system of Case Study One. The centrality of judgment in appraising the status of information militates against the modular approach and recommends the use of a methodology sensitive to the appreciation of global patterns.

Serial decision trees are a mature technology, and have provided a basis for the development of useful expert systems. However, the subtleties of expertise seem to preclude decision trees' universal utility, either for decision support, or for substantial cognitive modeling. Much is required before the implementational consequences implied by the latter two case studies reach similar maturity. And whether human expertise is essentially elusive remains, as before, a fascination.

REFERENCES

Alvey, P. L. (1985). An analysis of the problems of augmenting a small expert system. In Bramer, M.A. (Ed.), *Research and development in expert systems*, CUP.

Bolger, G., Wright, G., Rowe, G., Gammack, J. G., & Wood, R. (1989). LUST for life: Developing expert systems for life assurance underwriting. In Shadbolt, N. (Ed.), *Proceedings BCS Conference on Expert Systems*, London, CUP.

Bliss, J., Monk, M., & Ogborn, J. M. (1983). *Qualitative data analysis for educational research: A guide to the use of systemic networks*. London: Croom Helm.

Boose, J. H. (1986). *Expertise transfer for expert system design*. Amsterdam: Elsevier.

Bounds, D. G., Lloyd, P. J., Mathew, B., & Waddell, G. (1988). A multi-layer perceptron network for the diagnosis of low back pain. *Proceedings IEEE 2nd International Conference in Neural Networks*, San Diego, Vol II, p. 481-5.

Breuker, J. A., & Wielinga, B. J. (1987). Knowledge acquisition as modelling expertise: The KADS methodology. In T. R. Addis (Ed.), *Proceedings First European Workshop on Knowledge Acquisition for Knowledge Based Systems*. Reading University.

Checkland, P. B. (1981). Systems thinking, systems practice. Chichester: Wiley.

Chignell, M. H., & Peterson, J. G. (1988). Strategic issues in knowledge engineering. *Human Factors, 30*, 381-394.

Collins, II. M. (1987). Domains in which expert systems could succeed. *Proceedings 3rd International Conference on Expert Systems*. London: Learned Information.

Collopy, F., & Armstrong, J. S. (1989). Knowledge acquisition methods: A computer aided approach. Paper presented at SPUDM-12, Moscow.

Cooley, M. (1989). Human centred systems: An urgent problem for systems designers. *AI and Society Journal*, Vol 1.

Farr, R. M. (1984). Interviewing: An introduction to the social psychology of the interview. In: C. L. Cooper & P. Makin (Eds.), *Psychology for managers* (2nd ed.). London, Macmillan, 182-200.

Fox, J., Myers, C. D., Greaves, M. F., & Pegram, S. (1987). A systematic study of knowledge base refinement in the diagnosis of leukaemia. In: Kidd, A. L. (Ed.), *Knowledge acquisition for expert systems: A practical handbook*. New York: Plenum.

Gammack, J. G. (1987a). Modelling expert knowledge using cognitively compatible structures. *Proceedings 3rd International Conference on Expert Systems*. London: Learned Information.

Gammack, J. G. (1987b). Different techniques and different aspects on declarative knowledge. In: Kidd, A. L. (Ed.), *Knowledge acquisition for expert systems: A practical handbook*. New York: Plenum.

Gammack, J. G. (1988). Eliciting expert conceptual structure using converging techniques. Unpublished doctoral dissertation, University of Cambridge.

Gammack, J. G., & Anderson, A. (1990). Constructive interaction in knowledge engineering. *Expert Systems: The International Journal of Knowledge Engineering, 7*(1), 19-26.

Gammack, J. G., Battle, S. A., & Stephens, R. A. (1989). A knowledge acquisition and representation scheme for constraint based and parallel systems. *Proc. IEEE Conference on Systems, Man and Cybernetics*, Vol III, 1030-1035, Cambridge, MA.

Gill, S. P. (1988). On two AI traditions. *AI and Society Journal, 2*.

Gill, S. P. (1989). A dialogical approach to the design of KBS for insurance underwriting. *Human Centred systems workshop*, Sept. SEAKE Centre, Brighton Polytechnic.

Gill, S. P. (1990). A dialogical framework for participatory KBS design. *Proc. 10th European Meeting on Cybernetics and Systems Research*, Vienna. London: World Scientific Publishing Co.

Gregory, D. (1986). Delimiting expert systems. *IEEE Transactions*, SMC-16 834-843.

Gregory, D. (1987). Philosophy and practice in knowledge representation. In: J. Zeidner (Ed.), *Human productivity enhancement*. New York: Praeger.

Johnson, L., & Johnson, N. E. (1987). Knowledge elicitation involving teachback interviewing. In: Kidd, A. L. (Ed.), *Knowledge acquisition for expert systems: A practical handbook*. New York: Plenum.

Johnson, N. E. (1989). Mediating representations in knowledge elicitation. In: D. Diaper (Ed.), *Knowledge elicitation: Principles, techniques, and applications*. Chichester: Ellis Horwood.

Kidd, A. L., & Cooper, M. B. (1985). Man-machine interface issues in the construction and use of an expert system. *International Journal of Man-Machine Studies, 22*, 91–102.

Loftus, E. F., & Palmer, J. C. (1974). Reconstruction of automobile destruction: An example of the interaction between language and memory. *Journal of Verbal Learning and Verbal Behaviour, 11*, 770–777.

Long, J. A., & Neale, I. M. (1989). Validating and testing in KBS—A case study. *Proc. 2nd International Conference on Industrial and Engineering Applications of Artificial Intelligence and Expert Systems* (IEA/AIE-89) Univ. of Tennessee Space Inst, Knoxville, TN., Assoc. Computing Machinery, 875–880.

Michalski, R. S., & Chilausky, R. L. (1980). Knowledge acquisition by encoding expert rules versus computer induction from examples: A case study involving soybean pathology. *International Journal of Man-Machine Studies, 12*, 63–87.

Nazareth, D. L. (1989). Issues in the verification of knowledge in rule-based systems. *International Journal of Man-Machine Studies, 30*, 255–271.

Neale, I. M. (1988). First generation expert systems: A review of knowledge acquisition methodologies. *The Knowledge Engineering Review, 3*, 105–145.

Patel, V. L., & Groen, G. J. (1986). Knowledge based solution strategies in medical reasoning. *Cognitive Science, 10*, 91–116.

Suchman, L. A. (1987). *Plans and situated actions: The problem of human-machine communication*. Cambridge: CUP.

Turban, E. (1988). *Decision support and expert systems*. New York: Macmillan.

Welbank, M. (1987). *A review of knowledge acquisition techniques for expert systems*. Ipswich: Martlesham Consultancy Services.

Wright, G., & Ayton, P. (1987). Eliciting and modelling expert knowledge. *Decision Support Systems, 3*, 13–26.

Wright, G., & Ayton, P. (1989). Psychological aspects of forecasting with statistical methods. In: M. C. Jackson, P. Keys, & S. C. Cropper (Eds.), *Operational Research and the Social Sciences*. London: Plenum.

Young, R. M., & Gammack, J. G. (1987). Converging techniques and the role of intermediate representations in knowledge elicitation. In: T. R. Addis (Ed.), *Proceedings First European workshop on knowledge acquisition*. Reading University, U.K.

CHAPTER 10

Human Expertise, Statistical Models, and Knowledge-Based Systems

Dominic A. Clark

INTRODUCTION

The focus of this chapter is the provision of decision support modeled, at least in part, on human expertise. This chapter is divided into sections, each concerned with some aspect of the relationship between human expertise, statistical modeling, and knowledge-based systems, in particular expert systems. The first section provides a comparison of human expert judgment with statistical models, particularly linear regression models, concluding that statistical techniques have been shown to be more accurate than human experts given knowledge of which variables to include in the analysis and the relevant data. The second section provides a brief introduction to expert systems and a comparison of the accuracy of expert systems with human experts. Like statistical models, some expert systems have been shown to be more accurate than human experts. The third section discusses the circumstances under which symbolic representation of

Dominic A. Clark • Advanced Computation Laboratory, Imperial Cancer Research Fund, Lincoln's Inn Fields, London WC2 3PX, England. Research for this chapter was supported by the United Kingdom Science and Engineering Research Council and the Imperial Cancer Research Fund.

Expertise and Decision Support, edited by George Wright and Fergus Bolger. Plenum Press, New York, 1992.

knowledge (as rules or frames) or purely statistical approaches are likely to be more useful in building decision aids. Since the utility of a decision support system is a combined function of both the cost of system development and the change in performance of the decision maker(s) using the system, this analysis necessarily raises considerations relating to knowledge engineering and utility of system explanations as well as that of accuracy. The final section summarizes the relative merits and demerits of statistical and symbolic styles of reasoning, emphasizing the complementarity of the two approaches, and provides a brief illustration of how statistical and symbolic reasoning may be combined within a knowledge-based decision support system.

Various chapters in this volume have discussed the nature of expertise, its elicitation, validation, and improvement. In this chapter the question of what constitutes an expert in a particular field is not directly addressed and an operational definition is adopted whereby the term "expert" means the person or people identified as experts in the studies reported. The principal focus of the chapter is, instead, on the provision of decision support modeled, at least in part, on human expertise. Here the question to be answered is: If time and resources are to be invested in the development of a decision support system with expert level performance, what is the most appropriate representational formalism to adopt?

Many representational formalisms have been employed in expert systems and other decision technologies (Kline & Dolins, 1989). For tasks that involve reasoning under or the management of uncertainty, at least two approaches have been taken for modeling expert judgment. These are statistical modeling and symbolic (or knowledge-based) approaches. Statistical modeling typically involves either (1) determining from the expert which information (or case features) is relevant in analysis and then producing a statistical model that best represents the relationship between this information and an independent gold standard by the analysis of sets of test cases; or (2) taking the judgment of an expert as the gold standard to be replicated and statistically modeling the relationship between features of cases and these gold standard judgments, using either parameters derived from test cases or the subjective estimates of the expert. The more recent technology of knowledge-based systems and particularly expert systems, in contrast, employ more elaborate and generic methods of knowledge representation which can combine heuristic reasoning with quantitative analyses though with different knowledge engineering requirements.

This chapter outlines the basics of the two approaches, reviews some comparisons of the two technologies with expert judgment, discusses criteria for selecting between symbolic and statistical styles of reasoning within knowledge-based applications, and provides a brief example of how statistical and symbolic reasoning may be combined within a single application.

STATISTICAL MODELS AND EXPERT PERFORMANCE

The most comprehensive comparison of expert performance with statistical models is the comparison of prediction under uncertainty with simple linear (regression) models. In this type of modeling task, the value of a criterion (dependent) variable (either the judgment of an "expert" or the outcome of a process) is modeled as a weighted linear combination of a number of predictor (independent) variables represented as a regression equation of the form:

$$Criterion = \sum_{i=1}^{N} weight_i \, Predictor_i + constant \qquad (1)$$

where $Predictor_i$ is the value of the ith predictor variable and $weight_i$ is the weight of the ith predictor variable in the linear model.

In Equation 1, if normalized, the value of the constant term can be interpreted as a measure of prior (or default) tendency and weights may be positive or negative depending upon the nature of the correlation between the corresponding predictor variable and the criterion variable. In the simplest, binary prediction, situation, values for the criterion variable would be coded as 0 or 1. In *proper linear models,* weights are optimized by minimizing a variance function (e.g., least-squares) in the training data for which the criterion and predictor variables are known. Other kinds of weight assignment, *improper linear models,* such as uniform or random weights are discussed below.

Linear models have been employed in two types of analyses of human performance: (1) assessing the external validity of experts' judgments by comparing them with the output of a proper linear model; and (2) using linear models to capture the policy of an expert judge, by using the expert's judgments as the criterion for variance minimization.

Expert Judgment versus Linear Models

Many different task domains have been employed in comparison of expert judgment with simple linear models. One classic study (Meehl, 1959) focused on the ability of clinical psychologists to classify psychiatric patients as either neurotic or psychotic on the basis of their MMPI (Minnesota Multiphasic Personality Inventory) profiles. A MMPI profile consists of a set of scores on 11 personality scales which are assessed by the degree to which patients' answers to the inventory questions match those of a reference set of patients suffering from well-defined psychopathologies. The *true* classification of the patient as neurotic or psychotic was provided by the psychiatric staff of the relevant institution on the basis of more extensive data. In Meehl's study, 29 clinicians (13 Ph.D. clinical psychologists and 16 advanced graduate students) gave predictions for 861 patient MMPI profiles collected from 7 hospitals and clinics. In this study a simple linear model was found to be more accurate than the human experts.

One of the important aspects of this clinical task is that "the differences between psychotic and neurotic profiles are considered in MMPI lore to be highly configural in character" (Meehl, 1959) so that there is no a priori reason to expect that simple linear models would be particularly suited to this task.

The first comprehensive review of the literature on the comparison of the accuracy of expert judgment with simple linear models was conducted by Meehl (1954) who summarized evidence from some 20 studies which compared the judgments of expert clinicians with regression analyses for the same data. In all cases the statistical method was found to be at least as accurate as clinical judgments leading to the conclusion that simple linear weighting of information outperform the intuitive judgments of clinical experts. In a later review, Meehl (1965) came to the same conclusion. Subsequent assessments have not led this view to be substantially revised (Dawes, 1979) and superiority of linear models to expert judgment has been demonstrated in a broad range of tasks including clinical diagnosis (Goldberg, 1970), graduate university admissions (Dawes, 1971), and economic forecasting (Armstrong, 1978).

More recently, using large data sets in four diverse prediction tasks (e.g., predicting neurotic/psychotic tendencies from MMPI profiles, predicting the success of graduate students from their Graduate Record Exam (henceforth GRE), undergraduate grade point average and the quality of their undergraduate college), Dawes and Corrigan (1974) identified four common structural characteristics of tasks in which superiority of linear models over expert judgment had been observed:

Conditional Monotonicity

The relationship between predictor and criterion variables tends to be conditionally monotone. That is, the ordinal relationship between each predictor variable and the criterion variable is independent of the values of the remaining variables and there is a monotone relationship between predictor variables and the criterion variable. As an illustration, in predicting the success of graduate students, no matter how they score on other variables, they are more likely to do better the higher they score on the GRE, and so on. Non-monotone relationships (e.g., single-peaked) may, of course, be converted to monotone relationships by the appropriate transformation (e.g., rescore by taking the absolute value from the peak).

Criterion Error

Error in the data for the criterion variable does not effect the relative values of the weights for the predictor variables, it merely means that the overall model will account for less variance.

Predictor Error

When error is added to the measurement of predictor variables that have a nonlinear (e.g., curvilinear or step-function) relationship to the criterion variable, the relationship between the predictor and the criterion tends to become more linear, with the implication that linear models are more for modeling relationships between variables for which data is characterized by a high degree of error.

Sensitivity

In sensitivity analyses the optimal weights of the proper linear models were replaced with (1) uniform weights (i.e., using only the signs of the optimal weights +1 or −1); and (2) normally distributed random weights (with the appropriate sign). The finding was that the predictive performance of the linear models was fairly robust across these changes in weights. Indeed, in some cases the improper linear models with uniform weights were more accurate than the proper linear models (due to the small number of observations). The implication is that the magnitude of the weights applied to the predictor variables has little effect on the external validity of the resulting predictions and therefore that even if the weights in a linear model are non-optimal, the performance can be expected to be robust. To summarize, Dawes and Corrigan explained the high accuracy of linear models in terms of their conditional monotonicity in the tasks in which they had been assessed, their insensitivity to error, and the flat maximum of the optimum weight function.

Previous studies had shown that regression models with optimized weights were more accurate than human judgments. By comparing the external validity of expert judgments with improper linear models with (1) equal weights and (2) random weights (from normal and rectangular distributions), Dawes and Corrigan (1974) demonstrated that for all their data sets the accuracy of human experts was inferior to improper linear models with uniform weights and equal or inferior to improper linear models with random weights. Subsequent studies have supported this finding.

Comparisons of expert performance with other statistical techniques (principally Bayesian) have yielded similar results to studies with linear models.

Essentially, given sufficient data and knowledge of the relevant variables to consider, Bayesian systems can outperform individual human experts. In one well-known example, a Bayesian decision aid correctly diagnosed the cause of acute abdominal pain in approximately 90% of test cases, whereas physicians achieved only 80% accuracy (DeDombal, 1975).

Expert Judgment as Linear Models

A related line of research to the comparison of expert judgment with linear models is the modeling of expert judgment as linear models. In this paradigm the predictor variables in the regression analysis are the variables (e.g., MMPI profiles) that the expert uses as the basis for judgment. In contrast to comparisons of expert judgment with linear models, however, the criterion variable in these studies is the expert's judgment itself. This line of research was initiated by Hoffman (1960), who termed such linear equations intended to simulate experts' judgments *polymorphic linear representations*.

The major finding of studies of such *polymorphic linear representations* (e.g., Yntema & Torgenson, 1961; Bowman, 1963; Wiggins & Kohen, 1961; Goldberg, 1970; and others reviewed in Dawes & Corrigan, 1974), was the intriguing and pervasive observation that the resulting polymorphic models had higher external validity than the judge him/herself, even though the model was based on the behavior of the judge. This phenomenon was termed *bootstrapping* (Yntema & Torgenson, 1961).

Explanations of this phenomenon based on expert inconsistency have been proposed (Goldberg, 1970). More recently these explanations have been augmented and subsumed by the demonstrations of Dawes and Corrigan (1974), discussed above, concerning the robustness of improper linear models with random weights and their ability to outperform human judges. Essentially, the robustness of improper linear models in the tasks under consideration means that the source of the weights (e.g., from experts) are relatively unimportant because similar results can be achieved with random weights. In fact, on average, Dawes and Corrigan found that the external validity of predictions from improper linear models with random weights was greater than for the predictions from linear polymorphic representations. What is important, however, is that the factors relevant to the construction of such models be identified.

Overall, studies employing statistical modeling have demonstrated that statistical models can outperform human prediction even when the statistical model is based largely on the behavior of the human expert. It should also be emphasized, however, that prediction from multiple cues is only one role performed by human experts. In addition to the evaluation of evidence human experts must typically formulate hypotheses, adjust these in the light of new data, learn from past cases, avoid catastrophies, communicate their ideas, elicit feedback, and perform various other important tasks (Shanteau, 1987).

EXPERT SYSTEMS

The technology of expert systems and its parent discipline, artificial intelligence (henceforth AI) has attracted much attention in recent years. In part, because of the high level of problem solving performance that has been achieved by some programs (Reddy, 1988), but also because of the breadth of scientific and commercial domains in which the technology is potentially applicable.

Several definitions of expert system have been proposed which differ in their emphases. Some emphasize expert systems as computer simulations of human expertise while others stress expert level performance usually operationalized as accuracy (see Shafer, 1987). While these are both aspects of expert system technology, expert systems can, in general, be distinguished from conventional computer programs by five characteristics (identified by Buchanan & Smith, 1988) with particular applications differing in the degree to which each characteristic is represented. These five characteristics are:

1. The use of symbolic as well as mathematical reasoning.
2. The use of domain specific heuristic knowledge (as well as algorithmic knowledge).
3. Expert level performance.
4. Facilities to explain the reasoning strategy and justification of inferences.
5. Flexibility for modification and extension.

Under this characterization a computer implementation of a linear model would not be considered an expert system, even if it were capable of expert level performance.

While some of these characteristics may be present in well-designed conventional software, it is their combination that characterizes and distinguishes expert system from conventional software. Further, in contrast to the kinds of quantitative representation and evaluation that are the basis of statistical modeling techniques, it is the characterization of expert systems by: (1) the use of symbolic reasoning; and (2) heuristic methods for the representation and manipulation of information that mark expert systems as AI programs (Buchanan & Smith, 1988, p. 23) that distinguishes them from purely statistical approaches. In this respect, expert systems may be said to draw more inspiration from models of human reasoning than do statistical models.

Symbolic knowledge for reasoning is typically represented in terms of *frames* (Minsky, 1975) or *rules* (Buchanan & Shortliffe, 1984) or hybrid formalisms combining both.

Frame-Based Systems

Frame-based systems consist of structured sets of facts organized around objects. These facts typically consist of attribute-object-value tuples such as those shown in Figure 1 for the frame PERSON. In this simple example, the attributes (or slots) of the frame PERSON are date_of_birth, father, mother, occupation, marital_status, no_of_children, nationality, and age. For a particular person John Smith, these slots might have the slot values 4.10.1960, Paul Smith, Clare Smith, student, single, 0, British, and 9.8.29 (29 years, 8 months, and 7 days), respectively (assuming that current date is 13 June 1990). Note that values of attributes may themselves be objects with an associated frame (such as John Smith's father and mother who are also people and therefore have values corresponding to each of the attributes in the frame PERSON).

Symbolic reasoning in frame-based systems has no necessary features but is usually based on procedural attachments which manage mechanisms such as the assignment of default values to slots (e.g., where unspecified the default value of no_of_children is 0), the computation of slot values (e.g., the value for age is computed by subtracting a person's date of birth from the current date), the inheritance of slot values from more general frames (e.g., a person inherits the value of the slot nationality from the corresponding slot in the frame of their

```
frame: PERSON (e.g. John Smith)
    date_of_birth: DATE.BIRTH (4.10.1960)
    father: PERSON (e.g. Paul Smith)
    mother: PERSON (e.g. Clare Smith)
    occupation: JOB (e.g. student)
    marrital_status: MARRITAL_STATUS (e.g. single)
    no_of_children: NUMBER default=0 (e.g. 0)
    nationality: NATIONALITY default=father.nationality (e.g. British)
    age: DAYS.MONTHS.YEARS: (e.g. 29years 8months 7days)
            constraint age < father.age
            constraint age < mother.age
            compute-age(PERSON,DAYS.MONTHS.YEARS)

compute-age(PERSON,DAYS.MONTHS.YEARS)
    DAYS.MONTHS.YEARS = current.date - PERSON.date_of_birth.
```

Figure 1. Example of a frame associated with the object PERSON and an associated procedure to compute the value of the slot "age" of the person by subtracting the person's date of birth from the current date. (Adapted from Kramer & Mylopoulos, 1987.)

father), and constraint propagation between slots (e.g., the age of a person must be less than the ages of both parents).

In expert systems, frame-based applications frequently employ some form of hypothesize-and-test as the principal form of abductive reasoning (Ramsey et al., 1986). In this paradigm, knowledge is divided into manifestations (symptoms) and causes (disorders). Each disorder includes in its frame a set of associated symptoms and each symptom includes in its frame a set of associated causes. Then, given a diagnostic problem with a set of manifestations, the inference mechanism identifies all the sets of disorders that could explain any of the manifestations, seeks further manifestations associated with these sets of disorders, and finally selects the most plausible set of disorders using some criteria of parsimony such as the set that explains (or covers) the greatest number of manifestations and has the smallest number of elements (minimum cardinality).

Rule-Based Systems

Representing knowledge as rules derived much of its impetus from Newell and Simon's (1972) work on human problem solving and is the principal form of knowledge representation employed in most expert systems. In rule-based systems, the primary form of knowledge representation is *condition* => *action* statements consisting of a number of conjunctive/disjunctive conditions (premises or antecedents) and one or more actions (conclusions or consequents). The action(s) may be assertions (e.g., about hypotheses), exhortations (e.g., drug administration) or control statements (see Figures 2 and 5) or any combination of these. The primitive action in rule-based systems is the firing of a rule.

Rules are most frequently used to represent strategic ("how to") knowledge (see Figures 2 and 5). For example, Figure 2 shows the top level (strategy) rule of Mycin (Shortliffe, 1976), often regarded as the prototypic rule-based system. The strategy embodied by this rule is to determine the set of organisms that need treatment, generate a short list of candidate treatment regimes, and then decide

---

If   (1) There is an organism which requires therapy
and (2) consideration has been given to possible existence of
         further organisms requiring therapy
Then (3) Compile a list of possible therapies which may be effective
         against the organisms requiring therapy
and (4) Determine the best therapy recommendations from the compiled list.

Figure 2. Mycin top-level strategy rule. (Adapted from Buchanan & Shortliffe, 1984, p. 104.) The strategy embodied by this rule is to determine the set of organisms that need treatment, generate a short list of candidate treatment regimes, and then decide among these.

among these. Mycin in fact used rules in a backward-chaining manner so that the top-level goal (determine the best therapy recommendation) would lead to the system firing other sets of rules which interpret existing data and request information from the user in the attempt to determine whether there was an organism that required therapy, and so on.

Rule-based systems have incorporated statistical as well as symbolic types of reasoning. In particular, the Mycin certainty factor (henceforth CF) formalism (Shortliffe & Buchanan, 1975; Buchanan & Shortliffe, 1984) provides a method for quantifying the strength of each rule, using a measure of the relative increase or decrease in belief given to the conclusion by the truth of the premises (Figure 3). This type of representation in which symbolic knowledge (rules) is combined with statistical weights appears to provide a method for both formalizing heuristic knowledge (as rules) and simultaneously allowing uncertainty to be combined by a formal calculus. In consequence the CF formalism has been very popular with expert system designers. However, it has been widely criticized on both formal and pragmatic grounds particularly because of its lack of semantic modularity (the degree to which changes (additions, deletions, or replacements) to functional units (rules) in the system have unanticipated effects or other functional units). Specifically, Heckerman and Horvitz (1988) showed that the strength of association between antecedents and consequents in rules with CFs was dependent upon the composition of the set of rules as a whole and not just the particular rule. This raises problems in changing the rule base.

Symbolic reasoning of a different kind was employed by Ellam and Maisey (1987) in an expert system designed to assist in medical image interpretation. Following Fox (1986a, 1986b), Ellam and Maisey characterized evidence features in this domain in terms of whether they were sufficient for, supporting (simply evidence for), detracting (simply evidence against), necessary for, or eliminating with respect to particular diagnostic categories. Rules were then used to characterize diagnostic hypotheses as either *possible, impossible, suspected,* or *likely* as a function of which types and how much evidence was present for each category (Figure 4). Determining whether the sum of the evidence for an hypothesis is greater than the sum against (as in the definition of *suspected*) can be achieved in a number of ways, such as using improper linear models with

---

> If   (1) the stain of the organism is gram positive,
> and (2) the morphology of the organism is coccus,
> and (3) the growth conformation of the organism is chains
> Then there is suggestive evidence (0.7) that the identity
>   of the organism is streptococcus.

Figure 3. English translation of a Mycin rule. (From Shortliffe & Buchanan, 1975.) The certainty factor (CF) of this inference is 0.7.

X is *possible*	if no necessary conditions for X are violated.
X is *impossible*	if an excluding condition for X is present.
X is *suspected*	if X is possible and at least one piece of evidence in favour of X is present.
X is *likely*	if X is possible and the sum of evidence for X is greater than the sum of evidence against X.

Figure 4. Uncertainty categories employed by Ellam and Maisey (1987). Evidence in this domain is characterized in terms of whether it is sufficient for, supporting (simply evidence for), detracting (simply evidence against), necessary for, or eliminating with respect to particular diagnostic categories. These rules assign diagnostic categories as possible, impossible, suspected, or likely by evaluating this evidence.

uniform weights or using dominance relationships, etc. Thus, as the characterization of expert systems above emphasized, it is possible to combine statistical and symbolic reasoning within the same application. Indeed, many of the more successful applications of AI techniques such as chess and other game-playing program employ symbolic techniques for control (move-generation and aspects of search) and quantitative scoring functions to evaluate the resulting possible game positions.

Further symbolic rules in the system then use these uncertainty categories for representing control strategies. The generic rule in Figure 5, for example, says that if there is evidence for a particular kind of object in the image (e.g., a certain kind of cell) then look for evidence of subclasses of that object which have not already been classified as impossible. This is effectively an hypothesis refinement rule, seeking evidence for subtypes of objects which already have supporting evidence.

Overall, it is the combination of statistical and symbolic methods for rea-

If   **Class** is *suspected* and **Subclass** is a type of **Class** and **Feature, Value** is evidence for **Subclass** and features include **Feature, Value** and **Subclass** is *not impossible* Then **Subclass** is *suspected*.

Figure 5. Hypothesis refinement control rule employing symbolic uncertainty constructs. (From Ellam & Maisey, 1987.) The rule states that when there is evidence for a particular diagnostic class, search for evidence associated with noneliminated subclasses of that class. Bolded expressions are variables, while italicized expressions are uncertainty terms defined in Figure 3.

soning about uncertainty that gives expert systems one aspect of their potential utility. Frames provide a natural method for representing descriptive knowledge whereas rules are useful for encoding strategic knowledge. Many systems combine the two.

Expert Judgment versus Expert Systems

Many expert systems are in routine use (see Rauch-Hindin, 1986; Buchanan, 1986; Walker & Miller, 1986; Harmon & King, 1985, for lists of examples) and some of the best known, such as R1 (also known as XCON) which configures Vax computers (McDermott, 1982), have been in commercial use for many years.

As the list of expert system characteristics outlined above suggests there are many ways in which expert systems may be evaluated. For example, it is possible to evaluate expert systems of the basis of performance (accuracy, severity, or errors), the manner in which conclusions are reached, acceptability to users in terms of ability to explain conclusions and lines of reasoning, efficiency, cost-effectiveness, brittleness (does the system degrade gracefully given a problem which borders on the fringes of what it knows), and meta-level capabilities (does the system know what it knows or will it try to provide a solution to a problem that is strictly outside its domain (Wyatt & Spiegelhalter, 1989, 1990). In a clinical context, for example, a complete evaluation would involve precise measurement of the full army of medical and nonmedical benefits and costs resulting from alternative diagnostic strategies applied to patients with specific signs, symptoms, and risk factors. The remainder of this section, however, reviews only the evaluation of expert system accuracy against human expertise. Some of the other aspects of expert system evaluation are discussed in the final section of this chapter.

Many expert systems are evaluated by comparing their performance with that of a relevant human expert in the absence of any true gold standard. In such situations the expert system can at best match the performance of the human expert but cannot better it. Moreover, in this paradigm if there is any error or inconsistency in the expert judgment, the expert system can only achieve 100% comparability by modeling this error. Logically, then, expert systems can only be shown to outperform human judgment either when there is some external gold standard against which both can be compared (such as a set of test cases) or using a form of *peer review,* analogous to Turing's test, illustrated below.

Using gold standards or peer review, some systems have been shown to perform at least as well as human experts (Duda & Shortliffe, 1983). These include PROSPECTOR and Mycin (Yu et al., 1979). The evaluation of Mycin provides a good illustration of the comparison of human experts with expert systems by peer review.

The evaluation of Mycin consisted of two principal stages. In the first a detailed clinical summary was compiled for ten patients with infectious meningitis, which were considered to be diagnostically challenging and had not been employed in the development of the Mycin system. The summaries were then input to Mycin and also presented to seven Stanford physicians with expertise in infectious diseases and one senior medical student. The physicians were asked to prescribe an antimicrobial therapy regimen for each case, or if they chose not to prescribe, to specify which laboratory tests they would recommend to determine the infectious etiology. There were no restrictions concerning the use of reference materials.

In the second stage, ten prescriptions were compiled for each case: Mycin's recommendation, the recommendations of the seven physicians and the student, and the prescription actually administered to the patient in the local hospital. These ten prescriptions for each case were then sent to eight independent infectious disease specialists at institutions other than Stanford who had all published clinical reports on the management of infectious meningitis. These evaluators were asked: (1) to make their own prescription for each case; and then (2) to assess for each of the ten prescriptions they received for each case whether it was equivalent to their own prescription, an acceptable alternative to their own prescription, or a nonacceptable alternative. These evaluators were blind in the sense that they were not aware of the source of each prescription.

Of the ten sets of prescriptions, analysis showed that Mycin's recommendation were classified as acceptable (equivalent or an acceptable alternative) by the evaluators on 65% of occasions compared with 57.5% for the actual therapy, a mean of 54.7% (range 42.5% to 62.5%) for the seven Stanford physicians and 30% for the senior medical student. This study therefore provides an example in which the accuracy of an expert system was found to be better (on the average) than the performance of a set of human experts using the standard of independent peer review. Similar results have been found in the domains of pediatric cardiology (Reggia et al., 1984).

These studies therefore demonstrate that expert systems can outperform individual human experts in tasks where performance is based on the assessment of percentage accuracy.[1]

EXPERT SYSTEMS VERSUS STATISTICAL MODELS

Given that both statistical modeling and expert systems can outperform human experts, which should one choose in developing a decision support sys-

---

[1]However, it should be borne in mind that other measures of performance, such as severity of errors and cost of data required, might lead to different results.

tem? There are few direct performance comparisons between expert systems, and such comparisons are of questionable utility because, as the preceding sections have emphasized, in many domains suitable for statistical modeling expert systems have been developed that are hybrid. That is, they have employed both statistical and symbolic reasoning. A more meaningful way of assessing the relative utility of statistical modeling and expert systems, therefore, is to determine the contexts in which symbolic styles of knowledge representation and reasoning (characteristic of expert systems and more typical of human reasoning) are likely to be more or less productive than statistical modeling in isolation.

Symbolic versus Statistical Reasoning

Some authors have compared symbolic and statistical approaches to the development of decision support systems. Fox et al. (1980) compared the performance of a rule-based system modeled on clinical thinking with a simple Bayesian system. The finding was of similar performance of the two on both the training data (78% to 76% in favor of the rule-based system) and on a subsequent test set of patient records (68% versus 66% in favor of the Bayesian system).

A comprehensive review of comparisons between different implementation techniques was conducted by Ramsey et al. (1986). They critically assessed the relative advantages and disadvantages of three different approaches to building expert systems: symbolic approaches employing rule-based deduction, symbolic approaches employing frame-based abduction, and statistical analyses (predominantly Bayesian) by surveying existing comparisons in the literature and conducting a set of targeted evaluations that assessed factors relating to performance, ease of implementation and run-time efficiency. Their analysis identified clear advantages and disadvantages for each method. The following paragraphs summarize these and are supplemented by observations from Clark (1990).

A problem associated with statistical techniques is the requirement for extensive case data or subjective estimates from which to determine the relevant statistical parameters. This may be problematic because of incompleteness in the relevant database and/or unreliabilities of subjective estimates.[2] If parameters are based on data frequencies, how are events with low frequency observations to be managed? Alternatively, if parameters are derived from human experts, how is consistency and comprehensiveness ensured? Finally, it may be necessary to make unreasonable assumptions such as independence of problem features and/or mutual exclusivity of outcomes during the development of the system.

---

[2]Spiegelhalter et al. (1989) have recently presented a method for refining possibly erroneous expert judgments with independent case data by estimating a hypothetical case sample size associated with the expert's judgment on the basis of the expert's confidence intervals and then combining the hypothesized sample set with the real data to produce a modified confidence interval and mean judgment.

Conversely, rule-based systems are excellent for representing strategic information (as in Figures 2 and 5), but are not always appropriate for representing descriptive knowledge, such as taxonomic information and other relationships which are more easily expressed as facts in frames. The interpretation of some problem features can also be highly context-dependent with the implication that a rule-based system would need to consist of many rules, each with many antecedent conditions. The resulting rules are suboptimal for knowledge engineering as they present difficulties for maintenance and debugging. Finally, there are many ways of organizing sets of rules and it is usually not clear a priori which is the best. Finding the most appropriate form of rule organization can be a matter of trial and error.

In contrast to rule-based and statistical approaches, frames provide a natural form of knowledge representation when the source information is largely descriptive, as in textbooks or published papers. Further, in diagnostic and other problems involving selection, abductive methods can work well when multiple solutions are involved. However, by virtue of their shorter history, frame-based systems are the most experimental of the three approaches.

Ramsey et al. concluded that all three methods can generally be applied to any problem involving the selection of different alternatives and have all been shown to be capable of high accuracy. However, on the basis of their review and analysis, they proposed a set of criteria for determining the utility of these three types of knowledge representation (statistical, rule-based, and frame-based) relating to:

1. The preexisting format of the application knowledge (textual/strategic, etc.).
2. The types of classification that are desired (mutually exclusive/multiple simultaneous).
3. The amount of context dependency in a problem as a function of interactions between input features (few/many).

Using these dimensions of comparison, they argued that statistical approaches are appropriate when: (1) the relevant data are available; (2) outcomes are mutually exclusive; (3) input features are relatively independent; and (4) predominantly probabilistic inferences are involved.[3] This kind of situation is characterized by limited-size problems involving selection of one outcome from a fixed

---

[3]Restrictions (2) and (3) might be relaxed if nontraditional Bayesian techniques are used. More recent Bayesian approaches, championed by Pearl (1986), Cheeseman (1985, 1986, 1988), Spiegelhalter (Spiegelhalter, 1986a, 1986b; Lauritzen & Spiegelhalter, 1988), and others, and variously described as influence diagrams, causal nets, belief nets, knowledge maps, relevance diagrams, and Bayesian networks, do not represent the relationship between input features and outcomes as a giant joint distribution table, but as a network of low-order probabilistic relationships represented as a directed graph, avoiding some of the problems of independence and exclusivity (see Clark, 1990).

set of alternatives, such as the studies discussed in the comparison of clinical and statistical judgment earlier in this chapter.

In contrast, Ramsey et al. concluded that rule-based inference is most appropriate when: (1) the underlying knowledge is already organized as rules or in a table format; (2) the required categorization is predominantly categorical; and (3) there is not a great deal of context dependency. This kind of situation would be characterized by "screening" or policy implementation type problems in which the appropriate strategy for each situation is well documented (such as the use of oncology protocols in management of cancer patients).

Finally, they concluded that frame-based representation should be considered when: (1) the underlying knowledge is descriptive (consists predominantly of facts); (2) there is a mixture of probabilistic and categorical classification required; (3) there is a large amount of context dependence; and (4) there are potentially multiple simultaneous outcomes (e.g., diseases or treatments) to be considered. This approach to knowledge representation would therefore be applicable to large diagnostic problems and is the technique most frequently employed in large knowledge-based systems application (e.g., O'Neil et al., 1989; Lenat & Guha, 1990).

A number of other recent papers have compared the two approaches (Carroll, 1987; Hammond, 1987). Carroll's (1987) argument is essentially that since expert systems are attempts to model human experts, they can at best perform as well as human experts, and since it has been demonstrated that for noisy decision problems human experts are outperformed by simple linear models, it follows that, given the degree of error that exists in the real world and the cost of developing expert systems, linear models are a more productive approach to modeling expert reasoning, while Hammond (1987) lists 15 differences between AI and psychological approaches to modeling judgment. Demonstrations of expert system superiority to the judgment of human experts (as in Yu et al., 1979, reviewed above) clearly make Carroll's position untenable. Additionally, however, against this view, Schwartz et al. (1989) have argued that:

1. The true cost of producing statistical models is not always less than that of producing expert systems because of: (a) the real cost of problem definition (determining which possible predictor and outcome variables are relevant); (b) data collection (e.g., a large and representative sample of patient records); and (c) experimentation (determining which predictors are conditionally independent and monotonically related to the criterion variables). In short developing linear models is not necessarily cheaper than developing expert systems since statistical models can require large-scale data collection and empirical analyses.

2. Expert systems are more efficient and general than linear models because: (a) whereas linear models require all parameters to be known,

expert systems, by interactively updating their database of case-specific facts can frequently make a decision on the basis of partial information; and (b) by operating interactively, expert systems are able to respond opportunistically to user intervention in the generation of decision options (see Fox et al., 1989, 1990) rather than being constrained to predefined sets.

Schwartz et al. conclude by arguing that expert systems and linear models are not designed to perform the same kinds of tasks and therefore should not be considered as alternatives. A more useful perspective is one of potential "unification" is which linear models are seen as one part of the more general knowledge contained in an expert system.

The factors identified by Ramsey et al. (1986) and Schwartz et al. (1989) above concerning the relative utility of statistical and symbolic methods can be complemented by a number of other observations relating to model-based reasoning, planning under uncertainty, and explanation.

Model-Based Reasoning

Earlier, it was argued that under some circumstances (such as conditional monotonicity, etc.) statistical approaches to knowledge combination can lead to high levels of accuracy. In many situations, however, conditional monotonicity is not present and model-based (or theory-driven) reasoning may be more appropriate. An illustration of such reasoning is in medical diagnosis, where it is often necessary to reason about the relationship between decision candidates (e.g., diagnostic candidates) as well as the relationship between the decision candidates and manifestations.

In diagnosis, for example, within the same patient some sets of diseases may co-occur whose collective signs and symptoms differ from the simple union of the set of signs and symptoms usually associated with each disease in isolation. As an example, a sign of renal failure is acid blood, whilst a sign of hyperventilation is alkaline blood. Therefore when both are present the patient's blood may have a high, low, or normal pH.[4] If blood pH is one of the variables in the analysis (as it should be if either renal failure or hyperventilation is suspected) and the pH is normal, a simple linear model that does not include the combination of renal failure and hyperventilation as a single diagnostic category would count this as evidence against both renal failure and hyperventilation in isolation.

Statistical systems can be made to treat combinations of outcomes as individual entities (e.g., "syndromes"); however, in any nontrivial application the

[4]This example is inspired by Patil et al. (1984).

potential explosion of combinations mitigates against such an enumeration. Conversely, using the appropriate deeper symbolic knowledge, an expert system can potentially reason about this possible association and infer that normal pH is not evidence against the conjunction of renal failure and hyperventilation (see O'Neil et al., 1989, for examples of such reasoning about the exclusiveness of candidates).

Finally, Schwartz et al. (1989) have pointed out that by contrast with statistical models, expert systems are generally employed in a highly interactive manner. This facility is particularly important for problems such as scheduling and planning under uncertainty where the order in which operations are to be performed is highly dependent upon interactive feedback (e.g., Smith et al., 1986). In such tasks statistical models may be used to evaluate particular sets of actions; however, reasoning about the components and order of execution of plans or schedules is best performed using symbolic reasoning.

Explanation

Earlier it was pointed out that a principal characteristic that distinguishes expert systems from conventional software is the capability for explanation. Teach and Shortliffe (1981) demonstrated empirically that explanation was the principal concern of American physicians with respect to computerized medical decision support systems. Here the ability of the system to justify its conclusions was rated more highly than than the possibility of diagnostic errors.

Where simple evaluation of alternatives is required, statistical systems are excellent at precise combination of numerical parameters. Statistical models can also provide an account of the sensitivity of judgments to particular input features and potential future information (Spiegelhalter, 1986b). However, because purely statistical systems compile strategic knowledge into numerical parameters, in multistage tasks involving strategic decisions as well as evaluations, knowledge relating to the problem solving or diagnostic process is lost and is therefore inseparable from the descriptive knowledge, with the result that the strategy being followed is not amenable to query or explanation.

The utility of a decision support system should not be evaluated simply on the basis of the external validity of the systems advice, but by the wider outcome of the effects the system's advice has on the performance of the decision maker using the system. Thus, human-factor considerations, such as the acceptability of the advice given by the system, are critical.

SUMMARY AND CONCLUSIONS

The sections above have shown that both statistical modeling and expert systems approaches to the development of decision support systems can be used to produce expert and above-expert level performance. Since expert systems frequently employ quantitative or statistical parameters, however, the most useful dimension for comparison between the two technologies concerns symbolic and statistical models of reasoning. In this respect the relevant dimensions of comparison identified above include:

1. Whether the domain of interest is characterized by extensive quantitative/case study data: if so, there is a strong argument in favor of a statistical analysis.
2. The predominant nature in which information is precoded. Is this (a) in terms of a branching logic or rules, such as policy decisions/legislation and of some protocol (as in the management of some diseases and fault analysis), which would suggest a rule-based approach; (b) primarily descriptive involving taxonomic and other relationships, which would suggest a frame-based approach; or (c) essentially statistical?
3. Whether model-based reasoning is required: that is, whether it is necessary to reason about which sets of decision candidates to consider as exclusive and which to consider as potentially complementary in a decision task, and then to determine the implications of different combinations of decision candidates for the parameters relevant to the decision. This would suggest use of a symbolic approach, such as rule or frames or both.
4. Whether it is important to be able to reason about control as in planning and scheduling tasks or to use symbolic constructs such as truth maintenance: this would suggest use of a symbolic approach, such as rule or frames or both.
5. Whether explanation, especially of strategic information, such as intermediate steps in an analysis is needed to enable to user to act upon the system's advice? This would suggest use of a symbolic approach or a hybrid symbolic/statistical approach.

Throughout this paper (and elsewhere: Schwartz et al., 1989; Fox et al., 1990; Clark et al., 1990) the complementary nature of statistical and symbolic techniques has been stressed. Indeed, the characterization of expert systems above suggests this is fundamental to the technology. The guidelines given above for determining the appropriateness of statistical and symbolic reasoning are relevant for assessing the relative utility of statistical modeling and expert systems approaches to the development of decision support systems. Essentially, if symbolic reasoning is required, then an expert system approach is likely to be the most productive. However, if a hybrid expert system which employs both statistical and symbolic reasoning is to be built, then the guidelines above are relevant to modularization of tasks within the system.

An example of such a hybrid decision support system that combines symbolic and statistical reasoning is provided by the Oxford System of Medicine,

OSM (O'Neil et al., 1989), a medical information and decision support system intended to provide a second opinion to general practitioners in a number of tasks in general medicine (such as diagnosis, selecting investigations, and treatment). The OSM employs rules, frames, and quantitative evaluation techniques (unweighted linear models). The high level reasoning strategy is represented as a set of general rules which are used to dynamically determine which sets of decision candidates to consider in each decision task (e.g., which diseases to consider in diagnosis, which tests to consider in investigation, which drugs to consider in treatment, etc.), whether these decision candidates are exclusive or potentially conjunctive (e.g., drugs with different modes of action can be combined within a therapy, but drugs that interact negatively cannot) and which evidence (e.g., signs/symptoms, counterindications, etc.) are relevant to their evaluation. The OSM's descriptive knowledge is represented as associated collections of facts (frames) containing taxonomic, causal, and other kinds of relationships among diseases, signs/symptoms, treatments, and investigations, while evaluation of sets of decision candidates is conducted by the use of statistical analyses, such as improper linear models using uniform weights. Some recent experiments have investigated the use of Bayesian analysis in the evaluation stage (Fox et al., 1990; Clark et al., 1990).

ACKNOWLEDGMENTS

I am grateful to John Fox (ICRF), Mike O'Neil (ICRF), Jeremy Wyatt (the Brompton Hospital/IBM Scientific Research Center, Winchester), and to George Wright and Fergus Bolger for comments on an earlier draft of this chapter.

REFERENCES

Armstrong, J. S. (1978). Long range forecasting: From crystal ball to computer. New York: Wiley.
Bowman, E. H. (1963). Consistency and optimality in managerial decision making. *Management Science, 9*, 310–321.
Buchanan, B. G. (1986). Expert systems: Working systems and the research literature. *Expert Systems, 3*(1), 32–51.
Buchanan, B. G., & Shortliffe, E. H. (1984). Rule-based expert systems: The Mycin experiments of the Stanford Heuristic Programming Project. Reading, Mass.: Addison-Wesley.
Buchanan, B. G., & Smith, R. G. (1988). Fundamentals of expert systems. *Annual Review Computer Science, 3*, 23–58.
Carroll, B. (1987). Expert systems from clinical diagnosis: Are they worth the effort? *Behavioral Science, 32*, 274–292.
Cheeseman, P. (1985). In defense of probability. In *Proceedings of International Conference on Artificial Intelligence*, Los Angeles, 1002–1009.
Cheeseman, P. (1986). Probabilistic vs. fuzzy reasoning. In Kanal & Lemmer, *Uncertainty in artificial intelligence*. Amsterdam: Elsevier North Holland.

Cheeseman, P. (1988). An inquiry into computer understanding. *Computational Intelligence, 4*(1), 58–66.

Clark, D. A. (1990). Numerical and symbolic approaches to uncertainty management in AI: A review and discussion. *Artificial Intelligence Review, 4*(2), 109–146.

Clark, D. A., Fox, J., Glowinski, A. J., & O'Neil, M. (1990). Symbolic reasoning for decision making. In Borcherding, K., Larichev, O., I., & Messick, D. M. (Eds.), *Current issues in decision making.* Amsterdam: Elsevier.

Dawes, R. M. (1971). A case study of graduate admissions: Application of three principles of human decision making. *American Psychologist, 26,* 180–188.

Dawes, R. M. (1979). The robust beauty of improper linear models in decision making. *American Psychologist, 34,* 571–582.

Dawes, R. M., & Corrigan, B. (1974). Linear models in decision making. *Psychology Bulletin, 81*(2), 95–106.

DeDombal, F. T. (1975). Computer assisted diagnosis of abdominal pain. In Rose, J. & Mitchell, J. (Eds.), Advances in medical computing. New York: Churchill Livingston.

Duda, R. O., & Shortliffe, E. H. (1983). Expert systems research. *Science.* 220, 261–268.

Ellam, S., & Maisey, M. N. (1987). A knowledge-based system to assist in medical image interpretation: Design and evaluation methodology. In Bramer, M. A. (Ed.), *Research and development in Expert Systems III.* Cambridge University Press.

Fox, J. (1986a). Knowledge, decision making and uncertainty. In Gale, W. A. (Ed.), *Artificial intelligence* and statistics. Reading, Mass.: Addison-Wesley.

Fox, J. (1986b). Three arguments for extending the framework of probability. In Kanal, L. N. & Lemmer, J. F. (Eds.), *Uncertainty and artificial intelligence.* Amsterdam: Elsevier B. V.

Fox, J, Barber, D, & Bardhan, K, D. (1980). Alternatives to Bayes. *Methods of Information in medicine, 19,* 210–215.

Fox, J, O'Neil, M, Glowinski, A., & Clark, D. A. (1989). Decision making as a logical process. In *Research and development in expert systems V.* Cambridge, University Press.

Fox, J, Clark, D. A, Glowinski, A., & O'Neil, M. (1990). Using predicate logic to integrate qualitative reasoning and classical decision theory. *IEEE: Trans Systems, man and cybernetics.*

Goldberg, L. R. (1970). Man versus model of man: A rationale plus some evidence for improving clinical inference. *Psychological Bulletin, 73*(6) 422–432.

Hammond, K. R. (1987). Toward a unified approach to the study of expert judgment. In Mumpower, J. et al. (Eds.), *Expert judgement and expert systems.* Heidelberg: Springer-Verlag.

Harmon, P., & King, D. (1985). Expert systems: Artificial intelligence in business. Chichester: Wiley.

Heckerman, D., & Horvitz, E. (1988). The myth of modularity in rule-based systems for reasoning with uncertainty. In Lemmer, J. F. & Kanal, L. N. (Eds.), *Uncertainty in Artificial Intelligence 2.* Amsterdam: Elsevier North Holland.

Hoffman, P. J. (1960). The paramorphic representation of clinical judgement. *Psychological Bulletin, 57*(2), 116–131.

Kline, P. J., & Dolins, S. B. (1989). *Designing expert systems.* Chichester: Wiley.

Kramer, B. M. & Mylopoulos, J. (1987). Knowledge representation. In Shapiro, S. C. (Ed.), *Encyclopedia of artificial intelligence.* Chichester: Wiley.

Lauritzen, S. L., & Spiegelhalter, D. J. (1988). Local computations with probabilities on graphical structures and their application to expert systems (with discussion). *Proceedings of the Royal Statistical Society, B, 50,* 157–224.

Lenat, D., & Guha, (1990). Building large knowledge based systems. Reading, Mass.: Addison-Wesley.

McDermott, J. (1982). XSEL: A computer sales person's assistant. *Machine Intelligence,* 10, 325–337.

Meehl, P. E. (1954). *Clinical versus statistical prediction.* Minneapolis: University of Minnesota Press.

Meehl, P. E. (1959). A comparison of clinicians with five statistical methods of identifying psychotic MMPI profiles. *Journal of Counseling Psychology, 6*(2) 102–109.

Meehl, P. E. (1965). Seer versus sign: The first good example. *Journal of Experimental Research in Personality, 1,* 27–32.

Minsky, M. (1975). A framework for representing knowledge. In Winston, P. (Ed.), *The psychology of computer vision.* New York: McGraw-Hill.

Newell, A., & Simon, H. (1972). *Human problem solving.* Englewood Cliffs, N.J.: Prentice-Hall.

O'Neil, M, Glowinski, A, & Fox, J. (1989). A symbolic theory of decision making applied to several medical tasks. In *Lecture Notes in Medical Informatics, 38: Proceedings* of the European Conference in AI in Medicine. Berlin: Springer-Verlag.

Patil, R. S, Szolovits, P., & Schwartz, W. B. (1984). Causal understanding of patient illness in medical diagnosis. In Clancey, W. J. & Shortliffe, E. H. (Eds.), *Readings in medical artificial intelligence: The first decade.* Reading, Mass.: Addison Wesley, pp. 339–360.

Pearl, J (1988). *Probabilistic reasoning in intelligent systems.* Los Altos, CA: Morgan Kaufmann.

Ramsey, C. L, Reggia, J. A, Nau, D. S., & Ferrentino, A. (1986). A comparative analysis of methods for expert systems. *International Journal of Man-Machine Studies, 24,* 475–499.

Rauch-Hindin, W. B. (1986). Artificial intelligence in business, science and industry: Volume II— Applications." Englewood Cliffs, N.J.: Prentice-Hall.

Reddy, R. (1988). Foundations and grand challenges of artificial intelligence. *AI Magazine,* Winter, 9–21.

Reggia, J, Tabb, R, Price, T, Banko, M., & Hebel, R. (1984). Computer-aided assessment of transient ischemic attacks. *Archives of Neurology, 41,* 1248–1254.

Schwartz, S, Griffin, T., & Fox, J. (1989). Clinical expert systems versus linear models. *Behavioral Science, 34,* 305–311.

Shafer, G. (1987). Probability judgement in artificial intelligence and expert systems. *Statistical Science, 2*(1), 3–16.

Shanteau, J. (1987). Psychological characteristics of expert decision makers. In Mumpower, J. et al. (Eds.), *Expert judgement and expert systems.* Heidelberg: Springer-Verlag.

Shortliffe, E. H. (1976). Computer-based medical consultations: Mycin. New York: Elsevier.

Shortliffe, E. H., & Buchanan, B. G. (1975). A model of inexact reasoning in medicine. *Mathematical Biosciences, 23,* 351–379.

Smith, S, Fox, M. S., & Ow P. S. (1986). Constructing and maintaining detailed production plans: Investigations into the development of knowledge-based factory scheduling systems. *AI Magazine,* Fall, 45–61.

Spiegelhalter, D. J. (1986a). A statistical view of uncertainty in expert systems. In Gale, W. A. (Ed.), Artificial Intelligence and Statistics. Reading, Mass.: Addison-Wesley.

Spiegelhalter, D. J. (1986b). Probabilistic reasoning in predictive expert systems. In Kanal, L. N. & Lemmer, J. F. (Eds.), *Uncertainty in artificial intelligence.* Amsterdam: North Holland.

Spiegelhalter, D. J., Franklin, R. C. G., & Bull, K. (1989). Assessment, criticism and improvement of imprecise subjective probabilities for a medical expert system. *Uncertainty in Artificial Intelligence 5,* Elsevier.

Teach, R. L., & Shortliffe, E. H. (1981). An analysis of physician attitudes regarding computer-based clinical consultation systems. *Computers in Biomedical Research, 14,* 542–558. Reprinted in Buchanan, B. G. & Shortliffe, E. (Eds.), Rule-based expert systems: The Mycin experiments of the Stanford Programming Project. Reading, Mass.: Addison-Wesley.

Walker, T. C., & Miller, R. K. (1986). *Expert systems 1986.* Madison, Ga: *SEAI Tech. Publ.*

Wiggins, N., & Kohen, E. S. (1961). Man vs model of man revisited: The forecasting of graduate school success. *Journal of Personality and Social Psychology, 19,* 100–106.

Wyatt, G., & Spiegelhalter, D. (1989). Evaluating medical expert systems: What to test and how? In Talmon, J. and Fox, J. (Eds.), *Systems engineering in medicine.* Heidelberg: Springer-Verlag.

Wyatt, G., & Spiegelhalter, D. (1990). Evaluating medical expert systems. *Proceedings AAAI Spring Symposium on AI in Medicine,* 211–215.

Yntema, D. B., & Torgenson, W. S. (1961). Man-computer cooperation in decision requiring common sense. *IRE Transactions of the Professional Group on Human Factors in Electronics,* 2(1), 20–26.

Yu, V. L., Fagan, M. L., Bennett, S. W., Clancey, W. J., Scott, A. C., Hannigan, J. F., Blum, R. L., Buchanan, B. G., & Cohen, S. N. (1979). An evaluation of Mycin's advice. *Journal of the American Medical Association, 242,* 1279–1282. Reprinted in Buchanan, B. G., & Shortliffe, E. H. (Eds.), *Rule-based expert systems: The Mycin experiments of the Stanford Heuristic Programming Project.* Reading, Mass.: Addison-Wesley.

CHAPTER 11

Synthesis of Expert Judgment and Statistical Forecasting Models for Decision Support

Derek Bunn

JUDGMENT, MODELS, AND DECISION SUPPORT

One of the characteristic features of decision-support systems that Keen and Scott-Morton (1978) envisioned was an interaction between computer-based models and the expert judgment of the managers who would use them. This objective had been motivated by the apparent lack of success at the everyday managerial level that twenty-five years or so of operations research and management science model building had achieved. The OR and MS tradition had been a scientific one with a reliance upon a comprehensive problem representation and mathematical techniques of solution. As such, a large part of the work remained in the domain of specialists, did not facilitate interaction with the expert judgment of managers, and was not as widely adopted as their designers had expected. Keen and Scott-Morton emphasized the use of simpler models, more intuitive to managers and an interactive style of usage. What the DSS models lacked in comprehensive problem representation was more than compensated for by the ease with which they could be run under alternative assumptions. The popularity of PCs at the managerial level and the development of friendly, generic software over the following decade greatly facilitated these ideas.

Derek Bunn • London Business School, Sussex Place, Regent's Park, London NW1 4SA, England. *Expertise and Decision Support*, edited by George Wright and Fergus Bolger. Plenum Press, New York, 1992.

Now, when we look at strategic decision-making models, we see much more of a focus upon their design for structuring qualitative judgment. Their use and relevance for *learning* about the business environment rather than for *solving* a particular problem is much more evident (Morecroft, 1984). The majority of recent OR/MS applications uniformly stress interactive decision-support capabilities and simulation seems to be more useful than optimization as a general technique for analyzing decisions. Thus, even if the content of DSS methods had not been novel in OR and MS terms, it has succeeded in focusing the design upon more intuitive and interactive models.

However, when we look at the development of forecasting methodology over recent years, it is surprising to see that it has not paralleled this DSS theme and has been slow to learn the lessons of OR and MS. In the 1970s, forecasting as a subject was concerned with establishing an objective and scientific basis to its methods and was increasingly becoming esoteric (e.g., the development of Box-Jenkins methods). Furthermore, this coincided with a theme in psychological research concerned with establishing the many ways in which human judgment could be fallible (e.g., Tversky & Kahneman, 1974). Because of these two factors, forecasting researchers were slow to reflect the DSS thinking on the intuitive interaction of model and judgment. Even now, several influential researchers have persisted in arguing against the routine use of explicit managerial judgment, except in special cases (e.g., Armstrong, 1985; Makridakis, 1988). The result of all this was that researchers on judgmental methods, by the mid-1980s (e.g., Lawrence et al., 1985), had been put strangely on the defensive in having to establish a case for judgment against statistical models. Essentially, in the decision-making sciences, one usually assumes that the onus is upon the model builders to show improvement on expert judgment (Simon, 1960).

The DSS influence is, nevertheless, beginning to show up in forecasting research. Fischhoff (1988) and Belsley (1988) have discussed the role of judgment in quantitative modeling and the observation that all serious forecasting involves some human judgment is not by itself controversial. Some of the PC software now available does enable both judgment and statistical extrapolations of data to be combined. An understanding of the *extent* to which there should be an explicitly formal interaction of expert judgment and statistical modeling and *how* that should be achieved are still, however, major issues. The purpose of this chapter is to review what we know about these issues in practice and to speculate upon how effectively some of the DSS ideas on interaction can be brought into the forecasting process.

JUDGMENTAL ADJUSTMENTS

Surveys of the practical use of models in forecasting have invariably shown a managerial inclination to use relatively simple models and subject them to considerable judgmental adjustment. For example, Edmundson et al. (1988), Huss (1986), and Mathews and Diamantopoulos (1989) have provided practical case studies of the effectiveness of this approach. In addition, Mathews and Diamantopoulos (1990) have demonstrated from their sales forecasting data that in exercising discretion upon which model-based forecasts to adjust and which to leave, managers have generally chosen well. A similar conclusion has been reached by Willemain (1989) from experimental studies showing that judgment generally improved "bad" quantitative forecasts, but was not detrimental to "good," i.e., near-optimal, ones. It seems that, while well-specified time-series models can be most effective in filtering out noise and projecting past patterns in the data, expert intervention will pay off in practice when there is extra information about new untypical circumstances.

However, the intervention should comprise some real expertise and be undertaken with concern for quality:

- Studies using students in university laboratories have been more equivocal than those of experts in real tasks. Issues of substantive knowledge and motivation clearly apply. As O'Connor (1989) observes, studies of experts in tasks which make use of their actual professional knowledge, for which they have been well trained and where important payoffs are involved, have generally shown a higher quality of judgment than those of student experiments.
- Evidence that can be justified rather than untested conventional wisdom is more reliable. Guerts and Kelly (1986) give an interesting example of ineffective "conventional wisdom" in practical sales forecasting in a case study where various factors which salesmen believed were important in actual fact did not really influence sales at all significantly. Thus, the basis of any judgmental adjustment needs to be made explicit and defensible.
- Where there is potential for feedback and training in the use of expert knowledge, its quality is likely to improve (see Fischhoff, 1988).
- Where there is the possibility of graphic aids, or a decomposition approach to providing a structure to the judgmental reasoning (e.g., by breaking up the time series with trends, seasonals, and residuals, as in Edmundson, 1990), the quality of the intervention will again improve.
- Where the evidence for particular adjustment has been assessed together with disconfirming evidence in an attempt to take a balanced view (cf. Einhorn & Hogarth, 1978), expert performance is less likely to be biased. It is a common observation in psychological research that individuals tend to selectively search for evidence to support their views at the expense of seeking contrary evidence which might then provide the basis of a more balanced judgment.

With an emphasis upon the use of "best practice" (as above) in the use of expert judgment, much of the "heuristics and biases" psychological research of the 1970s can be considered less pessimistic for judgmental forecasting. Rather than looking at how poorly individuals do under unfavorable circumstances (as in Tversky & Kahneman, 1972, or Lichtenstein, 1977), several researchers (e.g., Phillips, 1987; O'Connor, 1989; Beach et al., 1987) have contrasted the evidence of "best practice" and found that individual judgments are indeed reliable in real forecasting situations. When Hogarth and Makridakis (1981) warned against the use of judgment in forecasting, they were extrapolating from the "heuristics and biases" theme in psychology at that time which was largely based upon artificial experiments. Today, empirical and case-study research seems to give us more grounds for confidence.

With more complicated forecasting models, such as the multiple econometric equations used for economic forecasting, judgmental adjustment by the producers is equally prevalent in practice. McNees and Perna (1891), Corker et al. (1986), Wallis et al. (1984–1988), and Turner (1990) all discuss this process in detail. Turner (1990), in particular, provides an extensive analysis of this process on the major U.K. econometric models. Adjustments take the form of subjective projections of the residuals of some of the variables in the model. The residuals are the differences between the actual values of particular variables in the past (e.g., manufacturing exports) and the values "fitted" by the model. For a well-specified model, the residuals should just reflect random variation and would not therefore have any systematic effect on the forecasts. If, however, the forecaster believes that the model is inadequate in some way, then he, or she, will often make a "residual adjustment" to one or more of the variables by projecting forward a systematic pattern of residuals.

Figure 1 shows the residual adjustments made to the forecasts in 1988 by the London Business School (LBS) and National Institute of Economic and Social Research (NIESR) for manufacturing exports. The data series up to the second quarter of 1988 shows an average (but periodic) pattern of underestimating this variable. Looking beyond the second quarter of 1988, the LBS forecasters clearly decided to project out a constant residual adjustment of about 6% to compensate for this, whereas the NIESR evidently saw the misspecification getting progressively worse and included an increasing adjustment. Both LBS and NIESR noted these adjustments as being caused by recently unreliable data and a probable misspecification of the U.K. elasticity with respect to world trade.

Similarly, Figure 2 shows the LBS and NIESR residual adjustments to consumer expenditure. In this case, both were noted as being caused by a recent change in the savings ratio: LBS saw this as a misspecification due to financial deregulation whereas NIESR saw it as an omitted variable in terms of mortgage equity withdrawals. Again, LBS projected the residual error at a fairly constant value, but NIESR took the view that its effect would attenuate.

Of course, the added difficulty with adjusting one variable in a system of equations is caused by the interrelationships with the variables. Thus, for exam-

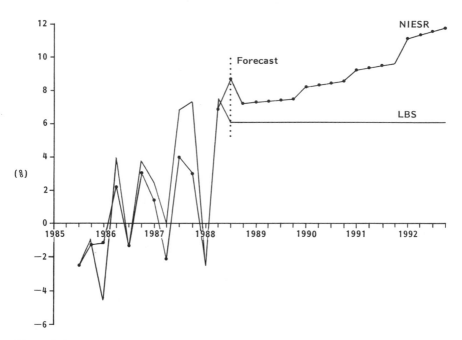

Figure 1. Single-equation error/residual adjustment on manufacturing exports, as a percentage of level of variable in 1988:2. (From Turner, 1990. Reprinted by permission.)

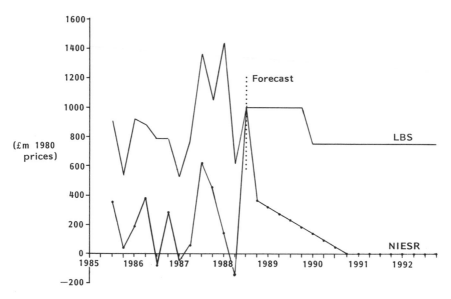

Figure 2. Single-equation error/residual adjustment on consumer expenditure. (From Turner, 1990. Reprinted by permission.)

ple, the LBS consumer expenditure adjustment takes the 1989 GDP growth from 3.4% to 1.4%. As Turner (1990) observes, generally less than half of the endogenous variables are adjusted, but their effects are extremely significant. Furthermore, from the perspective of a *user* of these forecasts, very little background to the adjustment is normally given and no sensitivity analysis performed on the effect of other possible adjustment assumptions. This is a real concern for users of these models. However, in a series of retrospective studies, Wallis (1984–1988) has shown that these adjustments have, overall, produced more accurate forecasts than if they had not been undertaken.

It is clear, therefore, that as with business forecasting, *adjustment* is an integral part of the economic forecaster's craft and, again, with apparently very little formal structure. At the very least, a documentation of the evidence for adjustment would seem to be required in both cases. This should improve the quality and credibility of the process. We have already noted the concern of users of economic forecasts for greater understanding of the impact and rationale of the residual adjustments. Armstrong (1985) refers to this documentation as an "audit trail" and quotes the example of Glantz (1977) in which the U.S. government was sued by a group of farmers for forecasting and issuing directives for a drought which did not occur. The forecast had been based upon a judgmental adjustment to a quantitative model, which the suit contended represented unprofessional practice. Clearly an explicit process of adjustment needs to be undertaken, not just to be defensible to adversarial challenge, but also to better communicate the reasoning in the forecast. To point simply to the availability and incorporation of some "extra information" is not enough.

To be more specific, judgment is needed where, for example:

1. *Theories are inadequate.* Exchange rate forecasts in econometric models are essentially judgmental interpretations of government policies. Theory is currently inadequate to set up these rates as endogenous variables determined similarly to the other economic variables.
2. *There are some omitted variables.* We have seen an example of this in Figure 2 where NIESR adjusted the consumer expenditure residuals to account for a lack of modeling mortgage withdrawals.
3. *Data quality is suspect.* We have seen examples of this in Figure 1 where both NIESR and LBS chose to adjust the manufacturing export residuals because of lack of quality in the recent data.
4. *Continuity in forecasts is necessary.* Period by period forecasting is often required to show consistency. Short, medium or long-term forecasts need to show a consistent profile for reasons of credibility.
5. *Misspecification of dynamic relationship,* e.g., government incentives on unemployment, new market behavior in business forecasting.
6. *Change in coefficients,* e.g., new market share, or savings ratio.

7. *Forecast outcomes are partially controllable.* In business situations where the forecasts may be treated more as targets, or part of the budgetary process, then subjective intervention may be performing the function of introducing an asymmetric loss function rather than expert information (e.g., Willemain et al., 1991) or anticipating commitment to achieve outcomes (e.g., Brown, 1988).

8. *Political background.* This is the major source of judgmental input to economic forecasts, as such models are essentially conditional upon a particular policy framework.

The value of a documented audit trial is at least threefold:

- The quality of the expert judgmental input should be improved through becoming less casual. If the adjustment is a group effort, the explicit reasoning should improve group communication and consensus formation.
- The adjustment becomes more credible to users and appears less arbitrary. The information content of the forecast is more evident.
- With background assumptions more evident, multiple simulations and sensitivity analysis can be facilitated on the part of users. This DSS aspect is particularly important in the use of economic forecasts, where users may wish to make alternative political scenarios to those taken as background to the adopted forecasts.

To go beyond a *documented audit trail* and develop an *adjustment decomposition structure* is still more of an ideal than an established practice. Various methods have been developed to help structure purely judgmental forecasts, and provide a process of integrating quantitative and qualitative data, but there have been very few applications concerned specifically with adjustment of statistical forecasts.

STRUCTURAL APPROACHES

Wolfe and Flores (1990) have used the so-called analytical hierarchy process to adjust statistical earnings forecasts. This is a relatively simple process of subjectively rating the impact of various factors (such as economic, competitive, supply) for possible change in the underlying trend extrapolation. The method appeared to perform well. In principle, however, various other techniques which have been found useful in decomposing and making explicit the reasoning behind judgmental forecasts could be used in this way.

The "hierarchical inference" framework which developed most conspicuously around several political risk forecasting tasks (e.g., Barclay et al., 1977) is very similar in its visual setup and type of assessment process to the analytical hierarchy process. However, it has a stricter Bayesian way of handling the uncertainty assessments as conditional probabilities which makes it slightly less flexible to use, but this could be a strength if it were to be developed as a basis for modeling the adjustment process of a statistical time-series forecasting model.

Figure 3 shows an example from the political risk context where the focus of interest was upon whether a particular country would develop a nuclear capability within the subsequent five years. The hierarchical structure models the relationship between the various activities deemed necessary for this to happen and the indicative data which have so far been observed. The assessments are made by "backward induction" which means that assessments of the probabilities of data in the hierarchy are made conditional upon its being assumed that the activities above are actually true. The reasoning proceeds, therefore, by

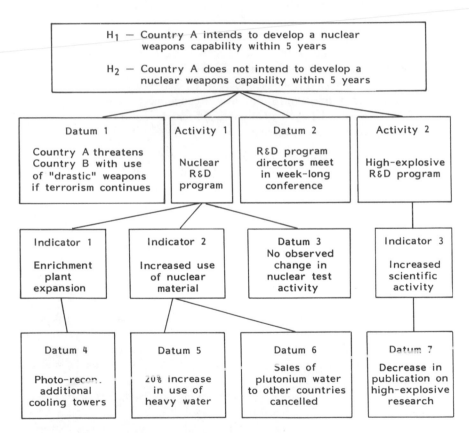

Figure 3. Hierarchical structure for nuclear weapons development program. (From Barclay et al., 1977. Reprinted by permission.)

assuming in this example that it is true that the country is developing a nuclear capability and then asking for assessments of the conditional probabilities of the various data and activities in the second row of the hierarchy.

After all of the conditional probabilities have been so assessed by going down all of the branches of the hierarchy, a simple manipulation of the probabilities then reverses the conditional nature of the assessment to give the probability of the event under consideration (e.g., the country going nuclear) conditional upon the activities and data explicitly modeled in the hierarchy. This type of reasoning is quite distinct from the more commonly adopted "forward induction" which involves thinking through what has just happened and what might happen next in an iterative way to build up various "scenarios" or "causal maps" (see, for example, Nilsson, 1989). Most researchers on this topic suggest a joint process of forward and backward induction to obtain a full representation of the hierarchical structure (e.g., Jungermann, 1985).

The problem with the hierarchical type of decomposition is that it may overconstrain the way that individuals think about the various factors in order to make them fit into this structure. More recently, the modeling technique of "influence diagrams" (as in Smith & Oliver, 1990) has been found to be useful in providing a similar explicit and systematic representation of the judgmental process, but in a much more flexible way both with respect to structure and the assessment of conditional probabilities. Figure 4 shows an example from McNamee and Celona (1987), concerned with new product forecasting, where the various nodes (events) and directed arrows (influences) can be developed interactively without being constrained to a hierarchical or decision-tree format. Probability assessments on the influences can then be processed according to the various rules of conditional probabilities.

Software is now available to help all of these judgmental decomposition techniques and their subsequent analysis to give subjective probability forecasts. However, while these can clearly provide more structure to a forecasting adjustment process, from our perspective, they would still represent an ad hoc treatment of the output from a basic statistical model without any real interaction with the model.

The ultimate ideal would be to develop a fully *interactive decomposition structure,* whereby the specification of the subjective evidence and the statistical model are both part of an overall coherent modeling effort. This would provide the most defensible and credible approach. We only really have clues to the future here. State space methods (e.g., Harvey, 1984) are amenable to both qualitative (e.g., "influence diagrams") and statistical (e.g., "structural models") specifications and would seem to be the most promising. The purely subjective decompositional software of Edmundson (1990), which allows judgment to be incorporated on trend, seasonal, and residual components has so much structural similarity to common statistical decomposition methods that some synthesis

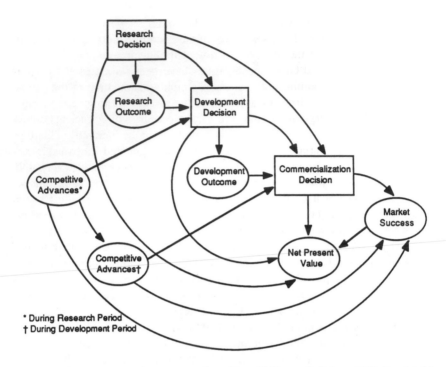

Figure 4. Influence diagram for a new product. (From McNamee & Celona, 1987. Reprinted by permission.)

must be attractive. The ideal is to have interaction of judgment and quantitative modeling at the level of components in an overall model, rather than at the level of ad hoc adjustment of statistical model outputs.

When expert knowledge is sufficiently substantial to provide an alternative forecast, then a key issue is whether a *combination* of the separate statistical and subjective forecasts should be undertaken in preference to using the subjective knowledge to *adjust* the basic statistical model.

COMBINATIONS OF JUDGMENTAL AND STATISTICAL FORECASTS

When we have several reasonably good separate forecasts of a particular outcome, then the evidence now is quite well established that a linear combination will, on average, produce more accurate forecasts than trying to select the best. This applies to combining either statistical, judgmental, or both types of forecast (e.g., Lawrence et al., 1986; Bunn, 1989). By "reasonably good," we generally mean that the forecasts should be unbiased and comparable in terms of accuracy. Most methods of combination have been statistically developed, assuming that a history of the relative performance of the separate forecasts has been available. Bates and Granger (1969) are usually credited with starting this theme whereby the combining weights are estimated as being proportional to the inverse of the individual forecast error variance.

We now have a large number of statistical approaches from the dozen or so heuristic variations on the original Bates and Granger (1969) approach, to a variety of regression-based methods (Granger & Ramanathan, 1984; Diebold & Pauly, 1987). Also, the multiobjective formulation of Reeves and Lawrence (1982) offers scope for combinations subject to several criteria, beyond just accuracy, possibly of a more subjective nature. Where the forecast errors are likely to be positively correlated, efficiency in practice requires a robust method of combination, and equal weighting is often hard to beat in this situation, providing the individual models are in themselves good predictors. Differential weighting, on the other hand, is often required to devalue the impact of "poor" models. Where differential weighting schemes are being used, there is a strong requirement that they be adaptive in order to deal with the nonstationary nature of relative performance in the forecasting models.

Outside the use of statistical or equal-weighting combinations, the method of assigning judgmental "outperformance" probabilities by the forecaster across the set of models has shown useful, if limited, applicability (Bunn, 1975, 1977, 1985; Bessler, 1987; Gupta & Wilton, 1987). This limited use of judgment in encoding belief across quantitative models (rather than on events) is quite surprising when we think of the large body of research in combining expert forecasts using subjectively assigned weighted on the experts (see Lock, 1987, for a recent review).

Outperformance probabilities are assessed by the analyst as the chances that each forecast, in turn, will perform best over the horizon being considered. Such an interpretation of subjective probability weights has the advantage of being:

- *assessable* (i.e., avoiding issues of model truthfulness);
- *flexible* in allowing interpretations of "performance" to be based on issues other than accuracy;
- *robust* in that these weights are not unduly influenced by outliers, nonnormality of errors, etc.;
- *adaptive* when a past history of performance is available—they can be updated by a Bayesian process; and
- *efficient* in that when an accuracy criterion is being used and a simple nonparametric interpretation of accuracy is taken (e.g., which method performed best) then linear combinations based upon outperformance have performed well in comparison to the more parametric statistical methods.

Despite their limited application so far, they do offer a formal process of integrating judgment and quantitative evidence at the level of combining separate forecasts.

However, the methodology of combining forecasts represents a pragmatic response to a form of modeling failure. In seeking to form a combination of the outputs of several models rather than a coherent synthesis of all the input data and hypotheses, we are responding to the multivariate difficulties in performing the latter. For example, in dealing with regression and time-series models, a coherently synthesized model would incorporate all the exogenous variables, together with the time series, into one large estimation task. It is the statistical intractability of this estimation which motivates a robust combination of separate models.

Similarly, if we are dealing with subjective forecasts or experts' opinions, then a synthesized model would require a cognitive decomposition of each expert and a consensus developed over all of the input assumptions that each individual uses. Again, the pragmatic response is to develop a clinical combination over the stated forecasts as in Ashton and Ashton (1985). Nevertheless, this pragmatism seems to pay off, and as a strategy for incorporating judgment with a statistical model, combinations work well (see also Lawrence et al., 1986; Bunn, 1985; Bunn & Seigal, 1983; Pereira et al., 1989).

But we lose several virtues of model building in this pragmatic pursuit of efficiency and accuracy. The combined model is not so lucid in structure and generates less insight into the overall relationships between input variables. Essentially, the combined forecast can be a mixture of different perspectives, assumptions, and hypotheses for extrapolating the data. As such, it does not embody a single theory and does not provide an internally consistent model of all the inputs to the output variable. Thus, it may not be so useful for policy simulation or communication with other decision makers. It does not fit in well with current thinking·on the structure of decision support systems where the overall impact of separate future scenarios should be evaluated in outcome terms for decision flexibility and robustness, not synthesized prior to decision analysis. From a DSS perspective, there is a move away from seeking an optimal analysis to a process of developing a multiplicity of perspectives. In such circumstances, the judgmental tasks are not ones of model combination, but of creating disparate, yet coherent scenarios.

Thus, while it might seem that the combination of forecasts can provide the framework for evaluating the interaction of judgmental and statistical forecasts, the question of whether such a pragmatic solution is really appropriate must be considered. A more coherent model of the judgmental and quantitative factors may be preferable, which portrays in lucid terms an overall structure of interaction with possibly less emphasis on predictive accuracy and more on communications.

SYNTHESIS AND DECISION SUPPORT BY ADJUSTMENT
OR COMBINATION

Thus, although we must remember that our ideal is to develop a coherent and comprehensive model, in practice we will choose to use expert knowledge and statistical models either in *combination,* or with one performing the function of an informative *adjustment* of the other. In the latter case, it is suggested that in practice, a simple statistical model should provide the baseline from which special expert knowledge can be used to suggest how far the extrapolation of the past trends may in fact be different in the future. However, we should note that sometimes, the judgmental forecasts can provide the baseline, either because they are more organizationally established or because the quantitative data are *peripheral* and not be itself sufficient to form a more reliable separate forecast. In this case, the quantitative data can sometimes effectively be used to adjust the subjective forecasts, through calibrating past errors and thereby "debiasing" the forecasts (e.g., Clemen & Winkler, 1987; Fildes, 1989).

Adjustment is clearly the preferred approach when one source of information is indeed *peripheral,* or secondary. When expert and model provide, separately, equivalently good forecasts, then a combination is the usual practice, although one should be clear of the criteria.

1. If *accuracy* is the main objective, a combination may be the most efficient. Indeed, the literature on combining is now so supportive that the baseline method should now be taken as a simple combination. Discussion should then proceed as to why the combining weights should be different.

2. If the forecasting model is to be the basis of *policy simulation,* then coherent relationships of input to output variables are of essential importance (such relationships can get obscured, or even biased, in simple combinations of models based only upon outputs). This seems to suggest a case for an interactive decompositional structure, based upon formal adjustment as discussed above. Certainly, the idea of an overall coherent model renders the forecast more *defensible to adversarial criticism,* or more easily *communicated* to others than is often the case with a combined forecast, which can sometimes appear to be a pragmatic mixture of different perspectives.

If we look at some of the current thinking in decision support systems, we would expect to see a tendency towards using quite simple models, run many times under various assumptions with straightforward attempts at listing and rating the judgmental factors not modeled statistically. This suggests a form of hybrid approach with adjustment of simple models ultimately leading to a combination if forecast accuracy is the objective, or to a sequence of multiple alternative scenarios if policy evaluation is the objective. What is to be seen as simple will evolve as more effort is expended in making various statistical methods more friendly and understandable to users. Certainly, it will be a continuing goal of software designers to bring more thorough methods of data analysis and model building into general use by nonspecialists.

In these terms, recent microcomputer software has both facilitated and inhibited judgmental interaction. Interactive packages allow considerable modeling insights to be gained through easy, visual experiments on respecifications, and the range of facilities offered gives the user wide access to different types of models. The statistical graphics packages have been especially successful in this way. However, while this certainly opens up new scope for judgment as to the appropriate models and their respecifications, it does tend to encourage a restricted choice of general purpose, "off-the-shelf" models, rather than the building of models from personal insight and belief.

For example, in modeling a new product's growth and saturation, the software-package approach would be to fit various forms of logistic curves to the data and find which fits the early observations best. There would be no theory, just goodness of fit. A more informative approach might be to consider what factors may cause saturation, what factors cause adoption and repurchase, and examine the implications of such a relationship. Such behavioral model building would generate more insight, but it is less likely in a software-package environment. The introduction of "intelligent front ends" and "automatic" model identification procedures clearly further inhibits the scope, in practice, for this type of judgmental interaction.

Thus, as Fischhoff (1988) notes, modeling the decision processes of expert forecasters into automated expert forecasting systems presents new judgmental challenges. Technical feasibility issues aside, how should one expert system be chosen from a range of alternatives on offer to the consumer? Belsley (1988) is particularly critical of attempts to automate the specification of statistical models. Within his framework for reliable model building, quality is achieved through the attainment of fit, meaning, and diagnostics, all of which, but especially that of being meaningful, requires the exercise of critical judgment.

We must await the incorporation of the current judgmental software for influence diagrams, hierarchical inference, and "soft" systems modeling onto basic time-series methods to see interactive software helping both judgmental and statistical analysis. Certainly, the impact of influence diagrams, and their inherent connections to state space modelling provide a useful modeling synergy in this respect with the type of subjective decomposition support that Edmundson (1990) has developed for structuring expert judgment on trends, seasonal, and noise components. Thus, interactive software is going to be the key to making quite thorough statistical forecasting methods simple and reliable to professional forecasters, and in facilitating a coherent synthesis of their judgments within the statistical models, but these methods must remain open and flexible to suit individual needs. The commercial pressures of featuring software packages as "intelligent," "expert," or "automatic" will not necessarily foster this type approach where it is needed most: to support regular managerial functions.

CONCLUSION

Much of the emphasis of this chapter has been in the synthesis of expert judgment, model specification, and the process of forecast and error adjustment. In terms of the acquisition of data, there are important judgmental issues involved with data selection that do not usually get discussed in the forecasting literature. Connolly and Porter (1990) discuss the need to understand the incentives behind the contributions to voluntary data bases and the consequent care that must be taken in their use by third parties for other purposes. Dennis (1985) looked at the selection of data in a multiperson context and points to the need to examine disconfirming evidence as a basis for mediation between different viewpoints.

It is a great oversimplification to see the majority of forecasting tasks in the context of single, or multiple equation, statistical models and some extramodel information. In many environmental and strategic forecasting models, the "model" is a connection of relatively poorly supported causal theories based upon controversial assumptions and equivocal interpretations of various sorts of data. Experts are required to take a view on various aspects of the model and its defensibility is often based around the thoroughness with which disconfirming evidence has been explicitly addressed. In terms of structure for these types of models, we again note the promise of systems dynamics or influence diagram technology, although their value in this case would be in providing a structure for separating out areas of relative expertise or controversy.

Finally, in terms of research in this area, one of the great difficulties in assimilating published work from a variety of perspectives and disciplines is the multiplicity of confounding factors in methodology and experimental situations. As we have discussed, in methodology, it is important to know how quality was achieved as *best practice* in the judgmental and statistical model specifications, whether the judgments were *individual or group, holistic or decomposed, with or without the aid of interactive graphics,* whether the statistical models had good *fit, meaning, and diagnostics,* whether any adjustments were *formally explicit,* and how any combinations were effected. In the experiment or case study, it is likewise important to establish the status of the *subjects,* their *information bases,* whether the tasks were *real-world or laboratory,* the existence of *feedback* and what form it takes, the extent of any *influence* that practicing forecasters might have on the outcomes, and the way in which their *success* is assessed. Such a taxonomy seems essential in being able to compare research results and thereby establish practical guidelines.

REFERENCES

Armstrong, J. S. (1985). *Long-range forecasting*. New York: Wiley.

Ashton, A. H., & Ashton R. H. (1985). Aggregating subjective forecasts: Some empirical results. *Management Science, 31,* 1499–1508.

Barclay, S., et al. (1977). *Handbook for decision analysis*. McLean, Virginia: Decisions and Designs Inc.

Bates, J. M., & Granger, C. W. J. (1969). The combination of forecasts. *Operational Research Quarterly, 20,* 451–468.

Beach, L. R., Christensen-Szalanski, J., & Barnes, V. (1987). Assessing human judgement: Has it been done, can it be done, should it be done? In Wright, G., & Ayton, P. (Eds.), *Judgemental forecasting*. Chichester: Wiley.

Belsley, D. A. (1988). Modeling and forecasting reliability. *International Journal of Forecasting, 4*(3), 427–447.

Bessler, D. W., & Chamberlain, P. J. (1987). On Bayesian composite forecasting. *Omega, 15,* 43–38.

Brown, L. D. (1988). Comparing judgmental to extrapolative forecasts: It's time to ask why and when. *International Journal of Forecasting, 4*(2), 171–173.

Bunn, D. W. (1975). A Bayesian approach to the linear combination of forecasts. *Operational Research Quarterly, 26,* 325–329.

Bunn, D. W. (1977). Comparative evaluation of the minimum variance and outperformance methods for the linear combination of forecasts. *Operational Research Quarterly, 28,* 653–663.

Bunn, D. W. (1985). Statistical efficiency in the linear combination of forecasts. *International Journal of Forecasting, 1,* 81–193.

Bunn, D. W. (1987). Expert use of forecasts: Bootstrapping and linear models. In Wright, G. & Ayton, P. (Eds.), *Judgemental Forecasting*, Wiley: Chichester.

Bunn, D. W. (1989). Forecasting with more than one model. *Journal of Forecasting 9*(3), 161–166.

Bunn, D. W., & Siegal, J. P. (1983). Forecasting the effects of television programming upon electricity loads. *Journal of the Operational Research Society, 34,* 17–21.

Clemen, R. T., & Winkler, R. L. (1987). Calibrating and combining precipitation probability forecasts. In Viertl, R., (Ed.), *Probability and Bayesian statistics*. New York: Plenum.

Connolly, T., & Porter, A. L. (1990). Discretionary databases in forecasting. *Journal of Forecasting, 9*(1).

Corker, R. J., Holly, S., & Ellis, R. G. (1986). Uncertainty and forecast precision. *International Journal of Forecasting, 2*(1), 53–70.

Dennis, R. L. (1985). Forecasts and mediation: Colorado and the clean air act. *International Journal of Forecasting, 1*(3), 297–308.

Diebold, F., & Pauly, P. (1987). Structural change and the combination of forecasts. *Journal of Forecasting, 6*(1), 21–40.

Ebert, R. J., & Kruse, T. E. (1978). Bootstrapping the security analyst. *Journal of Applied Psychology, 63,* 110–119.

Edmundson, R. H. (1990). Decomposition: A strategy for judgemental forecasts. *Journal of Forecasting* (in press).

Edmundson, R. H., Lawrence, M., & O'Connor, M. (1988). The use of non-time-series information in sales forecasting: A case study. *Journal of Forecasting, 7*(3), 201–212.

Einhorn, H. J., & Hogarth, R. (1978). Overconfidence in judgment: Persistence of the illusion of validity. *Psychological Review, 85*, 395–476.

Fildes, R. (1989). Efficient use of information in the formation of subjective industry forecasts. Working paper, Manchester Business School, England.

Fischhoff, B. (1988). Judgemental aspects of forecasting: Needs and possible trends. *International Journal of Forecasting, 4*, 331–339.

Glantz, M. H. (1977). Consequences and responsibilities in drought forecasting. *Water Resources Research, 18*, 3–13.

Granger, C. W. J., & Ramanathan, R. (1984). Improved methods of combining forecasts. *Journal of Forecasting, 3*, 197–204.

Guerts, M. D., Kelly, J. P. (1986). Forecasting retail sales using alternative models. *International Journal of Forecasting, 2*, 261–272.

Gupta, S., & Wilton, P. C. (1987). Combination of forecasts: An extension. *Management Science, 33*, 356–372.

Harvey, A. (1984). A unified view of statistical forecasting. *Journal of Forecasting, 3*(3), 245–276.

Hogarth, R. M., & Makridakis, S. (1981). Forecasting and planning: An evaluation. *Management Science, 227*, 115–138.

Huss, W. R. (1985). Comparative analysis of company forecasts and advanced time-series techniques using annual electric utility energy sales data. *International Journal of Forecasting, 1*(3), 217–239.

Jungermann, H. (1984). Inferential processes in the construction of scenarios. *Journal of Forecasting, 5*, (4).

Keen, P. G., & Scott-Morton. (1978). *Decision support systems: An organisational perspective.* Mass.: Addison-Wesley.

Kunreuther, H. (1969). Extensions of Bowman's theory on managerial decision-making. *Management Science, 15*, 415–439.

Lawrence, M. J., Edmundson, R. H., & O'Connor, M. J. (1985). An examination of the accuracy of judgemental extrapolation of time series. *International Journal of Forecasting, May*, 14–25.

Lawrence, M. J., Edmundson, R. H., & O'Connor, M. J. (1986). The accuracy of combining judgemental and statistical forecasts. *Management Science 32*, 1521–1532.

Lichtenstein, S. Fischhoff, B., & Phillips, L. D. (1977). Calibration of probabilities: The state of the art. In Jungermann, H., & de Zeeuw, G. (Eds.), *Decision making and change in human affairs.* Amsterdam: Reidel.

Lock, A. (1987). Integrating group judgements in subjective forecasts. In Wright, G., & Ayton, P. (Eds.), *Judgemental Forecasting.* Chichester: Wiley.

Makridakis, S. (1988). Metaforecasting. *International Journal of Forecasting, 4*(3), 467–491.

Mathews, B. P., & Diamantopoulos, A. (1989). Judgemental revision of sales forecasts: A longitudinal extension. *Journal of Forecasting, 8*(2), 129–140.

Mathews, B. P., & Diamantopoulos, A. (1990). Judgemental revision of sales forecasts: Effectiveness of selection. *Journal of Forecasting, 9*(4).

McNamee, P., & Celona, J. (1987). Decision analysis for the professional with supertree. Redwood City, Cal.: *The Scientific Press.*

McNees, S. K., & Perna, N. S. (1981). Forecasting macroeconomic variables: An eclectic approach, *New England Economic Journal, May/June*, 15–30.

Morecroft, J. (1984). Strategy support models. *Strategic Management Journal, 5*(3), 715–229.

Nilsson, G. (1989). The credibility of inflation-related scenarios of different lengths. In H. Montgomery & O. Svenson (Eds.), *Process and structure in human decision making.* Chichester: Wiley.

O'Connor, M. (1989). Models of Human Behaviour and Confidence in Judgement. *International Journal of Forecasting, 5*, 159–169.

Pereira, B., Coqueiro, R., & Perrota, A. (1989). Experience in combining subjective and quantitative forecasts of open market rates. *Journal of Forecasting, 8*(3), 331–342.

Phillips, L. (1987). On the adequacy of judgmental forecasts. In Wright, G., & Ayton, P. (Eds.), *Judgmental Forecasting,* Chichester: Wiley.

Reeves, G. R., & Lawrence, K. D. Combining multiple forecasts given multiple objectives. *Journal of Forecasting, 1,* 271–280.

Simon, H. A. (1960). *The new science of management decision.* New York: Harper & Row.

Smith, J. Q., & Oliver, R. N. (1990). *Influence diagrams, belief nets and inference.* Chichester: Wiley.

Turner, D. (1990). The role of judgement in macroeconomic forecasting. *Journal of Forecasting, 10.*

Tversky, A., & Kahneman, D. (1974). Judgment under uncertainty: Heuristics and biases. *Science, 185,* 1124–1131.

Wallis, K. F., et al. (1984–8). Models of the UK economy: Reviews 1–5. Oxford: *Oxford University Press.*

Willemain, T. R. (1989). Graphical adjustment of statistical forecasts. *International Journal of Forecasting, 5,* 179–185.

Wolfe, C., & Flores, B. (1990). Judgemental adjustment of earnings forecasts. *Journal of Forecasting* (in press).

Wu, L. S-Y., Ravishanker, N., & Hosking, J. R. M. (1991). Forecasting for business planning: A case study of IBM product sales. *Journal of Forecasting, 11,* (in press).

Index